Acknowledgements

This project was conceived at Lund University, carried out at Malmö University and continued at Stockholm University. The results have been discussed at a number of seminars and workshops in various contexts, and the final push in finishing a draft manuscript was made at the University of Illinois, Urbana-Champaign.

Accordingly, there are many scholars and colleagues who have been involved along the way and to whom I am indebted. First and foremost, I would like to thank Professor Sven-Axel Månsson who generously invited me to become a postdoctoral researcher in the research group Gender, Sexuality and Social Work at Malmö University. Thanks to this invitation, I was eligible for and later granted funds from the Swedish Research Council. My years working with this group have been among the best of my professional career. I would like to thank Sara Johnsdotter, Aje Carlbom, Lars Plantin, Pernilla Ouis, Lotta Holmström, Eva Elmerstig, Lotta Löfgren-Mårtenson, Pernilla Nigård, Gunnel Brander and Niklas Eriksson, and last but not least Sven-Axel Månsson, for not only providing valuable feedback, access to empirical data and advice on my work, but for simply being great colleagues.

During the project's conception at Lund University, my closest colleagues met my idea of working on the history of Swedish pornographic films with much enthusiasm and little prejudice. Lars-Gustaf Andersson, Ann-Kristin Wallengren, Erik Hedling, Olof Hedling, Mats Jönsson and Anders Marklund encouraged me in my scholarly pursuits. At Stockholm University, I had the benefit of working at the largest Cinema Studies program in Northern Europe, thus encountering several excellent international researchers. In particular Maaret Koskinen, Malin Wahlberg and Laura Horak (now at Carleton University) were very helpful, as were the rewarding scholarly exchanges with Ingrid Ryberg. Other scholars with whom I have worked, and who share my research interests, are Klara Arnberg and Elisabet Björklund, whose interactions have always proved fruitful.

I spent the spring semester of 2014 at the University of Illinois, Urbana-Champaign, as a visiting scholar at the Media and Cinema Studies department and scholar-in-residence at the EU Center. I would like to thank Anna Stenport, who not only made this stay possible but also helped in numerous other ways and gave me vital feedback on the Introduction. In addition, Angharad Valdivia, James Hay, Sasha Mobley, Paula Treichler, Larry Smith and several others were kind enough to offer feedback on my work, and were generally very welcoming (for instance, recruiting me for the soccer team Hot Mamas). They provided such an invigorating environment that it became possible for me to make that final leap and finish the first full draft. Moreover, Tommy Gustafsson (Linneaus University) and I exchanged reader comments on our respective work, and his suggestions for my manuscript were extremely valuable.

I would also like to thank those interviewees who are anonymous but whose stories were vital for this project. If you read this, you will know who you are and that your memories were invaluable. Archivists and librarians have also been instrumental, with special mention to Shawn Wilson and Liana Zhou at the Kinsey Institute, and Magdalena Salomonsson at the Swedish National Archive. Erick Janssen helped me apply for access to the Kinsey Institute's archive, and Ulf Dalquist at the Swedish Media Council answered all my questions regarding the censorship processes of the National Board of Film Censors

Funding for the project came initially from the Swedish Research Council, and I have also been supported by Stockholm University.

Finally, and as always, my most sincere love and gratitude go to my family: Olle, Albert, Martha, Pinge and Kinsey the boxer dog.

The Swedish Porn Scene

The Swedish Porn Scene
Exhibition Contexts, 8mm Pornography and the Sex Film

Mariah Larsson

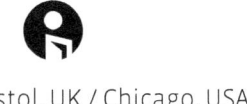

intellect Bristol, UK / Chicago, USA

First published in the UK in 2017 by
Intellect, The Mill, Parnall Road, Fishponds, Bristol, BS16 3JG, UK

First published in the USA in 2017 by
Intellect, The University of Chicago Press, 1427 E. 60th Street,
Chicago, IL 60637, USA

A catalogue record for this book is available from the
British Library.

Cover designer: Emily Dann
Copy-editor: Michael Eckhardt
Production manager: Katie Evans
Typesetting: Contentra Technologies

Print ISBN: 978-1-78320-682-7
ePDF ISBN: 978-1-78320-683-4
ePUB ISBN: 978-1-78320-684-1

This is a peer-reviewed publication.

Contents

Introduction

The history of pornography in the 1960s and 1970s may seem a simple narrative of increasingly liberal censorship and obscenity laws; a developing industry producing ever more (both in terms of numbers and explicitness) films, advancing both technically and in relation to its content, its distribution and exhibition; and a pornography that enters the public sphere only to eventually withdraw from it. However, this study tries to draw attention to the complexities in this history to discuss issues of genres and formats; of exhibition contexts and gendered sexual space; of censorship, content and ideology; and of highly permeable national boundaries.

During this time period, two Scandinavian countries became emblematic of being liberal in relation to both sexual morals and moving images capturing these liberal sexual ideas.[1] Denmark and Sweden had already begun to gain this reputation in the 1950s, with the much publicized sex reassignment surgery of American Christine Jorgensen performed in Denmark in 1951, and with mandatory sex education in Swedish schools starting in 1955. In 1969, Denmark legalized pornography and in 1971, Sweden followed suit. In the 1970s, both countries can be said to participate in what is sometimes referred to as 'the golden age of porn', producing narrative, feature-length porn films (both softcore and hardcore) as well as 8mm hardcore porn.

The focus for this book is Sweden. However, the history of Swedish sex films, 8mm pornography and their respective exhibition contexts is inextricably entangled with the development in Denmark and, accordingly, cannot be written without keeping at least an intermittent eye on the development in the neighbouring country. The perception of these two Scandinavian countries had to do with several things. Of course, the news of sex reassignment surgery and sex education in schools were two reasons. Other reasons had to do with the dissemination of ideals of Scandinavian beauty in *Playboy*, where tall, blonde women who were both elegant and sexual embodied a Nordic feminine ideal,[2] with exported films like *Hon dansade en sommar/One Summer of Happiness* (Arne Mattsson, 1951), *Sommaren med Monika/Summer with Monika* (Ingmar Bergman, 1953) and *Jag är nyfiken – gul/I am Curious (Yellow)* (Vilgot Sjöman, 1968), but also with American films like *Sexual Freedom in Denmark* (John Lamb, 1970) or the Italian-American *Svezia, Inferno e Paradiso/Sweden, Heaven and Hell* (Luigi Scattini, 1968).[3]

Still other reasons had to do with the fact that Sweden and Denmark actually had a scene of sexually explicit material and entertainment. Sex stores had been established already in the 1960s, and more or less clandestine sex clubs offered entertainment in the form of striptease, live shows (couples performing intercourse onstage) and screenings of pornographic films.

Swedish politicians complained that foreigners came to Stockholm for sex tourism, and in Denmark, the first porn trade fair, Sex 69, was held in October 1969.[4] One example of the notoriety of the sex clubs in Scandinavia is the somewhat famous photograph of classic rock group Led Zeppelin standing around a podium on which a live-sex couple is performing. It is taken at Chat Noir in Stockholm in 1973. In the picture, the band members seem a bit uncomfortable or even bored with the situation. Notwithstanding the liberal 1970s and, in this case, the ostensibly abundant sex lives of rock stars, the notion of making public something that is regarded as private might still be experienced as awkward, embarrassing and shameful; a kind of paradox inherent in this time period's relation to sexuality, pornography and sexual consumption in the public sphere.

Perhaps somewhat surprisingly considering the reputation generated during this time period in Scandinavia, this particular section of the history of pornography has not been thoroughly researched. One of the objectives of this study is to begin to remedy that. This will be done through two micro-historical case studies: one on the exhibition of pornographic films in the city of Malmö, in southern Sweden, between 1971 and 1976; and the other on the hardcore 8mm films that were produced, distributed and exhibited during this time. These two case studies are framed by more comprehensive chapters that detail both the stratification of sexually explicit moving image material (in accordance with format and degrees of explicitness), and the historical situation for the relationship between the sexually explicit film and the Scandinavian welfare states, as well as a discussion of pornographic and sexually explicit film as a regional, national and transnational cinema. By moving from the macro to the micro and then back to macro level, the purpose is to map out the Swedish 'porn scene' during the period. The first case study looks at the venues for consumption of pornographic films and other sexual entertainment, thereby placing the films in a context of urban sexual space, and discerning (some of) the uses and functions of pornographic moving image material. The second case study describes and discusses the 8mm films that were sold, rented out and exhibited via mail order or in such venues. By focusing on the substandard films, the notion of a 'golden age of porn', consisting of feature-length, narrative hardcore films, can be challenged and nuanced, as the substandard fare was no less common as a mode of consumption of pornographic moving image material than films of the 'classic' (or golden) type.

The three comprehensive chapters place the two case studies in context, which is significant since much knowledge about pornographic film during this time period comes from the United States. By describing the particular situation in Sweden both in relation to the national issue of the welfare state and in relation to the perception of pornography as a film genre, the specifics of the exhibition contexts, as well as of the censorship that has given me much of the material for the case study on 8mm film, can be explained, understood and thus compared to other national situations. However, it is quite clear that pornographic film today (as well as during these pioneering years) cannot be fully understood without taking its seemingly inherent transnationality into account. Transnational cinema within a political context is often understood as a way to unite people across national borders, and is presented as 'distinctly other from mainstream or Hollywood cinema'.[5] *Transnationality*, on the other hand, refers to movements across national borders in general; for various reasons, pornography appears to have a strong tendency towards such movements. The final chapter in this book provides a tentative discussion of this pornographic characteristic; however, I believe more pan-European and transatlantic research is ultimately called for in order to uncover the full extent of sexually explicit images' capacity to travel.

Background

'Of all the political and social revolutions that were either promised or striven for in the tumultuous era of the late sixties and seventies, it is the sexual one that in the end wrought the biggest change', claims Linda Williams in the introduction to *Screening Sex* (2008).[6] Obviously, this is a bold statement, but although it could be argued that the various revolutions are more or less inextricable from one another, and that the civil rights movement and the anti-war movement held at least equal weight to the struggle for change in sexual morals and ideas, the impact of the sexual revolution cannot be denied. Discussions about sexuality, sexual orientation, sexual freedom, contraceptives, sexually explicit materials, sex education – in addition to the research that had been performed and influenced the discourse (Wilhelm Reich and Alfred C. Kinsey are two names that Williams mentions), and that continued to be carried out during the 1960s by William Masters and Virginia Johnson[7] – led to momentous changes in legislation, censorship and policy, as well as to important gender and sexual rights movements, such as the women's movement and the LGBT movement. This applied to both the United States and to Scandinavia, where Kinsey's first volume of work, *Sexual Behavior in the Human Male* (1948), had been translated into Swedish in 1949, and proved influential in the coming debates about sexuality during the 1960s.[8]

During the late 1960s and the 1970s, pornography was more or less legalized in a number of western countries. Censorship regulations changed and the concept of obscenity became more liberalized. Not only are the 1970s sometimes described as 'the golden age of porn' because of the comparatively high-budget, narrative pornographic feature films that were produced, but also because more adult and graphic material was incorporated into non-pornographic films – from *The Graduate* (Mike Nichols, 1967) to European art film *Ultimo tango a Parigi/Last Tango in Paris* (Bernardo Bertolucci, 1972) and Japanese-French art film *Ai no korida/In the Realm of the Senses* (Nagisa Oshima, 1976), more risqué stories found their way on to the screen. The somewhat misleading epitaph 'golden age of porn' includes classics like *Deep Throat* (Gerard Damiano, 1972) or *Behind the Green Door* (Mitchell Bros., 1972),[9] but as American film scholar Eric Schaefer points out in his account of the rise of the pornographic feature:

What has become increasingly evident is that the feature-length hardcore narrative constituted merely an entr'acte between reels of essentially plotless underground stag movies in the years 1908 to 1967 and the similarly plotless ruttings of porn in the video age (emerging in the mid-1980s and continuing to the present).[10]

Although narrative, feature-length hardcore films did not disappear after the 1970s, they are first and foremost associated with this time period, and make up the 'gold' of the golden age. Nonetheless, one of the significant arguments of this volume is that the hardcore narrative feature was never the only kind of porn available to consumers, but that more or less 'plotless ruttings' distributed on 8mm or 16mm made up a large share of the pornography which was consumed during this decade. Just how large is hard to determine, however, but from looking at the venues for pornographic exhibition in my case study, it is quite apparent that narrative has never been the dominant attraction for pornography.[11]

Moreover, from a consumer perspective, it might just as well be argued that the breakthrough of the VCR in the late seventies led to swifter and easier production, as well as more widespread consumption of porn; or that the digital revolution, with its dissemination of a large amount of free and readily available material on the Internet, constitutes a more significant golden age for porn than the 1970s. At the other end of the timeline, recent research has shown that an increase in the production of pornographic material (in the specific study magazines) in Sweden came in the late 1960s, and thus preceded the legalization.[12] Random samples from advertisements in the tabloid *Kvällsposten* prove that so-called 'sex stores' were established in Malmö at least as early as the late 1960s.

Nevertheless, certain factors distinguish the seventies. There is no other time frame in modern history in which pornography enjoys such a legal freedom.[13] Pornography may seem ubiquitous today, and has influenced iconographies of advertisements and music videos, but the proximity of sex and sexual expressions in everyday public life has nevertheless also decreased since the 1970s. In Sweden, this period is bracketed between legalization in 1971 and the prohibition of child pornography in 1980, although the backlash starts in the mid-seventies. Thus, for ten years, pornography is nearly completely uninhibited by legal constraints. This is also a transitionary period in which pornography (or 'adult entertainment') teeters on the edge of the industrial development towards large, multinational conglomerates, but still mainly consists of small, entrepreneurial businesses.[14] Furthermore, a resistance against pornography develops during the seventies which does not pick up its arguments from a moral-religious discourse (which nevertheless continued to protest pornography),[15] but rather from a burgeoning women's movement, and, especially in a Swedish context, social workers, police authorities and journalists.

One important delimitation for this study is the time frame, chosen to envelope the period between the legalization of pornography in Sweden in 1971 and the year 1976, when the public inquiry into sex crime law was published.[16] Although eventually scrapped, the proposals of the sex crime inquiry expressed a sexually liberal ideology that many regarded as too extreme (for instance, a more narrow definition of rape and a loosening of the definition of incest), while the outcry it provoked led to a change in public discourse. Laws pertaining to pornography, sexual entertainment and prostitution in Sweden since then have become more restrictive rather than the other way around. More particular to my case study of Malmö, however, is another significant event in 1976. In the mid-seventies, the local police authorities undertook a large-scale investigation into the sex clubs, which were suspected of being places for procuring sex, unlicensed liquor sales and miscellaneous crimes. In 1976, several club owners were indicted on these accounts and most sex clubs were closed down as a result. Thus, the period 1971 to 1976 can be regarded as a brief period of extreme sexual liberation in Malmö and Sweden, a parenthesis containing what literature scholar Walter Kendrick has called the 'post-pornographic', by which he means that pornography is no longer defined by being obscene or censored.[17] The term 'post-pornographic' comes across as contradictory, but since Kendrick defines pornography as that which is deemed obscene and therefore censored or forbidden, this period is precisely post-pornographic due to legalization and liberalization. Accordingly, the 'post-' does not refer to the end of pornography, but rather to a proliferation of sexually explicit materials that are not placed in 'secret museums', but are allowed to exist in the public sphere instead, the 'off/scene' taking place 'on/scene', as Linda Williams phrases it.[18]

Since Williams' seminal and pioneering study *Hardcore: Power, Pleasure, and the 'Frenzy of the Visible'* was published in 1989, porn studies have slowly developed into a somewhat established research field, recently consolidated through the first issue of *Porn Studies Journal* in 2014.[19] Nevertheless, although a number of studies have been made thus far, there are still several white spots on the map, not least because the field has focused to a large extent on the situation and history of pornography in the United States, and to a lesser extent the United Kingdom and Europe. In addition, as Williams observes in her article in the first issue of *Porn Studies Journal*, much research has focused on other kinds of pornography than the mainstream, heterosexual one.[20] Moreover, for all its reputed morals with regards to sexuality, Sweden has not yet figured prominently in the studies made.[21] By looking at exhibition contexts in one town in Sweden, the aim is to capture the practices of watching pornography: how were the films regarded; who went to see them; why did people see them; what they were surrounded by; and how did the legal exhibition of pornographic and sexual entertainment in various forms shape the impression of the urban landscape. These practices – although belonging to mainstream, heterosexual pornography – can be discussed in terms of marginality, deviance and male-to-male sexuality. The emphasis on exhibition contexts entails an inclusion of a national and regional perspective in relation to which films were screened, how censorship worked, and how the national judiciary and political institutions regarded them. However, it also places Sweden – particularly the Swedish town of Malmö – in an international, or rather transnational, context which is highly relevant to the history of pornography.

Moreover, the Swedish 'porn scene' of the 1970s is a mythologized part of the national imagination, the collective sense of Swedish cultural history and the perception of Swedish film history. As anyone who has studied film history in Sweden knows, film production in the seventies to a large extent consisted of what is usually referred to as more or less pornographic films and, somewhat in a stark contrast, children's films. Additionally, with the patina of age, these films have received cult status, are revered or joked about on websites and in magazines, and disseminated by various distribution companies, most notably KlubbSuper8. On the one hand, these films are well remembered by many; on the other, Swedish film scholars seem in a sense to negate the existence of these films. With a few exceptions,[22] they are rarely treated in scholarship dealing with national film history, and in the most widely read film-history volume, Leif Furhammar's *Filmen i Sverige*, they are described as many – one fifth of the domestic output of feature-length theatrically released films in the decade – but have been almost expelled from the history of national cinema with the explanation that they were mostly made for export.[23] At the same time, this type of film influences the perception of the 1970s enough to warrant – like children's film, documentaries and the films of the decade in general – an essay in the introduction to the official filmography of the 1970s, *Svensk filmografi 7: 1970–1979*.[24]

This brief outline of the position of the Swedish sex film within the national historiography illustrates two issues that recur with increasing urgency while examining this particular group of films. The first issue has to do with the national identity of the films. Although Furhammar's claim about the export of these films may seem like an attempt to exonerate the national cinema of the 1970s, their national status is ambiguous to say the least. National cinema is of course difficult to define even when looking at the mainstream film industry (popular genre as well as art cinema). Several scholars have discussed the concept of national cinema, but it is usually used for films that are produced in a particular country and directed by a person of that particular nationality – the 'who' and 'where' of the films.[25] However, many of the films discussed in this book are co-produced with companies from other countries, some of them are directed by directors from other countries, and others so clearly made to function in other national markets that the issue of a 'national' cinema almost becomes moot. At the same time, they carry their Swedishness like a torch.

The other issue has to do with genre – can these films be described as 'porn films', even with the qualification 'more or less advanced pornography'?[26] The production of 35mm feature films with sexually explicit content does not necessarily fall into the category of 'pornography', at least not as it is understood today. Rather, it seems that the genre of pornography has been stratified in accordance with exhibition venues, targeted audiences, film gauge and production, and thus an attempt to study the Swedish 'porn scene' of the 1970s has to take all of these into account. This entails including the substandard films, that is, 8mm and 16mm films which were a common way to consume moving image pornography.

8mm films were screened not in cinemas, but in sex stores, sex clubs and private homes. As far as I have been able to judge, their generic designation is a lot easier than the theatrically released 35mm films because they are hardcore pornography in a way that reminds one of porn today. (Paradoxically, they are rarely called 'porn films' in the advertisements.) Compared to 35mm films, 8mm films are difficult to research since they are not listed in *Svensk filmografi* (a list of all theatrically released, feature-length films produced in Sweden), nor among the titles in *Långfilm i Sverige* (a list of all films theatrically released in Sweden).[27] Neither have they been systematically archived. However, many of them did go through the Swedish film censorship system and records from the National Board of Film Censors are available. Moreover, a selection of them is listed in *Filmårsboken* from 1972 and 1973.[28] This selection shows that there were two categories of such films: (1) those which showcased nudity but no sex, and which received the censorship ruling 'general' [*barntillåten*]; and (2) those which showed intercourse in various forms and received the ruling 'restricted' [*barnförbjuden*], which had an age limit of fifteen.

Even non-pornographic 8mm films are hard to research given that, as the foremost material of amateur film-makers, they have flown under the radar, so to speak, and are rarely found in archives and registers. In 'Plain Brown Wrapper: Adult Films for the Home Market, 1930–1969', Eric Schaefer points to the new-found interest within film studies for what is sometimes called 'orphan films' – home movies, holiday films, travel films, anything made on substandard film.[29] These films are not included in commercial or artistic film production; they have never been shown in cinemas. Their main venue has been the homes of the people who made them. Nevertheless, the pornographic 8mm films were not only screened in people's private homes, but also in sex stores and sex clubs. Much of the pornographic moving image material of the period was consumed in more or less public spaces; spaces which not only were constructed by the entertainment provided in them, but that also, in turn, influenced the perception of that material.

Mapping sexual space

Pornography constructs its own space, oscillating between the spectacular and the mundane, but always containing the element of explicit sex. The space constructed by pornography – the 'pornotopia' as some would call it – is not only intrinsic to the film, but affects the spectator and the space surrounding the spectator as well.[30] Linda Williams has famously termed pornography, horror and melodrama as 'body genres' because they affect the actual body of the spectator, causing a kind of mirroring effect whereby the body of the spectator mimics the body or bodies of the performers on-screen.[31] For instance, in horror, the spectator is scared like the characters in the film; in melodrama, the audience cries with the characters; and in pornography, the sexual arousal of the performers is reflected by the person who watches them. As Williams observes, this has a bearing on how these genres are perceived: 'what may especially mark these body genres as low is the perception that the body of the spectator is caught up in an almost involuntary mimicry of the emotion or sensation of the body on the screen'.[32] This seemingly immediate relation between what the bodies on-screen experience and the bodies among the audience experience is furthermore confirmed by the fact that pornographic film clips are used to elicit a response of arousal from medical sex research subjects. Porn clips are used simply because they work better than, for instance, asking subjects to imagine a sexual situation or letting them read an erotic story.[33] Although this usage can and should be discussed, Linda Williams' notion of body genres thus seems to have a bearing in actual situations, utilized by a science which is ultimately not interested in genres or cinema.

Although the kernel was already there in Williams' famous piece on body genres in 1991, the past ten years or so have seen affect become an important new theoretical paradigm, implying a shift in focus from representation to what that representation does to the spectator.[34] Susanna Paasonen argues convincingly for the usefulness of affect theory in porn studies, and coins her own phrase for the effects of (in her case, online) porn on consumers: carnal resonance.[35] The term 'resonance' is very illustrative: just as the body of the guitar responds to the vibrating strings, the body of the spectator or consumer can be thought of as responding to the images.

Paasonen and other film scholars point to how films may be perceived not only visually, but by providing tactile sensations as well. Terming it 'haptic cinema', 'haptic media' or 'haptic space', in reference to Gilles Deleuze, these scholars highlight aspects of cinema which influence the body in various ways.[36] As such, the 'embodied spectator' is a spectator which experiences a film tactilely. For me, the various spaces in which pornographic films were screened were spaces which were constructed as much *for* the consumption of sexual entertainment as they were *by* that sexual entertainment itself. Accordingly, the different venues in which pornographic films were screened were also affected by which films these were. This will be further elaborated in Chapters 3 and 4, which deal with the construction of sexual space. Yet it also forms an important undercurrent in the discussions of genre in Chapter 2, as well as the discussion of the 8mm pornographic films in Chapter 5.

However, it is not merely a simple causal relation that the films perform on the spectator's body. The social setting – or what might be called the 'scenario' – of the clubs and stores plays an important role in influencing the perception of space. Entering into a store, a club or a porn cinema brings with it certain behaviour as well, dependent on codes, norms and expectations. Such a scenario can be understood through the use of sexual script theory, presented by sociologists John H. Gagnon and William Simon in the early 1970s, and further developed in several articles since then.[37] The term 'script' in this case should be understood in light of the use of theatrical metaphors within sociology, perhaps most famously in the work of Erving Goffman and his 1959 book *The Presentation of Self in Everyday Life*.[38]

According to Gagnon and Simon, scripts are what enable us to act sexually – the how, why, when and with whom we have sex – and exist at three levels: (1) the intrapsychic (within each individual); (2) the interpersonal (between people); and (3) the cultural (i.e. the general scenario in society). These three levels cooperate in each given situation, providing permission as well as access to sexual behaviour, but also allowing particular outcomes of that behaviour.[39] Since sexuality is rarely dealt with explicitly, the sexual scripts are learned through various realizations, misapprehensions, more or less inadvertently communicated taboos, as well as through cultural expressions.[40]

These scripts can thus be understood both as providing a set of norms of behaviour to follow within the settings of sexual entertainment and consumption, and as telling the client/consumer/spectator how to act and respond. In addition, they signify what to do and how to feel about the images and live performances in these settings.

Pornography and the anti-porn movement in Sweden

In Sweden, the United States and many other western countries, the liberalization of censorship and obscenity laws, and the legalization of pornography coincided with the rise of the women's movement. Although there was a debate around 'sex roles' in the early to mid-1960s, in Sweden, which had a politically liberal perspective on gender, the rise of second-wave feminism with a socialist approach to gender equality came about in the late 1960s. As Klara Arnberg demonstrates in her study of the pornographic press in Sweden, pornography was heatedly debated in Sweden in the 1970s, mainly from a feminist standpoint. Pornography was regarded as an obstacle on the road to equality and emancipated female, and to a certain extent male, sexuality.[41] Simultaneously, the legalization of pornography was a result of sexual liberation and the general liberalization of sexual issues in the 1960s. The existence of porn compels a paradox between a need for emancipation, liberalism and openness on the one hand, and a production which was considered deeply problematic regarding what it depicted, how it affected its consumers and how it had been produced on the other.

As a result, another paradox, or rather another conflict, of pornography appears; one which was not explicitly touched upon in the discourse of Sweden in the 1970s, but is present in the so-called 'sex wars' in America in the 1980s. This conflict deals with the kinds of sexuality which are accepted, and which are thus possible to choose from, in a given society.[42] During the 'sex wars' – that is, the sometimes very aggressive debates between anti-pornography feminists on the one side and pro-sex or anti-censorship feminists on the other – pornography became a key issue in which various perspectives on sexuality and gender conflicted. The anti-porn establishments argued that pornography was, essentially, a male domination of women; that its production exploited and objectified women; that its representations of sexuality were violent, degrading and harmful; and that it resulted in the consumer's internalization of male dominance and an intrinsically misogynistic gender hierarchy. Whilst these same arguments were used in the Swedish feminist discourse of the 1970s, 1980s and 1990s, the arguments of the pro-sex or anti-censorship feminists did not permeate Swedish debate until sometime in the second half of the 1990s. American pro-sex or anti-censorship feminists argued that, among other things, the anti-pornography stance was a move towards censorship and towards sexual repression, privileging sexual practices that fell within a certain norm.[43] In the feminist discourse of 1970s Sweden, the ideal sexual relation was based on equality, and took place within a steady relationship characterized by mutual respect. It could be lesbian or heterosexual, but it seems as if within mainstream Swedish feminism, the heterosexual alternative was the most common.[44]

The conflict between the women's movement and pornography was perhaps the most apparent one, and has also received the most attention. However, there were also discrepancies between the worlds of pornography and sexual entertainment and the Swedish model welfare state, both in the manner of how the clubs and stores were started, managed and organized, and in the destitution and exploitation that many thought characterized the environment. Furthermore, there was a conflict between the clubs and stores and the people who lived in the neighbourhoods where these were located.

Accordingly, although pornography during this time was freer than ever from legal restraints, it was also under attack from the women's movement, from police and social authorities, and in some sense from the general public. The public sexual space is the subject of conflicts and negotiations regarding its borders – the tangible, geographical borders, but also the limits as to what can be shown, and when and where it can be shown – its conditions, its gender ('by men, for men'), its sexuality (homo- or heterosexual), its adjustment to what is simultaneously a liberal society and a social democratic welfare society, and its relation to the rest of society and urban space. The reason why this conflict surfaces during the 1970s has to do with the fact that pornography and sexual entertainment at this point in time occupies a share of the public space, but also because pornography's prominence in society coincides with a general economic development, namely the recession following the oil crisis in 1974.

Researching the clandestine – or streetwalking on a ruined map

As mentioned above, this study is located at the intersection of film history, film theory, sociology, sexuality studies and urban studies. For material and point of departure, I have first and foremost used the advertisements contained in *Kvällsposten*, a local tabloid evening newspaper. Various inquiries and other official documents have been of use as well. An academic inquiry by two sociologists, published as a report with the title *Svarta affärer*/'Shady Business' has provided an insight into how the clubs worked, whereas public inquiries of the government, such as the inquiry on film censorship (1969), the freedom of speech inquiry (1969), the sex crime inquiry (1976) and the prostitution inquiry (1980), have provided some further information.[45]

Furthermore, I have conducted a handful of interviews with men who frequented establishments such as sex shops, sex clubs and porn cinemas. These interviewees are more or less randomly selected, since I have for the most part let people get in touch with me.[46] In addition, I have been allowed access to interviews made in the 1970s with female sex workers in Malmö, some of whom worked at the sex clubs. These interviews were made for a research project related to prostitution, and focused to a large extent on the women's reasons for selling sexual services, the effects of doing so, and the motivations for ceasing. However, some of the interviews provide unique glimpses into what it was like to work in the clubs at the time, and is thus an invaluable historic source material.[47]

For the chapter on 8mm films, the censorship records in the archives of the National Board of Film Censors has supplied a large material of metadata – the titles, lengths, production companies, nationality, brief descriptions and censorship verdicts – on the more than one thousand pornographic small-gauge films that were submitted between 1971 and 1976. I could identify and see only a fraction of these films in the archive at the Kinsey Institute, from both their stag film collection and their Swedish Erotica collection.

Nonetheless, my study is partly based on highly fragile, not to mention slippery, material. Relying on sources such as random reminiscence and films which cannot be tied to a specific time and place is clearly problematic. If it is difficult to ascertain whether a film was screened or not in these establishments, the memories of my informants may be more or less unstable as well. However, to add to the knowledge of the more or less clandestine history of the 8mm pornographic film, its screening contexts and its possible audience, it is unavoidable that the material used for research in many instances is just as shaky as the screening contexts themselves.

This volume has six chapters. The first chapter, 'Sexually explicit films and the welfare state(s)', contextualizes the legalization of pornography in Sweden. Thus, the chapter provides a comprehensive historical overview, positioning sexuality and film in relation to the welfare state. In addition, it discusses one of the paradoxes of porn in this particular context: on the one hand, a need for emancipation, liberalism and openness; on the other, a production that was considered deeply problematic regarding what it depicted, how it affected its consumers and how it was produced. Furthermore, it discusses how (some of) these films thematically relate to ideas of the welfare state. Accordingly, the chapter not only traces a development of liberalization in the 1960s, but continues with the changing perception of sexually explicit material and sexual commerce in the 1970s. Focus here is on the historical situation regarding sexuality, sexually explicit material and pornography in general in Scandinavian welfare countries from the early 1960s to 1980.

Next, in 'Mapping the genre: The boundaries of pornography', I point to the complexities involved in designating a corpus of films as 'pornographic', and demonstrate how varied the output actually was. This is significant because there was quite clearly a stratification of materials in relation to their format (35mm, 16mm or 8mm), their production context, and, consequently, their distribution and exhibition. Accordingly, the production, distribution and exhibition of sexually explicit moving image material need to be discussed in relation to genre and format.

With a starting point in Rick Altman's genre theory, as well as Walter Kendrick's notion that the boundaries of pornography dissolved in this 'post-pornographic' period, the chapter moves on to discuss possible generic designations of theatrically released 35mm films. Even with a contextual definition of pornography (i.e. pornography is whatever people in a given context understand as pornography), the designation of what I propose to call 'sex films' as more or less pornographic is not completely beneficial to our understanding of the Swedish porn scene in the 1970s. In order to see how the genre is 'discursively constructed'[48], the chapter provides an overview of the specific production contexts of 35mm films, and presents sample analyses of advertisements, critical reception, censorship records and the films themselves.

Chapter 3 – 'Constructions of sexual space: The case of Malmö' – and Chapter 4 – 'Exhibition venues in Malmö' together deal with the first case study which zeroes in on Malmö as an urban site for the exhibition of pornographic films. At the time, Malmö can be described as a city (unknowingly) entering into post-industrial decline, with the large civilian shipyard Kockums losing its once firm grip on the market from 1974 onwards. The inner city was characterized by areas of urban decay, with buildings both projected to be taken down, and large, empty blocks where buildings had been demolished but not replaced. Moreover, there were both female-to-male and male-to-male prostitution streets, albeit in different parts of the city.

Pornographic films were exhibited in four different public contexts: regular cinemas, porn cinemas (only one in Malmö – Spegeln), sex clubs and sex stores. These contexts exhibited different kinds of films and were constructed as sexual spaces in different ways. Many clubs and stores were located in (or in the vicinity of) those areas of urban decay that coloured the perception of the city and the activities going on in the clubs. The allegation that the clubs were places of prostitution and the notion of solitary masturbation in the stores added to the sense of a space with gendered access. A few of these establishments are given particular attention. Chapter 4 concludes with a discussion of the notion of 'lived space' and the cleaning up of such spaces, inspired by Marilyn Adler Papayanis' discussion of the zoning out of pornography in New York.[49]

The second case study is presented in Chapter 5 – 'Size does matter: The substandard pornographic films of the 1970s'. The spaces of the exhibition contexts were to a large extent constructed by the sexual material and entertainment that were consumed on the premises. Depending on the particular establishment (store or club), magazines, sex toys, striptease shows and live shows were on offer alongside film screenings. The line between store and club was vague, but both showed films. Even though many of these – especially in the clubs – were 16mm, this chapter focuses on the 8mm films which were screened, sold and rented out. Already before the legalization of pornography, 8mm hardcore films showed explicit close-ups of genitals during intercourse. They were short (between five and twenty minutes long), and could contain a developed narrative or present a brief set-up which contextualized the depicted sex. Many of them were produced in Denmark or Germany.

The 8mm films are singled out for this chapter because they had their own production, distribution and exhibition circuit; they were a significant format for porn consumption during the time period; and, in addition, their prevalence calls into question the dichotomy of a golden age of narrative feature-length porn versus hardcore sex scenes in compilation videos of the 1980s onwards. The purposes of this chapter are, on the one hand, to provide a descriptive and empirically based account of these films, and, on the other, to discuss the impact of censorship and legislation on the actual content. There is still a dearth of research on 8mm porn, primarily due to the format's problematic conditions for preservation and archiving; in other words, they are 'doubly orphaned'.[50] Thus, this chapter's significance lies in what this empirical material discloses about the impact of censorship and legislation on the actual content, but also, conversely, in what the material may say about the impact of the actual content on those sexual spaces where these films were screened.

Finally, in 'A regional, national and transnational cinema?' I discuss both the domestic 35mm narrative sex films which were widely exported, and which used several strategies in order to enhance their exportability; and the 8mm hardcore pornographic films which were quite obviously tied to one national location (Denmark), but which travelled easily and were produced with covers containing three different languages. The argument of this chapter widens the discussion of the previous chapters and points forward in time to the contemporary situation. If porn today is either produced on an extremely small scale (i.e. home videos or as part of a cottage industry) or on a much larger one (such as part of a multinational conglomerate), and disseminated widely on the Internet, the transnational character of porn was already in place in the late 1960s and early 1970s. This is evident both in the 35mm and 8mm films, and comes out of porn's particular conditions for existence, namely its ambiguous status in relation to morals, politics and (historically) the law.

Notes

1 Jack Stevenson, *Scandinavian Blue: The Erotic Cinema of Sweden and Denmark in the 1960s and 1970s*, Jefferson, NC: McFarland, 2010; Eric Schaefer, "'I'll Take Sweden!" The Shifting Discourse of the "Sexy Nation" in Sexploitation Films', in Eric Schaefer (ed.), *Sex Scene: Media and the Cultural Revolution*, Durham, NC & London: Duke University Press, 2014.

2 Erika Jackson, 'Swedish Beauties or Feminists with Dragon Tattoos? A History of Sexualizing Nordic Feminine Qualities in American Popular Culture', Paper presented at Society for the Advancement of Scandinavian Studies, San Francisco, May 2–4, 2013.

3 Elisabet Björklund & Mariah Larsson (eds), *Swedish Cinema and the Sexual Revolution: Critical Essays*, Jefferson, NC: McFarland, 2016; Schaefer, 2014.

4 Klara Arnberg, 'Synd på export: 1960-talets pornografiska press och den svenska synden', *Historisk Tidskrift*, vol. 129, no. 3, 2009; Stevenson, 2010.

5 Quotation from Pietari Kääpä, 'Transnational Approaches to Ecocinema: Charting an Expansive Field', in Tommy Gustafsson & Pietari Kääpä (eds) *Transnational Ecocinema: Film Culture in an Era of Ecological Transformation*, Bristol: Intellect, 2013, p. 26. See also for instance Elizabeth Ezra & Terry Rowden, *Transnational Cinema: The Film Reader*, London: Routledge, 2006; and Mariah Larsson, 'A National/Transnational Genre: Pornography in Transition', in Tommy Gustafsson & Pietari Kääpä (eds), *Nordic Genre Film: Small Nation Film Cultures in the Global Marketspace*, Edinburgh: Edinburgh University Press, 2015, pp. 217–29.

6 Linda Williams, *Screening Sex*, Durham, NC: Duke University Press, 2008, p. 8.

7 Williams, 2008, p. 8.

8 For the influence of Kinsey on the Swedish sex debate, see Lena Lennerhed, *Frihet att njuta: Sexualdebatten i Sverige på 1960-talet*, Stockholm: Norstedts, 1994. Nevertheless, Kinsey's second volume, *Sexual Behavior in the Human Female* (1953), was not translated until 1968.

9 Linda Williams, *Hardcore: Power, Pleasure, and the 'Frenzy of the Visible'*, Berkeley, CA & London: University of California Press, 1999 [1989]; Eric Schaefer, 'Gauging a Revolution: 16mm Film and the Rise of the Pornographic Feature', in Linda Williams (ed.), *Porn Studies*, Durham, NC & London: Duke University Press, 2004; see also *Boogie Nights* (Paul Thomas Anderson, 1997); Wikipedia, 'Golden age of porn', http://en.wikipedia.org/wiki/Golden_Age_of_Porn [Accessed August 26, 2011].

10 Schaefer, 'Gauging a Revolution', 2004.

11 Cf. Peter Lehman, 'Revelations about Pornography', in Peter Lehman (ed.), *Pornography: Film and Culture*, New Brunswick, NJ & London: Rutgers University Press, 2006, pp. 87–98.

12 Klara Arnberg, *Motsättningarnas marknad: den pornografiska pressens kommersiella genombrott och regleringen av pornografi i Sverige 1950–1980*, Lund: Sekel bokförlag, 2010.

13 Arnberg, 2010, p. 225ff.

14 Cf. Phil Hubbard, Roger Matthews, Jane Scoular & Laura Agustín, 'Away from Prying Eyes? The Urban Geographies of "Adult Entertainment"', *Progress in Human Geography*, vol. 32, no. 3, 2008.

15 Arnberg, 2010, pp. 239–41.

16 SOU 1976:9, Sexualbrottsutredningen, *Sexuella övergrepp: förslag till ny lydelse av brottsbalkens bestämmelser om sedlighetsbrott: betänkande/avgivet av Sexualbrottsutredningen*, Stockholm, 1976.

17 Walter Kendrick, *The Secret Museum: Pornography in Modern Culture*, Berkeley, CA: University of California Press, 1996 [1987], pp. 213–40.

18 Linda Williams, 'Porn Studies: Proliferating Pornographies On/Scene: An Introduction', in Linda Williams (ed.), *Porn Studies*, Durham, NC: Duke University Press, 2005.

19 Williams, 1999. To only name a few significant works here: Thomas Waugh, *Hard to Imagine: Gay Male Eroticism in Photography and Film From Their Beginnings to Stonewall*, New York: Columbia University Press, 1996; Laura Kipnis, *Bound and Gagged: Pornography and the Politics of Fantasy in America*, New York: Grove Press, 1996; Jane Juffer, *At Home with Pornography: Women, Sex, and Everyday Life*, New York: New York University Press, 1998; Williams, 2004; Peter Lehman (ed.), *Pornography: Film and Culture*, New Brunswick, NC: Rutgers University Press, 2006; Clarissa Smith, *One for the Girls!: The Pleasures and Practices of Reading Women's Porn*, Bristol: Intellect, 2007; Tristan Taormino, Celine Parreñas Shimizu, Constance Penley & Mireille Miller-Young (eds), *The Feminist Porn Book: The Politics of Producing Pleasure*, New York: The Feminist Press, 2013; *Porn Studies Journal*, vol. 1, nos 1–2, 2014; Tim Dean, Steven Ruszczycky & David Squires (eds), *Porn Archives*, Durham, NC & London: Duke University Press, 2014; Enrico Biasin, Giovanna Maina & Federico Zecca (eds), *Porn After Porn: Contemporary Alternative Pornographies*, Mimesis International, 2014.

20 Linda Williams, 'Pornography, Porno, Porn: Thoughts on a Weedy Field', *Porn Studies Journal*, vol. 1, no. 1–2, 2014.

21 Some exceptions are Stevenson (2010) and Schaefer (2014), although these two works focus foremost on general sex films rather than specifically pornography. This is also true of Elisabet Björklund & Mariah Larsson (2016).

22 For instance, Mats Björkin, 'Fäbodjäntan: Sex, Communication and Cultural Heritage', in Alf Björnberg (ed.), Frispel: festskrift till Olle Edström, Göteborg: Institutionen för musikvetenskap, 2005; Per Olov Qvist & Tytti Soila, 'Eva – den utstötta/Swedish and Underage', in T. Soila (ed.), The Cinema of Scandinavia, London: Wallflower Press, 2005.

23 Leif Furhammar, Filmen i Sverige: En historia i tio kapitel, Höganäs: Wiken, 1991, pp. 328–29.

24 Lena Lennerhed, 'Fäbodjäntan och hennes systrar', in Lars Åhlander (ed.), Svensk filmografi 7: 1970-1979, Stockholm: Norstedts (SFI), 1989.

25 See, for instance, two notable authorities on the subject: Andrew Higson, 'The Concept of National Cinema', in Alan Williams (ed.), Film and Nationalism, New Brunswick, NJ: Rutgers University Press, 2002, pp. 52–53; and Thomas Elsaesser, European Cinema: Face to Face with Hollywood, Amsterdam: Amsterdam University Press, 2005, p. 37.

26 Furhammar, 1991, pp. 328–29.

27 Bertil Wredlund & Rolf Lindfors, Långfilm i Sverige 7: 1970–1979, Stockholm: Proprius, 1983.

28 Bertil Wredlund & Torsten Jungstedt, Filmårsboken: 1971/72, Stockholm: Proprius, 1972; Bertil Wredlund & Torsten Jungstedt, Filmårsboken: 1973/74, Stockholm: Proprius, 1974.

29 Eric Schaefer, 'Plain Brown Wrapper: Adult Films for the Home Market, 1930–1969', in Jon Lewis & Eric Smoodin (eds), Looking Past the Screen: Case Studies in American Film History and Method, Durham, NC & London: Duke University Press, 2007, p. 202.

30 The concept of 'pornotopia' is used by Steven Marcus in The Other Victorians: A Study of Sexuality and Pornography in Mid-Nineteenth Century England, London: Weidenfeld & Nicolson, 1966, although with a different meaning than what is implied here. However, 'pornotopia' has since been used in various contexts with various significances.

31 Linda Williams, 'Film Bodies: Gender, Genre, and Excess', Film Quarterly, vol. 44, no. 4, 1991.

32 Williams, 1991, p. 4.

33 Cf. Erick Janssen, Deanna Carpenter & Cynthia A. Graham, 'Selecting Films for Sex Research: Gender Differences in Erotic Film Preference', Archives of Sexual Behavior, vol. 32, no. 3, 2003.

34 Susanna Paasonen, Carnal Resonance: Affect and Online Pornography, Cambridge, MA: MIT Press, 2011, pp. 8–15.

35 Paasonen, 2011, pp. 16–19.

36 Vivian Sobchack, Carnal Thoughts: Embodiment and Moving Image Culture, Berkeley, CA: University of California Press, 2004; Paasonen, 2011; Ingrid Ryberg, Imagining Safe Space: The Politics of Queer, Feminist, and Lesbian Pornography, Stockholm: Stockholm University, 2012.

37 John H. Gagnon & William Simon, Sexual Conduct: The Social Sources of Human Sexuality, Chicago, IL: Aldine Pub. Co., 2005 [1973].

38 Erving Goffman, The Presentation of Self in Everyday Life, London: Penguin, 1990 [1959].

39 William Simon & John H. Gagnon, 'Sexual Scripts: Permanence and Change', *Archives of Sexual Behavior*, vol. 15, no. 2, 1986.

40 Gagnon & Simon, 2005.

41 Arnberg, 2010.

42 Gayle Rubin, 'Thinking Sex: Notes for a Radical Theory on the Politics of Sexuality', in Carol Vance (ed.), *Pleasure and Danger: Exploring Female Sexuality*, Boston, MA: Routledge, 1984; Jane Gerhard, *Desiring Revolution: Second-wave Feminism and the Rewriting of American Sexual Thought, 1920 to 1982*, New York: Columbia University Press, 2001.

43 Cf. Lisa Duggan & Nan D. Hunter, *Sex Wars: Sexual Dissent and Political Culture* (10th anniversary edition), New York: Routledge, 2006. A discussion of the Swedish relationship to the American debate can be found in Per Båvner, 'En reproducerad debatt. Svenska ståndpunkter om pornografi' in *Res Publica*, vol. 43, no. 1, 1999.

44 Cf. Ebba Witt-Brattström, *Å alla kära systrar!: historien om mitt sjuttiotal*, Stockholm: Norstedt, 2010; Gunilla Thorgren, *Grupp 8 & jag*, Stockholm: Norstedt, 2003.

45 SOU 1969:14, Filmcensurutredningen, *Filmen – censur och ansvar: betänkande*, Stockholm, 1969; SOU 1969:38, Kommittén för lagstiftningen om yttrande-och tryckfrihet, *Yttrandefrihetens gränser: sårande av tukt och sedlighet: brott mot trosfrid: betänkande*, Stockholm, 1969.

46 I made it known that I was interested in interviewees in various ways: when I gave public talks, on my blog and when I spoke to journalists.

47 The interviews were used in two dissertations which were published in the early 1980s: Sven-Axel Månsson, *Könshandelns främjare och profitörer: om förhållandet mellan hallick och prostituerad*, Lund: Doxa, 1981; and Stig Larsson, *Könshandeln: om prostituerades villkor*, Stockholm: Skeab förlag, 1983.

48 Rick Altman, *Film/Genre*, London: BFI Publishing, 1999.

49 Marilyn Adler Papayanis, 'Sex and the Revanchist City: Zoning Out Pornography in New York', *Environment and Planning D: Society and Space*, vol. 18, 2000.

50 Schaefer, 'Plain Brown Wrapper', 2007.

Chapter 1

Sexually explicit films and the welfare state(s)

The international reputation of Scandinavian countries has been accounted for and understood in terms of an ambivalent sense of fascination with and anxiety surrounding sexuality and the welfare state – not to mention as mysterious countries in Northern Europe with midnight sun, Vikings and *smorgasbord*.[1] Sexuality became a symbol for how the welfare state – situated geographically, as well as ideologically, ambiguously between the blocs of the Cold War – removed all traces of individuality and privacy from citizens by appropriating and colonizing that which is most intimate and personal.[2] Conversely, from a progressive perspective, Scandinavian sexuality could be regarded as an ideal of modernity.[3]

Nevertheless, the national, internal logic of the development of a particularly liberal relationship to sexuality is harder to pinpoint. This is because the image of Sweden and Denmark as more or less void of sexual repression is paradoxically both incorrect (obviously, there was and still is repression in both of these countries) and the result of reflections on developments that took place mainly after World War II. In addition, and as I will try to demonstrate throughout this book, the notion of sexual liberation carries with it several inherent contradictions or tensions. Michel Foucault has criticized what he terms the 'repression hypothesis' – i.e. that sexuality is a natural force that is repressed in society and sexual liberation thus emancipates that natural force.[4] Sexuality, repression and power are all produced in and by an intricate network of discourse; accordingly, 'liberation' is just as constructed by a social discourse as repression is. Although this is to some extent a problematic explanatory framework that does not really take sides with reproductive rights, gay rights or laws against marital rape and abuse, for instance, it has the advantage of being able to contain the various paradoxes that keep appearing as one continues to study the history of sexuality, obscenity and pornography.

One example is how homosexuality has been constructed institutionally. Although homosexuality was decriminalized in Sweden in 1944, it was classified as a mental illness until 1979, and the age of consent for homosexual acts remained eighteen until the 1980s, whereas for heterosexual acts it was fifteen. In 1987, as a response to the fear of the spread of HIV, the so-called 'sauna law' [*bastulagen*] was passed, criminalizing sauna clubs for men who had sex with men. This law remained until 2004.

As in the case of pornography, Denmark preceded Sweden by decriminalizing homosexuality in 1933, and making the age of consent for heterosexual and homosexual acts the same in 1977. Although Scandinavian legalization occurs earlier than in many other western countries (for example, Great Britain and East and West Germany did not legalize homosexuality until the late 1960s), homosexuality is quite invisible within Swedish sex films, which are blatantly heterosexual. *Mera ur kärlekens språk/More About the Language of Love* (Torgny Wickman, 1970), the sequel to the successful sex education film *Kärlekens språk/Language of Love* (Torgny Wickman, 1969), presented homo- and bisexuality as well as transvestism. However, as the first film exclusively represented heterosexual relations and the second film concluded with heterosexual intercourse, thereby 'reestablishing the idea that heterosexuality is the signifier of natural sexuality', the films still quite clearly follow a heteronormative logic.[5] In 1977, a 21-minute documentary called *Bögjävlar/Damned Queers* (Gunnar Almér et al.) was produced, describing life in a gay collective in Stockholm. A few lesbian films were also made, but gays and lesbians were sorely underrepresented in feature-length films, except in girl-on-girl scenes in heterosexual material.[6] Of the 8mm films, some titles among the censorship records indicate that they depict male-to-male sex, but these are quite rare compared to the mass of heterosexual films. While Sweden was perceived of as a sexual paradise (or nightmare), this perception was also heterosexual, and could even be described as an international male gaze at a femininely gendered nation/object, where female models and actresses embodied the projection of the national.

The welfare state's relationship to sexuality, sexual liberation and sexually explicit film is the subject of this chapter. In *Porno? Chic!*, Brian McNair argues that the same development that legalized pornography led to greater progress with women's and gays' civil rights.[7] Consequently, he argues, to be open to sexual imagery goes hand in hand with being open to gender equality and sexual citizenship. Trying this argument against the Swedish case, it is correct that the same discussions that led to legal and free abortion in Sweden in 1975, and to changing views on homosexuality, also led to the legalization of pornography. It is also interesting to note that the removal of the obscenity clause predated the other changes. However, when porn was decriminalized, many pro-porn intellectuals in Sweden were disappointed because they had thought that by being openly and legally available to everyone, pornography would somehow improve.[8] The disillusionment with which they witnessed the expansion of clubs, stores, prostitution and pornography would colour much of the debate on pornography in the late 1970s and 1980s, and may have also contributed to the staunch anti-porn movement in Sweden during the 1980s and 1990s. When McNair contends – and, in my opinion, he is somewhat right – that the proliferation of pornographies today comes out of the legalization of porn and more liberal attitudes towards it, he seems to be confirming the utopian vision that the pro-porn intellectuals in Sweden had in the 1960s; it is just that it took much longer than they expected. Pornography became the catalyst for the women's movement, which in turn, through its criticism of porn's sexism, objectification and exploitation, eventually spawned a radical activist movement that attempted to create a feminist pornography. This process could be described as a kind of dialectics of pornography. As McNair observes, a climate that allows pornography also allows discussion about sexual issues in general. This discussion is not unusually provoked by pornography. As with the sex wars that took place in the United States in the 1980s, they were sparked by pornography but came to deal with many other things, such as freedom of expression, women's, gays' and lesbians' rights, and various variations of sexuality such as fetishism and BDSM.[9]

In the Swedish context, the welfare state's relationship to pornography initially developed through a rational yet utopian perspective by which sexual liberation is a good idea (at least theoretically) as long as it is accompanied by the dispersal of knowledge and common sense. In the early 1970s, legalization in itself led to disenchantment with how prostitution, exploitation and human misery seemed to follow in its wake. The women's movement reacted strongly to the presence of sexual objectification in public space, and took on a struggle against pornography as the 'most extreme deformed variety of oppression' that extended over several decades.[10]

Sexual utopianism, film as art and the potentials of pornography

There is an element of utopianism in the Swedish sexuality debates of the 1960s. In the 1930s, when RFSU – the Swedish Association of Sexuality Education – was formed, the issues that concerned educators and activists were information and availability of birth control, limiting the spread of venereal disease and the right to sex education.[11] Although informing about birth control and distributing condoms or diaphragms remained illegal, the early sex debates focused to a large extent on incorporating education and access to contraceptives into the welfare state's project for improving the lives of the poor and the working classes. The discussion led to changes in legislation. For example, in 1938, it became legal to inform about birth control and in 1946 pharmacies became obliged by law to carry contraceptives. In 1955, sex education in schools became mandatory.

However, in the early 1960s, Katarina Ahlmark-Michanek, in the book *Jungfrutro och dubbelmoral*/'Virgin Belief and Double Standards', attacked this education because, as she claimed, it disseminated a double standard regarding gendered sexual behaviour.[12] Ahlmark-Michanek was only one of several participants in the sex debates of the 1960s. As the topic of her book illustrates, these debates concerned different issues than those of the 1930s. Other books discussed the rights of sexual minorities, including Henning Pallesen's *De avvikande*/'The Deviants', and Lars Ullenstam's *De erotiska minoriterna*/*The Erotic Minorities: A Swedish View*.[13] Journalists, young politicians, students of medicine, sociologists and other intellectuals participated in these discussions, as well as discussions on the right to abortion and the censorship of sexually explicit material.

As historian of ideas Lena Lennerhed has observed, men dominated the debate about sexuality in Sweden in the 1960s. Ahlmark-Michanek was one exception. Another important exception was Nina Estin, who made an attempt at promoting a (softcore) porn magazine for women, *Expedition 66*. *Expedition 66* can be regarded as an experiment that combined the sex debate with another public discussion that loomed large around the same time: sex roles. The liberal and emancipatory perspective of the sex roles debate would only be superseded a few years later by second-wave feminism,[14] which grounded its analysis of patriarchy in socialist thought and Marxist ideas. Estin's experiment questioned the notion that only men liked to watch, that only men were allowed to take sexual initiatives, and that men could not be objects of desire for women. The magazine combined photographs with articles discussing gender political issues, but struggled both with finding a readership and with finding male models, so was discontinued after only four issues.

Nevertheless, the sex debate was largely held by men. What can be added to this characterization of the participants in the debate is that not only were they men, they were decidedly educated, middle class and (at least openly) heterosexual – even those writing about sexual minorities. Again, there are some exceptions, such as Lars Görling, the author of *491*, the 1962 novel that was adapted into the film *491* (Vilgot Sjöman, 1964). Görling had a criminal record and raged against the censorship of the film because it was, as he called it, a 'prohibition of reality'.[15] Nevertheless, Görling can be said to be at the margins of the sexuality debates, because although the film *491* became important in the liberalization of film censorship of sexually explicit material, his direct contribution to the debate focused more on the censoring of a raw and brutal reality than on sexuality per se.

In addition, the discourse was liberal in tone, expressing a kind of rationality that exuded an attitude which might most accurately be described as superior. The men who discussed sexuality did so with science on their side – references to Kinsey's research results are common – and with a detached and disinterested distance. For instance, as Don Kulick has observed, the idea of state brothels was discussed as a possibility. Young men would save time, worn-out housewives would get relief from their needy husbands, and people with disabilities or lonely people would find an outlet for sexual needs and comfort.[16] If the brothels were run by the government, they would be controlled environments and decrease the risk of sexually transmitted infections. Although these ideas were met with scepticism by public opinion, their mere occurrence in the public debate is telling of the discourse of the time,[17] where rationality, common sense, scientific references and a notion of a utopian welfare world where all needs are taken care of characterized the debate.

Nonetheless, the high-minded liberalness of the debaters was grounded in what comes across as a sense of paternalism: they are not explicitly speaking on behalf of themselves, but for other less-fortunate fellow men. Moreover, the arguments are strikingly void of any analysis of subject-object relations, perceptions of unequal power balance (most apparent in the discussions of paedophilia), and reflections on gender and gender equality.

Censorship and obscenity

Simultaneously, an attack on the National Board of Film Censors was orchestrated, more or less consciously, by Ingmar Bergman and Harry Schein, the head of the Swedish Film Institute. Started in 1963 as the result of a new Swedish film policy, the Swedish Film Institute's objectives were to stimulate the production of quality films; to create a good film cultural climate; to promote Swedish film abroad; to work to preserve Swedish film heritage; and to do research on issues surrounding film. Essentially a foundation that received its money (at this point in time) from a 10 per cent fee on admission charges to practically all cinemas in Sweden, the Swedish Film Institute can be regarded as a consolidation of the perception and acceptance of film as a potential art form. Schein had argued that Swedish film needed more film-makers like Ingmar Bergman in order to thrive, whose critical success abroad generated both box-office revenues and cultural capital. Consequently, successful exportation of films could compensate for the small domestic market.[18]

This might seem far removed from the production of the sexually explicit films that would begin from the mid-sixties onwards. However, with the appreciation of film as an art form came the presumption that art should not be censored. Although produced and released before the new Swedish film policy, Bergman's *Jungfrukällan/The Virgin Spring* (1960) stirred up controversy due to its violent imagery, some of it in connection to the rape of the young titular virgin. The greatest injury to the National Board of Film Censors, however, came with Bergman's *Tystnaden/The Silence* in 1963 and Sjöman's *491* the same year. *The Silence* was passed with no cuts, even though it featured masturbation and casual sex, and it would become 'SF's biggest success ever up to that time. It was not until his immensely popular TV series *Scenes from a Marriage* [*Scener ur ett äktenskap*, 1973] that Bergman was to reach such a large audience, and this for his most inaccessible film to date'.[19] The debate surrounding the censorship decision led to publicity which in turn attracted spectators, and although most 'intellectual heavyweights'[20] seemed to be in agreement that the scenes were borne out of a narrative and thematic logic, and thus not speculative or motivated by a wish to profit on them, Maaret Koskinen demonstrates convincingly that Bergman was very aware of the effects of the sex scenes.[21]

As mentioned earlier, the film *491* was adapted from a novel by Lars Görling, and although directed by Vilgot Sjöman, was made on the initiative of Bergman.[22] Sjöman was a novelist and writer who ventured into film directing in the early 1960s. Bergman can be said to have functioned as Sjöman's mentor, helping him gain entry into film-making by placing him as a director's assistant on *Nattvardsgästerna/Winter Light* (1963), where he published a diary from the set. Although Sjöman is sometimes described as Bergman's disciple, he developed his own distinct directing style, as well as his own collection of themes and motifs. In *491*, the theme of forgiveness is explored – the title refers to the New Testament in the Bible, where Jesus explains that you should forgive your enemies not seven times, but seven times seventy (490) times. In both the novel and the film, the question is asked: what happens the 491st time? A group of juvenile delinquents are subject to an experimental treatment where they are allowed a certain measure of freedom. Nevertheless, they again and again transgress the boundaries for decent behaviour, and the film depicts drinking, homosexual abuse of the juveniles by the inspectors, rape and one instance of bestiality.

The National Board of Film Censors banned *491*, that is, the film was prohibited from public screening. This decision was appealed to the government, and after a few edits, the government gave the film permission to be screened. The prolonged process caused a long-lasting debate in Swedish media, even leading to the formation of a new political party – the Christian Democrats – who protested the deterioration of public morals.[23] Nonetheless, the fact that the film was banned by the National Board of Film Censors but allowed (with some changes) by the government became a precedent that suggested the government was more liberal than the Board.

The National Board of Film Censors had been introduced in 1911. Censorship of moving images became possible through the Cinema Act, which became an exception to the laws sustaining freedom of expression because film was regarded as so potentially harmful, particularly to young people. As such, the Board also rated films. To begin with there was only one age limit of fifteen; through the years, the age limits of eleven (1960) and seven (1978) were added. In 2011, the Board was abolished, but the rating of films for people younger than fifteen continues through the work of the Swedish Media Council (Statens medieråd). If a film is intended for an audience younger than fifteen, it has to go through the Swedish Media Council.[24]

Films were not only rated, but also cut if they were found to contain images that were perceived of as 'harmfully exciting' or 'brutalizing', or if they transgressed other laws and regulations; they could also be prohibited from public screening. Therefore, until 1971, any film containing obscene material would be censored or disallowed on the grounds that it would offend common morals ('såra tukt och sedlighet') in accordance with the Obscenity Law.[25] This was a limit that was pushed again and again during the 1960s, with reference to film as art and film as representing an authentic reality. That it could be pushed had both to do with an increasing regard and respect for the moving image as an art form and as potentially important social commentary, and with the debate occurring simultaneously around sexuality.

In 1964, the government instigated a public inquiry on the existence of film censorship, which would eventually be presented in 1969. In order to discover whether film censorship was necessary, a research group was formed by the newly-founded Swedish Film Institute. The leader of this group was Harry Schein, whose purpose was quite clear: film should not be subjected to censorship.[26] As he wrote in his reminiscence of the first seven years of the new Swedish film policy, *I själva verket: Sju års filmpolitik/*'In Fact: Seven Years of Film Policy':

> Obviously, research would be free – anything else would not have been accepted by the researchers and the members of the film research group. However, it was my opinion that, in light of the main objective of the research group, it would be a good thing if the researchers were radical.[27]

As Per Vesterlund has demonstrated, the research group ultimately concluded that Schein's anti-censorship view was correct.[28]

The results of the research group were incorporated into the public inquiry into film censorship, which found that sexually explicit material in films was on the whole probably quite harmless. For instance, a causal relationship between sexually explicit images and sex crimes could not be found, nor between such images and a 'disturbed sexual life'.[29] Nevertheless, the inquiry was careful to point out that there was not enough research on purely pornographic films to say anything about the possible effects on human beings.

Interestingly from a contemporary perspective, the inquiry stated that sexually explicit material in films was most likely not harmful to children either, at least not to 'well-adjusted' children.[30] However, the inquiry suggested that sexually explicit material, especially such material that might have 'a sadistic character', should be restricted, since it might counter the objective sex education that was striven for in schools and disturb the 'natural' sexual development of young people in puberty.[31] Violence, on the other hand, was deemed more potentially dangerous for mentally unstable individuals.[32] Nevertheless, on the whole, the inquiry proposed to abandon film censorship for grown-ups.

Simultaneously, another inquiry studied freedom of expression, proposing an abolishment of the obscenity clause that had been located in the penal code since 1964.[33] The public inquiry into freedom of expression had cooperated with the film censorship inquiry and had access to the results of the Swedish Film Institute's research group. In this inquiry, it was concluded that:

> There is no scientific evidence for the perception that the increased supply of pornography and representations with violent elements have a stimulating effect on crime, at least not for normal individuals. However, neither is there any evidence that pornography and representations of violence are absolutely harmless.[34]

Consequently, the inquiry proposed that the obscenity clause be removed, but that an 'outer limit' should be provided regarding the most violent and 'perverse' material.[35]

When these two inquiries were presented within only a couple of months of each other, they were, in accordance with the usual procedure, submitted for review by various organizations and groups who had a particular expert knowledge in the area, or whose activities might be influenced by the proposals. For some reason, the proposals of the inquiry into film censorship were discarded, whereas the proposal of the inquiry into freedom of expression was accepted – albeit to an even greater extent than the inquiry had suggested, with the outer limit being deemed unnecessary by the government.[36] In this manner, film censorship was retained, but the instructions of the Board meant that obscene material could no longer be censored with reference to the law.[37] During the 1970s, pornography and sexually explicit material was thus unrestrained by law, whereas the Board edited and disallowed films containing violence, particularly violence in connection with sexually explicit and pornographic material, which was considered 'brutalizing'.

So, while Ingmar Bergman made and encouraged the making of films that would challenge the film censorship institution and provide a precedent for later films, Harry Schein worked behind the scenes, so to speak, in order to provide the scholarly, scientific and political grounds for new legislation. Schein could do this since, as Vesterlund and Maaret Koskinen have both observed, he was a master of networking: not only was Schein a Social Democrat, he famously played tennis with Olof Palme, was friends with Ingmar Bergman and married to Ingrid Thulin, who acted in several Bergman films. Several of his fellow Social Democrats of the same generation held posts within the government, so Schein was well placed to blend the social/personal and the professional/political in an enterprise that was partly lobbying and partly executed on his own.[38]

Writing in this case not on censorship but Swedish film policy and the Film Institute, Vesterlund states that:

Social Democracy, the culture, and the industry – the three fields in which Schein was active gave him no doubt both proficiency and positions that could be transposed in his film policy program. [...] Above all, [in the carrying out of the new film policy] there are traces of Schein's ability to dissolve the borders between them as well as the borders between the private, the public, and the professional.[39]

The sex film in the welfare state

The debates around sexuality, the liberalization of film censorship and the initiation of the inquiries that led to the abolishment of the obscenity clause in the penal code all happened around the period 1962–65. Yet changes in legislation lagged behind both the opinion and the progression of sex stores, pornographic magazines and sexually explicit films that began to be established, published and released in the period between 1965 and 1970. The peak for pornographic magazines in Sweden came before pornography was legalized (1969–70).[40] Similarly, the peak for feature-length, theatrically released, sexually explicit 35mm films came in 1970.[41] The open climate and the knowledge of a forthcoming change in legislation allowed for the production of sex films, including sexploitation, softcore sex comedies and sex education films. With the Danish/Swedish film *Jag – en kvinna/I, a Woman* (Mac Ahlberg, 1965), a new kind of Swedish cinema began to be made. Between 1965 and 1975, a number of films were released which had sex and nudity as their main focus, and which took advantage of liberalized censorship. Some of them also took advantage of a sexually liberal discourse. Although *I, a Woman* was based on a Danish novel by Siv Holm, its narrative echoed themes from another film, *För vänskaps skull*/'For the Sake of Friendship' (Hans Abramson, 1965), written by Katarina Ahlmark-Michanek and based on her previously mentioned book *Jungfrutro och dubbelmoral*. In both films, a young woman attempts to live her erotic life outside of the social norms that govern women's sexual behaviour.[42]

This tendency to pick up themes in the contemporary sex debates is even more pronounced in Torgny Wickman's didactic films – that is, not just his sex education films in the *Language of Love* series, but films like *Eva – den utstötta/Swedish and Underage* (1969) and *Anita – ur en tonårsflickas dagbok/Swedish Nymphet* (1973) – which seem to align themselves with the same kind of plea for knowledge and tolerance that was made by the participants in the sex debate. By spreading knowledge and dispelling prejudice, puritan morals and double standards, and by preaching tolerance and understanding, sex debaters like Lars Ulvenstam and Henning Pallesen claimed that society would become a better place. Meanwhile, Wickman's *Kyrkoherden/The Lustful Vicar* (1970) makes fun of the clergy and can therefore, although less directly, be connected to a critique of religious bigotry and a sexuality inhibited by Christian morality.

What a film like *Ur kärlekens språk/Language of Love* (Wickman, 1969) (as well as the later films in the *Language of Love* series) demonstrate with all desired clarity, however, is the paradox that sexuality, pornography and sexually explicit material compelled within the welfare state. In her dissertation on sex education films in Sweden, Elisabet Björklund uncovers the production context of *Language of Love*, where repeated offers were made to the National Association for Sex Education (RFSU) to participate in the making of the film.[43] These offers were rejected, most likely because the organization was worried that they would have too little influence on its form and content, that it was a commercial enterprise and that it would too much resemble pornography.[44] Nevertheless, Maj-Briht Bergström-Walan – a well-established sex expert who was active in RFSU – decided to partake in the project, and was subsequently not re-elected for her post on the board.[45] Björklund relates this to RFSU's weakening position at that time. During the sex debates of the 1960s, RFSU did not have a strong voice, which had to do with a crisis within the organization. At the same time, however, RFSU was well-established and respected by official authorities, and also had a reputation to protect.[46]

Nonetheless, the refusal of RFSU to take part in the making of *Language of Love* may also have to do with a slowly surfacing suspicion that sexual liberation might not work as a sexual welfare project. Not only was RFSU reluctant to be associated with pornography, but the developing sexual landscape that came with the increasing liberalness of the late 1960s was distrusted by many later on. On the one hand, *Language of Love* was everything a national association of sex education could ask for: a popular feature length film that not only explained certain anatomical and medical facts about sexuality, but additionally sought to provide a sex-positive atmosphere. It had the potential to be – and would also become – a widely seen film that could spread knowledge and understanding to a large amount of people. Although the film by today's sex educational standards can be (and is) judged as extremely heteronormative, it encompasses several of the sexually radical ideas of the 1960s.[47]

In addition, revenues from the film were used to set up Svenska sexualforskningsinstitutet (the Swedish Institute for Sex Research), with Bergström-Walan as manager.[48] However:

> [...] at the heart of the controversy around the *Language of Love* films was not only the issue of explicit representations of sex or a traditionally negative view on the medium of cinema, but also a disbelief in the ability of the commercial market to provide reliable sex education.[49]

The right to speak, disseminate views and produce discourse on sexuality was by this time already beginning to be contested and defended. As Björklund phrases it: 'For the heads of the RFSU, it may have been crucial to guard their territory and their status as the "official" experts on sex, when a commercial film company with seemingly pornographic interests threatened to exploit their domain'.[50] The divide between the RFSU and the producers behind *Language of Love* can thus be said to point forward to the divide between what would be regarded as sexual welfare and what would be understood as exploitation; between social workers and prostitution; and between the feminist movement and pornography. At the same time, the participation of Maj-Briht Bergström-Walan indicates that this divide was not a simple one.

Commercial exploitation, social vulnerability and the objectification of women

In the 1977 foreword to *Svensk filmografi 6: 1960–1969*, Harry Schein wrote about the liberalization of film censorship:

> [T]he borders were stretched from female breasts to female genitalia, from just a penis to a fully erect one, to sexual intercourse. [...] As soon as a respected film-maker had conquered new territory this was occupied by a less regarded one. 'Why cannot I show what Bergman can show', was the eternal question that never could be answered.[51]

In this text, Schein seems to lament a change that he himself was an instrumental part of. Of course, writing with hindsight provides a different perspective. The proponents of the abolishment of censorship anticipated certain outcomes which ultimately they did not find realized. However, the disappointment cannot simply be ascribed to an undesired development of porn rather than the desired explicit art; it also had to do with shifting discourses that took their starting point in the pre-1960s' view of sexually explicit material for its own sake as trash, but which invested this view with political ideals such as gender equality and anti-exploitation.

By 1977, the work of social officers, debating and demonstrating feminists, journalists and politicians had led to a perception of all kinds of commercial sexuality as something bad and undesired in a welfare society. In the investigation *Svarta affärer* in 1976, sociologists criticized the 'commercialization of interpersonal relations'.[52] Journalist Göran Skytte published a series of articles in the 1979 book *Porrens profitörer*/'The Profiteers of Porn' which became an attack on prostitution and pornography.[53] Hans Nestius, who in addition to working for legal abortions in Sweden in the 1960s was an active supporter of the legalization of pornography, became chair of RFSU in 1979. His motto as chair was 'Death to pornography, long live the erotic image'. According to Nestius, legalization did not lead to 'an explosion of wonderful images, but the wave of porn that washed over us was porn by men for men, where woman served the man on his terms'.[54] In 1982, Nestius published a book entitled *I last och lust: sexuella bilder förr och nu*/'In Vice and Pleasure: Sexual Images Before and Now', juxtaposing commercial, pornographic and therefore 'bad' images of sex with artistic, erotic and therefore 'good' images of sex.[55] This book has recently (2014) been removed from the shelves of libraries since it contains child pornography (representing the bad kind of sexual imagery) and is thus illegal.[56] Nestius was extremely disappointed with the direction that pornography had taken in the 1970s.

In addition to – and probably also influencing – these examples, the women's movement had been adamant in its resistance to pornography since at least 1973. Although 'sex roles' had already been discussed in Sweden in the early 1960s – usually from a liberal, emancipatory perspective, which included both men and women – the starting point for the women's movement is most often claimed to be 1968, when Grupp 8 ('Group 8') was formed. Grupp 8 – and the other women's groups which followed – brought their inspiration from the left movement and grounded their analysis of patriarchy in socialism.[57] Patriarchy and capitalism were mutually dependent on one another, and only in a classless, socialist society would women be truly free and independent. Solidarity and sisterhood were key slogans. If Anglo-American feminists saw some kind of hope for sexual exploration and emancipation in the burgeoning experimental production of pornography and erotic films,[58] Swedish second-wave feminists were sceptical towards pornography early on, and after 1968, pornography began to be defined as 'degradation of women for profit', perpetually objectifying and reifying the female body, denying her an agency and a desire of her own.[59] The effects of pornography were regarded as so harmful that the Swedish women's movement adopted the Robin Morgan dictum that 'porn is the theory, rape the practice', eventually reborn in the 1980s as the statement that pornography provided a handbook for and instruction in violence against and oppression of women.[60]

When the obscenity clause in the penal code was removed, a prohibition of display replaced it, with the purpose of confining the visuals of pornographic and obscene material to the inside of stores and clubs. Such laws and regulations became an attempt in many other countries to contain the visceral nature of much sexual material, and offered a choice: you can consume it if you want to, but you should not have to see it if it is objectionable to you. An important concern for this containment in France and the United Kingdom was children.[61] In Sweden, however, children were not regarded as in need of protection from sexually explicit material to the same extent, and some groups initially found that the prohibition of display was not observed and offenders were not prosecuted.[62]

The book *Kvinnor och sex*/'Women and Sex' (1973) by Maud Hägg and Barbro Werkmäster claimed that pornography was 'woman splayed across the altar of patriarchy and capitalism',[63] while *Kvinnobulletinen*, Grupp 8's monthly journal, attacked the commercialism and capitalist exploitation of sexual entertainment and merchandise, which they called 'money between a woman's legs'.[64] The stage performance *Kärleksföreställningen* (a play with words that can mean both 'The Love Performance' and 'The Conception of Love') was produced by Suzanne Osten and Margareta Garpe in 1973, expressing a critique of pornography and young women's magazines as perpetuating false notions of love, sexuality and intimate relations. Romantic and sentimental imaginings of the women's magazines were juxtaposed with the brutal animalism of pornography, and both were explained as providing young men and women with incorrect and unrealistic conceptions of how to interact with one another, and how intimate relationships should be.[65]

The feminist or women's perspective gained momentum during the mid-1970s. In 1976, feminism won support as the public inquiry on sex crime was published, proposing, for instance, lowered penalties for rape, a more narrow definition of rape and a lowering of the age of consent to fourteen.[66] The sex crime inquiry claimed that the whole notion of *sedlighet* (morality, in keeping with good and common standards) was an old-fashioned, moralist concept, and that the law thus needed changing in order to keep up with the times. However, the critique of an old-fashioned sexual moral – that women should remain chaste and that sexuality was something inherently bad – was coupled with a perspective of male sexual privilege. Notions of women's agency and free will, as well as the aspect of power in relation to young people and children, were suspended. Accordingly, the sex crime inquiry seems to have been both a peak and turning point for sexual liberalization in Sweden. Upon publication, the sex crime inquiry was met with outrage not only by existing organised feminists but by other people as well, and public discourse began to question and renegotiate the meaning of sexual liberation. It was debated on the editorial pages in *Dagens Nyheter*, Sweden's largest daily newspaper, and the journalist Maria-Pia Boëthius wrote a series of articles in the evening newspaper *Expressen* (as well as a book) describing and discussing a number of women's experiences of rape.[67] Although some members of the inquiry committee attempted to defend the inquiry, it was eventually scrapped and a new sex crime inquiry committee was appointed.[68]

Consequently, 1976 seems like a watershed year, when the development of an increasing sexual liberation that started in the 1950s was replaced by one of increasing restrictions on sexuality and a questioning of previous ideas that had driven liberalization. As Boëthius wrote:

> We have, gratefully, become more liberal in our view of sexuality. Even though my opinion is that this 'liberal' view of sex in many cases has had the result that women have been exploited and ended up in the wrong place. But this – that we have a more liberal view of sex – should it mean that we also get a more liberal view of sexual abuse? Absolutely not, I think.[69]

Boëthius' conception of the increasingly liberal view of sexuality touches upon what was expressed by American anti-porn feminist Catherine MacKinnon and other feminists alike: that sexual liberation in a society of male domination created a situation whereby women were exploited and could not say no to sex.[70] Nonetheless, Boëthius does not reject the notion of sexual liberation but attempts instead to nuance it and describe where a reasonable line could be drawn; whilst a liberal view on sex between consenting adults may be problematic, it is nevertheless still beneficial, however, there should never be a liberal view of sexual abuse. In addition, Boëthius, like several other anti-porn feminists, saw pornography and prostitution as logically connected to rape, conveying the message, as did the sex crime inquiry, that women's bodies were available to an uncontrollable male sexuality.[71]

In the 1950s and 1960s, it had been the Christian and Free Church movements that had resisted and protested pornography on moral grounds.[72] To be against pornography during those years was to align oneself with puritanism and conservatism. However, as the women's movement formulated a different kind of criticism based on ideas of gender equality and an ideological analysis of patriarchal capitalism, the anti-porn movement became not only possible, but necessary for people who would describe themselves as radical or left-leaning to embrace. Interestingly, the equivalent shift in ideological discourse did not occur in Denmark, where a liberal conception of the freedom of expression was prioritized by the left and the women's movement.[73]

In the Swedish analysis, however, pornography became the ultimate expression of the commodification of the female body and sexuality. Through its production, it exploited, degraded and abused women; through its consumption, it taught men to regard women as dehumanized, available sex objects; through its distribution, it suffused public space with images of objectified, stereotyped women, creating an environment which was hostile to women. Focusing on the American and British anti-porn movement, Lynne Segal has argued that they privileged a very literal reading of pornography, basing their politics on 'assumptions of fixed identities and aspirations' without taking into account how 'a multiplicity of phallocentric and misogynistic discourses' in society outside of pornography – such as science and mainstream culture – shape 'our images of gender and sexuality'.[74] This literalness is quite evident in Swedish anti-porn feminism as well. Issues of identification, (hetero)sexual desire, objectification, male superiority, and power relations were taken at face value and seen as expressed most evidently, and therefore most dangerously, in pornography.

As previously mentioned, Brian McNair argues that freedom of pornography and women's and gays' rights seem to go hand in hand. In addition, he believes that pornography has become more diversified. Furthermore McNair points out that, as women and sexual minorities have gained a greater control over their lives, and as gender and sexual equality has increased, a shift in how pornography is perceived, consumed and produced has followed: the '*context* and therefore the *meaning* of sexual performance, and of sexual representation including pornography, are transformed at the point of consumption by the control exercised by women over the environment within which they occur and are disseminated'.[75] That statement can be read in reverse as well: in a society where women experience little control over sexual discourse and their own lives, the context and meaning of sexual performance and sexual representation is understood through that sense of little control. Comparing the 1970s to a contemporary situation, the conditions regarding gendered control over environment, gender, sexual equality and women's choices on the whole have changed radically, perhaps particularly in Scandinavia, but also in large parts of the western world more generally. Much of this radical change began to happen during the 1960s and 1970s. For instance, marital rape was criminalized in Sweden in 1965, while the right to abortion was granted in 1975. In 1974, maternity leave was reformed, extending the time period permitted to be away from work and introducing gender neutral parental leave (which was, however, still mainly used by mothers). During the 1970s, women also made strides in the work force. In the early 1960s, only 25 per cent of married women worked outside the home. In 1971, individuals rather than households were made the basic unit for taxation, which made it more profitable for both partners within a married couple to work. As childcare was expanded in the 1970s and new tax laws introduced, a new tradition of double-income families was established. From the late 1960s to the early 1980s, over half a million housewives began to work outside the home.[76]

Consequently, the 1970s can be regarded as an important transitionary phase for gender equality. At the same time, these legislative and attitudinal changes were sometimes precariously won as the result of long and hard struggles, despite some support from the Social Democratic Party. Much of what was gained during this time is taken for granted in contemporary welfare Sweden – from paid parental leave and guaranteed, state-subsidized childcare to legislation against sexual harassment in the workplace. The anti-porn sentiment within Swedish feminism in the 1970s must be understood in context, not only through the ideological context of the expanding women's movement, inspired by socialist thought and Marxist analysis, but also through the context of women's rights in society at the time.

To conclude, the welfare state's relationship to sexuality and sexually explicit material changed quite radically in the period between 1960 and 1980. At the outset, a liberal utopian ideal sought freedom from repression with rational arguments. All matters pertaining to sexuality would be improved with increased freedom and knowledge: Individuals would be able to fully enjoy life to a larger extent; pornography would become better; censorship would be abolished; art would find new ways of expressing the human condition; and people would, on the whole, be freed from prejudice and hypocrisy. However, this utopian vision did not include any particular analysis of power relations, be they related to age, gender, class or ethnicity. Rather, the male, middle-class perspective was quite pervasive. Furthermore, during the late 1960s, the left movement grew stronger, and ideas inspired by Marxism and socialist thought came to the fore in intellectual debate. This is also the background for the new women's movement (sometimes called second-wave feminism) in Sweden, which was begun in 1968 with the formation of Grupp 8.[77]

When pornography was legalized in 1971, the political climate had changed thusly. In addition, the pornography that was produced, marketed and sold did not meet the expectations of the utopian visionaries of the 1960s. At the intersection of the development of sexually explicit material, sexual commerce and the new political ideals, commercial sexuality became regarded as bad; that is, exploitative, objectifying, sexist and intrinsically connected to a patriarchal capitalism.

Notes

1 Cf. Lena Lennerhed, *Frihet att njuta: Sexualdebatten i Sverige på 1960-talet*, Stockholm: Norstedts, 1994; Nikolas Glover & Carl Marklund, 'Arabian Nights in the Midnight Sun: Exploring the Temporal Structure of Sexual Geographies', *Historisk Tidskrift*, vol. 129, no. 3, 2009; Elisabet Björklund, *'The Most Delicate Subject': A History of Sex Education Films in Sweden*, diss. Lund: Lund University, 2012; Klara Arnberg & Carl Marklund, 'Illegally Blonde: "Swedish Sin" and Pornography in American and Swedish Imaginations, 1950–1971', in Elisabet Björklund & Mariah Larsson (eds), *Swedish Cinema and the Sexual Revolution: Critical Essays*, Jefferson, NC: McFarland, 2016; Eric Schaefer, '"I'll Take Sweden!" The Shifting Discourse of the "Sexy Nation" in Sexploitation Films', in Eric Schaefer (ed.), *Sex Scene: Media and the Cultural Revolution*, Durham, NC & London: Duke University Press, 2014; Kevin Heffernan, 'Many of Your Finer Nudie Films: Saga Film, Swedish National Cinema, and Seventies Transnational Erotic Film', in Elisabet Björklund & Mariah Larsson (eds), *Swedish Cinema and the Sexual Revolution: Critical Essays*, Jefferson, NC: McFarland, 2016.

2 Lennerhed, 1994.

3 Schaefer, "I'll Take Sweden!", 2014, pp. 213–14.

4 Michel Foucault, *The Will to Knowledge – The History of Sexuality Volume I* (translated by Robert Hurley), London: Penguin, 1998 [1976], pp. 3–35.

5 Björklund, 2012, p. 230.

6 Ingrid Ryberg's work within her project on queer and feminist film cultures (Stockholm University and Gothenburg University) drew my attention to these films.

7 Brian McNair, *Porno? Chic!: How Pornography Changed the World and Made It a Better Place*, London: Routledge, 2013.

8 Cf. Mariah Larsson, 'Drömmen om den goda pornografin: Om sextio- och sjuttiotalsfilmen och gränsen mellan konst och pornografi', *Tidskrift för genusvetenskap*, nos 1–2, 2007, pp. 94–111.

9 Cf. Lisa Duggan & Nan D. Hunter, *Sex Wars: Sexual Dissent and Political Culture* (10th anniversary edition), New York: Routledge, 2006.

10 *Kvinnobulletinen*, nos 3–4, 1973, p. 3.

11 See Björklund, 2012, pp. 47–150.

12 Katarina Ahlmark-Michanek, *Jungfrutro och dubbelmoral*, Malmö: Cavefors, 1962.

13 Henning Pallesen, *De avvikande*, Stockholm: Bonnier, 1964; Lars Ullerstam, *De erotiska minoriteterna*, Göteborg: Zinderman, 1964 (translated version: *The Erotic Minorities: A Swedish View*, London: Calder & Boyars, 1967).

14 Lennerhed, 1994.

15 Lars Görling, 'Förbud mot verkligheten', *BLM*, no. 1, 1964, pp. 26–28.

16 Don Kulick, 'Four Hundred Thousand Swedish Perverts', *GLQ: A Journal of Lesbian and Gay Studies*, vol. 11, no. 2, 2005, p. 213.

17 Kulick, 'Four Hundred Thousand Swedish Perverts', 2005, p. 213.

18 The Swedish film reform, the establishing of the Swedish Film Institute and Harry Schein are described and discussed in several works: cf. Anders Åberg, *Tabu: Filmaren Vilgot*

Sjöman, Lund: Filmhäftet förlag, 2001; Mariah Larsson, *Skenet som bedrog: Mai Zetterling och det svenska sextiotalet*, Lund: Sekel bokförlag, 2006; Mikael Timm, *Dröm och förbannad verklighet: spelet kring svensk film under 40 år*, Stockholm: Bromberg i samarbete med Svenska filminstitutet, 2003; Lars Ilshammar, Pelle Snickars & Per Vesterlund (eds), *Citizen Schein*, Stockholm: Kungliga biblioteket, 2010.

19 http://ingmarbergman.se/en/production/silence-9015 [Accessed December 8, 2014].

20 Erik Hedling, 'Breaking the Swedish Sex Barrier: Painful Lustfulness in Ingmar Bergman's The Silence', *Film International*, vol. 6, no. 6, 2008.

21 Cf. Hedling, 2008; Maaret Koskinen, *Ingmar Bergman's The Silence: Pictures in the Typewriter, Writings on the Screen*, Seattle, WA: University of Washington Press, 2010, pp. 43–64.

22 Anders Åberg, *Tabu: Filmaren Vilgot Sjöman*, Lund: Filmhäftet förlag, 2001.

23 The case of *491* is extensively discussed in Åberg, 2001; Lennerhed, 1994; and Lena Lennerhed, '491 and the Censorship Controversy', in Elisabet Björklund & Mariah Larsson (eds), *Swedish Cinema and the Sexual Revolution: Critical Essays*, Jefferson, NC: McFarland, 2016.

24 Statens medieråd, 'History', http://www.statensmedierad.se/Om-Statens-medierad/Historik/ [Accessed April 18, 2014]. Cf. Ulf Dalquist, *Större våld än nöden kräver?: Medievåldsdebatten i Sverige 1980–1995*, Ph.D. diss. Lund University, Umeå: Borea, 1998; Björklund, 2012; Olle Sjögren, *Inte riktigt lagom? Om 'extremvåld', filmcensur och subkultur*, Uppsala: Filmförlaget, 1993; Arne Svensson, *Den politiska saxen: en studie i Statens biografbyrås tillämpning av den utrikespolitiska censurnormen sedan 1914*, Stockholm: Stockholm University, 1976; Mariah Larsson, '"Vem behöver *den här* yttrandefriheten?" Om filmcensur och rörliga bilders farlighet', in Sara Johnsdotter & Aje Carlbom (eds), *Goda Sanningar? Debattklimatet och den kritiska forskningens villkor*, 2010.

25 Cf. Tommy Gustafsson & Mariah Larsson, 'Porren inför lagen: Två fallstudier angående den officiella attityden till offentligt visad pornografisk film 1921 och 1971', *Historisk tidskrift*, vol. 129, no. 3, 2009.

26 Per Vesterlund, 'Instituted Sexploitation? The Swedish Film Institute and the research on effects of cinema in the 1960s', in Elisabet Björklund & Mariah Larsson (eds), *Swedish Cinema and the Sexual Revolution: Critical Essays*, Jefferson, NC: McFarland, 2016.

27 Harry Schein, *I själva verket: Sju års filmpolitik*, Stockholm: Norstedts, 1970, pp. 162–63 (my translation).

28 Vesterlund, 'Instituted Sexploitation?', 2016.

29 SOU 1969:14, pp. 35–37 (my translation).

30 SOU 1969:14, p. 47 (my translation).

31 SOU 1969:14, p. 48 (my translation).

32 SOU 1969:14.

33 SOU 1969:38.

34 SOU 1969:38, p. 60.

35 SOU 1969:38; cf. Klara Arnberg, *Motsättningarnas marknad: den pornografiska pressens kommersiella genombrott och regleringen av pornografi i Sverige 1950–1980,* Lund: Sekel bokförlag, 2010.

36 Arnberg, 2010, pp. 183–89.

37   Cf. Larsson, 2007, p. 103.

38   See Maaret Koskinen, 'P(owe)R, Sex, and *Mad Men* Swedish Style – Or How the Personal Can Become the Political', in Elisabet Björklund & Mariah Larsson (eds), *Swedish Cinema and the Sexual Revolution: Critical Essays*, Jefferson, NC: McFarland, 2016; Per Vesterlund, 'Vägen till filmavtalet – Harry Scheins politiska aktivitet innan filmavtalet 1963', *Nordisk kulturpolitisk tidskrift*, vol. 16, no. 1, 2013, pp. 45–47.

39   Vesterlund, 2013, p. 64 (my translation).

40   Arnberg, 2010.

41   Cf. Klara Arnberg & Mariah Larsson, 'Benefits of the In-Between: Swedish Men's Magazines and Sex Films 1965–1975', *Sexuality & Culture*, vol. 18, no. 2, 2013.

42   See Mariah Larsson, *Skenet som bedrog: Mai Zetterling och det svenska sextiotalet*, Lund: Sekel bokförlag, 2006, chapter 2.

43   Björklund, 2012, p. 177.

44   Björklund, 2012, p. 177.

45   According to Bergström-Walan, she was kicked off of the board. Björklund has gone through the minutes of the meetings but there are no existing records to prove that she was actually removed, and that it was in fact due to her involvement in *Language of Love*. Björklund, 2012, pp. 178–79.

46   Björklund, 2012, pp. 177–81.

47   As one of the professors at the master's programme in sexology at Malmö University, I have screened this film several times to the students and for the most part receive the response that it was interesting to see, but very old-fashioned and heteronormative.

48   Björklund, 2012, p. 198.

49   Björklund, 2012, p. 200.

50   Björklund, 2012, p. 181.

51   Harry Schein (1977, p. 29), translated and quoted by Hedling, 2008.

52   Sven-Axel Månsson & Stig Larsson, *Svarta affärer: utredning om vissa klubbars och näringsställens sociala betydelse och struktur*, Malmö: Socialförvaltningen, 1976, p. 14.

53   Göran Skytte, *Porrens profitörer: två reportage om porr- och kontaktbranschen*, Stockholm: Ordfront, 1979.

54   Hans Nestius quoted in Ira Mallik, 'Porr som vapen', in Stina Andersson & Silvia Sjödahl (eds), *Sex – en politisk historia*, Göteborg: Alfabeta/Anamma in collaboration with RFSU, 2003, p. 155.

55   Hans Nestius, *I last och lust: sexuella bilder förr och nu*, Stockholm: Prisma in collaboration with RFSU, 1982. Cf. Joakim Friberg, *Erotikens ideologi*, Stockholm & Lund: Symposium bokförlag, 1987.

56   For example, see Tomas Lindberg, 'Kungliga biblioteket har låst in barnpornografisk bok', sverigesradio.se, http://sverigesradio.se/sida/artikel.aspx?programid=106&artikel=5805061 [Accessed April 23, 2014].

57   Cf. Lennerhed, 1994; Cristine Sarrimo, *När det personliga blev politiskt: 1970-talets kvinnliga bekännelse och självbiografi*, Eslöv: Brutus Östlings bokförlag Symposion, 2000; Ebba Witt-Brattström, *Å alla kära systrar!: historien om mitt sjuttiotal*, Stockholm: Norstedt, 2010.

58 Cf. Elena Gorfinkel, 'Wet Dreams: Erotic Film Festivals of the Early 1970s and the Utopian Sexual Public Sphere', *Framework: The Journal of Cinema and Media*, vol. 47, no. 2, 2006; Jane Gerhard, *Desiring Revolution: Second-wave Feminism and the Rewriting of American Sexual Thought, 1920 to 1982,* New York: Columbia University Press, 2001.

59 Cf. Arnberg, 2010; Larsson, 2008.

60 This was one of the arguments put forth by Folkaktionen mot pornografi (People's Action Against Pornography) in the 1980s.

61 Baptiste Coulmont & Phil Hubbard, 'Consuming Sex: Socio-legal Shifts in the Space and Place of Sex-shops', *Journal of Law and Society*, vol. 37, no. 1, 2010.

62 Arnberg, 2010; Witt-Brattström, 2010. Cf. *Kvinnobulletinen*, nos 3–4, 1973.

63 Maud Hägg & Barbro Werkmäster, *Kvinnor och sex*, Göteborg: Författarförlaget, 1973, p. 74.

64 *Kvinnobulletinen*, nos 3–4, 1973, pp. 12–15.

65 Birgitta Johansson, *Befrielsen är nära: feminism och teaterpraktik i Margareta Garpes och Suzanne Ostens 1970-talsteater*, Stockholm: Östlings bokförlag Symposion, 2006; Margareta Garpe & Suzanne Osten, *Jösses flickor: Kärleksföreställningen: två kvinnopjäser*, Stockholm: Gidlund, 1977.

66 SOU 1976:9.

67 Leif Bylund, 'Skyddet mot våldtäkt', *Dagens Nyheter,* April 28, 1976; Inga-Lisa Sangregorio, 'Våldtäktslagen', *Dagens Nyheter,* May 9, 1976; Lars-Göran Engström, 'Svar på tal', *Dagens Nyheter,* June 23, 1976; Ulla Axelquist, 'Försvar för våldtäkt', *Dagens Nyheter,* July 3, 1976; Maria-Pia Boëthius, *Skylla sig själv: en bok om våldtäkt,* Stockholm: Liberförlag, 1976; articles in *Expressen* February 29, 1976; March 6, 1976; March 11, 1976; March 18, 1976.

68 For instance, the secretary, Lars-Göran Engström, in *Dagens Nyheter*, June 23, 1976. The new inquiry published its proposal in 1982, SOU 1982:61.

69 Boëthius, 1976, p. 41.

70 Cf. Catherine MacKinnon, *Feminism Unmodified: Discourses on Life and Law*, Cambridge, MA: Harvard University Press, 1987.

71 Boëthius, 1976, pp. 17, 41, 77 & 91–93.

72 Arnberg, 2010, pp. 49–136.

73 See Drude Dahlerup, *Rødstrømperne: den danske Rødstrømpebevægelses udvikling, nytænkning og gennemslag 1970–1985*, Copenhagen: Gyldendal, 1998.

74 Lynne Segal, 'Only the Literal: The Contradictions of Anti-Pornography Feminism', in Pamela Church Gibson (ed.), *More Dirty Looks: Gender, Pornography, Power*, London: BFI Publishing, 2004, quotations from pp. 63 & 67.

75 McNair, 2013, p. 94 (original emphasis).

76 Christina Axelsson, *Hemmafrun som försvann: Övergången till lönearbete bland gifta kvinnor i Sverige 1968–1981*, Stockholm: Institutet för social forskning, 1987, p. 46.

77 Lennerhed, 1994. Cf. Sarrimo, 2000.

Chapter 2

Mapping the genre: The boundaries of pornography

As Eric Schaefer observes in the introduction to *Bold! Daring! Shocking! True!*, exploitation films were not hardcore pornography, and illegal, pornographic stag film was quite different from exploitation in many respects. According to Schaefer, the stag film and the exploitation film would merge in the late 1960s to form the narrative hardcore film.[1] In a Swedish context, the first film in the *Language of Love* series can be said to be such a merging moment. Although the *I am Curious* films by Vilgot Sjöman (1967, 1968) had shown several intercourse scenes (among them, one in front of a sentinel guarding the royal castle), all of these were simulated, and any male genitalia in the film was flaccid.[2] The visual presentation of authentic, un-simulated intercourse in *Dom kallar oss mods/They Call Us Misfits* (Stefan Jarl & Jan Lindqvist, 1968) only disclosed rutting male buttocks, whereas *Language of Love* used a split screen to divulge not only close-ups of genitalia, but an intersection of penile-vaginal penetration and a line graph of the physical sensations of the act. When *Language of Love* was released, it was the first time Swedish audiences could legitimately see hardcore images in a cinema. Other films with such images – such as the ones famously shown by Eugen Vöhrman at his cinema Fenix in Stockholm in the late 1960s – had been screened within a kind of legal grey zone, while hardcore 8mm films were screened in sex clubs which utilized a loophole in the law by operating as 'members-only' establishments.[3]

The films in the *Language of Love* series have gone down in film history as pornography disguised as sex education. Swedish film historian Leif Furhammar writes that the first film, from 1969, was 'at least in form and *claimed* intent an educational film'.[4] As Elisabet Björklund shows in her study on sex education films in Sweden, the generic problem of the *Language of Love* films remains unresolved. In their finance and production, in the censorship processes and in the reception of the films, it is quite clear that they balance uncertainly on the border between pornography and sex education.[5] However, the emphasized ambivalence regarding the generic designation of the *Language of Love* films is actually relevant in relation to a large share of the complete output of Swedish sex films in the 1970s, most particularly in the early 1970s. Several of these films can be described as 'in-between' films, straddling the pornographic and the non-pornographic, seemingly seeking a balance between explicitness and acceptability where their depictions of sex could be sensational enough to attract an audience, but not graphic and sleazy enough to repel potential spectators.[6]

The conception of the pornographic film in Sweden during the 1970s is highly coloured by these 'in-between' films. According to standard Swedish film history, approximately one fifth of the production of feature-length films for theatrical release during the 1970s consisted of 'more or less advanced pornography'.[7] Going through the films listed in the Swedish filmography for the 1970s, *Svensk filmografi 7*, one can estimate that at least forty of the 205 films listed can be described as containing more or less explicit sex. However, explicit representations of sex do not automatically make something pornography, even with the qualifier 'more or less advanced'. As film scholar Rick Altman has observed, genres are discursively constructed (i.e. shaped by the discourses connected to them), either within the films themselves, or in their production, marketing and reception. Accordingly, 'genre' is not a fixed, unchanging entity, since conventions – i.e. narrative, theme and style, as well as in the production, marketing and reception – will alter over time.[8]

Additionally, as the obscenity clause in the penal code was removed, the clear categories of obscene and pornographic disintegrated, and thus definitions became more difficult. Consequently, a conflation of the pornographic and the explicit sex film has occurred which might be explained by a contextual definition of pornography: pornography is whatever is regarded as porn by its contemporary society. Such an explanation, however, immediately raises the question of whose context should be allowed to decide where the line be drawn between pornography and the sexually explicit. Additionally, it does not begin to describe the Swedish porn scene of the 1970s. I would argue that these films, although not hardcore porn nor even, in some cases, 'less advanced' porn, should be distinguished by being loosely labelled 'sex films'. At the same time, they should be included in the Swedish porn scene because they were regarded as porn by some at the time; they have been historicized as porn, and they eventually developed into softcore (which did not show close-ups of genitals during intercourse and contained no cum shots) and hardcore (which did show such close-ups and cum shots) pornography.

By focusing on what the concept of pornography signified in the relevant time period, how that relates to our understanding of the word, and how the sexually explicit 'in-between' films – the sex films – were regarded, the exhibition contexts under investigation in this study can be more clearly discerned. Calling them 'more or less advanced pornography' does not begin to explain how these various exhibition contexts were stratified, not only in relation to format (8, 16, and 35mm film) but also in relation to the content of the films and the context in which they were produced, distributed and marketed. Therefore, this chapter will deal with genre, and discuss how the sex film and the pornographic film both merge and differ from one another in 1970s Sweden using examples from production, marketing, reception and censorship.

The sex films discussed in this chapter are in a sense legendary, surrounded by myth and embraced by a cult audience.[9] They are part of a larger, more or less transnational, European popular film wave composed of the 'low' genres – spaghetti westerns, zombie films, sexploitation/softcore – while at the same time representing a unique part of the national film culture.[10] Their national status will be discussed further on in this volume, but here it will suffice to say that they are celebrated as cult films in the national imagination on the one hand, and swept under the carpet, marginalized and preferably forgotten on the other.

The pornographic and the post-pornographic

Literary scholar Walter Kendrick's contention that pornography through history is defined as that which is obscene, forbidden or censored in society at any given point in time is valuable here.[11] Kendrick calls the period under scrutiny in this study 'post-pornographic', which may sound paradoxical given that it is often regarded as the most pornographic period ever; in fact, some even call it the 'golden age of porn'. However, Kendrick's approach is that porn is defined by its legal limits, and when it is no longer defined by obscenity clauses and censorship, it becomes something other than porn. Eventually, according to Kendrick, a kind of social regulation of pornography restores it to its 'secret room'.[12] In a specifically Swedish context, Kendrick's perspective suggests that a disintegration of the formerly simple category of 'porn' or 'porn film' follows from the removal of the Swedish obscenity clause.

In one sense, one could say that modern pornography was born in the 'post-pornographic' era. If earlier pornography had been defined by its forbidden and obscene status, this meant there had been something inherently subversive about it, not least because many sexually explicit works functioned as political satire or social commentary.[13] As pornography was legalized during the latter half of the twentieth century, this subversive streak disappeared. What is left of pornography when literary, cultural, political and social values have been taken out is simply the sexually explicit with the intent to arouse.[14] Furthermore, this is also the time when pornography begins to be produced professionally – both in relation to how films are actually shot and edited, and in relation to how the market develops. Nonetheless, there are some factors which undermine this historiography. For instance, as Laura Kipnis argues so eloquently about *Hustler* in *Bound and Gagged*, pornography still contains several subversive, carnivalesque and satirical elements, simply through its 'gross-out', aggressive form of bad taste:

> At its most obvious, *Hustler* is simply allergic to any form of social or intellectual affectation, squaring off like some maddened pit bull against the pretensions and the earning power of the professional classes: doctors, optometrists, dentists, and lawyers are favored targets. It's pissed off by liberals and particularly nasty to academics, who are invariably prissy and uptight. [...] It rants against the power of government, which is by definition corrupt, as are elected officials, the permanent government, even foreign governments. Of course it smears the rich against the wall, particularly rich women, and dedicates many, many pages to the hypocrisy of organized religion.[15]

Although Kipnis' view of *Hustler*'s pornography can be contested – composed as it is in the mid-1990s to a certain extent as a defence of pornography, and a reaction to the criticisms raised by the women's movement, the American sex wars and the Meese Commission's investigation into the harmful effects of pornography – there is more than a grain of truth in it. Pornography (including its production and exhibition contexts) begins at 'the edge of the culture's decorum', and thus both reproduces and subverts the values of that society.[16] That is one of the paradoxes of porn: how it at once encompasses a dominant view of gender while at the same time challenges it; how it uses racial stereotypes in a racist way, but at the same time transgresses taboos around interracial sex; how it offers a sexual consumption of the female body, but those sites where this is offered may well function as sites for male-to-male sexual contacts; how some people involved in the production of porn may be abused and exploited whereas others find their work empowering. It is not considered art, but although it largely functions within the commercial, capitalist market space, it is not really a popular kind of entertainment either.[17]

In addition, there are ties back in time which makes the otherwise interesting theoretical construction of modern pornography somewhat precarious. For instance, it might be reasonable to implicate modern pornography with images rather than words, especially considering how porn today is usually associated with the visual, whereas the countless sexually explicit narratives (or pornographic short stories) that can be found on the Internet are usually referred to as 'erotic'. However, images depicting sexual acts have existed for a long time (for instance, as brothel paintings in ancient Greece or illustrations in the Kama Sutra). One could of course say that those images had other purposes than simply being arousing, but there are several examples of modern visual pornography that have purposes beside being sexually arousing. More significantly, as I will argue further on in this volume, there is also a continuation within pornographic moving images from the earliest stag films to present-day Internet clips, namely a very simple focus on sexual acts, sometimes in a context such as a narrative or an explanatory set-up, sometimes fragmented and isolated.

'Stag films' are usually defined as early pornographic films, which were often one-reelers. Some of them have been released on DVD[18] and some can be found in archives (there is a collection at the Kinsey Institute). The large majority of them, however, have been lost. Although this makes it very difficult to say something generally about them,[19] they are usually described as containing various intercourse scenes in different constellations (couples, threesomes or foursomes), some depicting cum shots and some depicting the use of strap-on dildos. Although unlike later pornographic films in that they were black-and-white, silent and for various technical reasons contained fewer close-ups of genitals (especially during intercourse), and in many instances have an amateurish quality to them, they were in other ways remarkably similar. In other words, the basic premise of showing explicit sexual acts has remained the same. One significant difference, however, is that these films were illegal.[20] They were clandestinely circulated and shown in exclusively male homosocial contexts and brothels. There is evidence that they were sometimes screened in movie theatres as well, after regular show times and to a secretly invited audience. In Sweden, for instance, one cinema owner was convicted of having shown an 'indecent' film at such a screening in 1921.[21] On such occasions, there could be women in the audience as well as men. For the most part, however, it seems that such films were screened to men in such contexts that the women who did see them were sex workers.[22]

Through time, sex on film has not been exclusive to the pornographic film, but through censorship institutions, concepts about art, and conventions on morality and obscenity, what could be seen outside of the illegal stag film has been limited in various ways. Parallel to the stag films, there were films which contained sexual innuendo as far as censorship would allow; there were also sex educational films like the German *Aufklärung* films[23] and American exploitation films.[24] Art film and the avant-garde film transgressed various taboos. In Sweden, one such particular case was the short film *Enligt lag*/'According to the Law' (Peter Weiss & Hans Nordenström, 1957), which caused a debate when the National Board of Film Censors decided to cut out a scene in which a young man is seen masturbating. The film was ultimately released without the scene, but with an intertitle at the beginning stating that 'This film has been censored by the state. We, who have made the film, have been obstructed in our freedom of expression. You, who see the film, were believed to be susceptible to harm by certain details of reality'.[25]

Beginning in the late 1960s with more liberal film censorship, and anticipating a legalization of pornography, a wave of Swedish sex films are released. This wave peaks around 1970, followed by the first hardcore narrative-led, feature-length 35mm film, *Bäddat för lusta*/'A bed made for lust' (Rune Ljungberg) in 1973, before a slowing down in production in the late 1970s. One important inspiration for the Swedish sex film is the Danish counterpart, the *Bedside* and *Zodiac* films, which were both commercially and, in their initial stage, critically successful. The year 1973 is a watershed: not only due to Ljungberg's *Bäddat för lusta*, but because this is the year that three significant American hardcore classics are released in Sweden: *Deep Throat*, *Behind the Green Door* and *The Devil in Miss Jones*.[26]

Considering these films from a production perspective does not perhaps answer any questions. However, it elucidates how the issues of national identity and genre are pertinent, as well as the ways in which they are further complicated. For instance, as I will discuss in-depth in the last chapter of this volume, the matter of the films' national identity (or identities) and their transnational potential becomes clearer if you consider how a complex network of companies produced and co-produced these films.[27] In addition, it makes it easier to distinguish between the various types of films that fit under the umbrella 'sex film'. Finally, the success of the Danish films seems to be an influence as well, in particular for the later 'quality porn' films from Filminvest. According to Jack Stevenson – and I would concur with this judgment – the Swedish films were not as successful as the Danish.[28]

The production of the Swedish sex film

The Swedish sex film was produced by numerous different companies.[29] Many of them only produced one or two films, and there was something of a Klondike entrepreneurial spirit to the early years of legalized pornography. A mapping of the 35mm companies illustrates how diverse the field of the sex film actually was, and also demonstrates the problems of lumping these films together under the label 'more or less advanced pornography'.[30] In general, the 1970s were not prolific years within the Swedish film industry. Domestically, the most successful Swedish films during this time were Jan Troell's *Utvandrarna/The Emigrants* (1971) and *Nybyggarna/The New Land* (1972), which were based on popular novels, as well as a number of children's films and the (political art) comedies by the duo HasseåTage.[31]

Looking at the box-office charts in the annual reports of the Swedish Film Institute, one can note that the crest of the wave of sex films actually took place slightly before the legalization of pornography, with a peak in the season 1970–71, just when the obscenity clause of the penal code was removed. In particular, the two Ivarson/Wickman films *Kyrkoherden/The Lustful Vicar* (1970) and *More About the Language of Love* were commercially successful. In the preceding year (1969–70), no less than three films in the domestic box-office chart were directed by Torgny Wickman: *Language of Love*, *Swedish and Underage* and *The Lustful Vicar*.

Although the box-office charts only include films that have gained an income above a certain amount of money (and not necessarily the same amount every year), they clearly show that those domestic films which contained more or less sexually explicit material did well commercially, and that foreign (read: Danish) films with such material fared even better. They also show that hardcore material needed a justification in order to sell cinema tickets, as in the *Language of Love* films, where the educational framework provided a motivation other than sexual arousal to go and see the film.

Most of the sex films were produced by companies that specialized in this particular product. Nonetheless, it should be noted that some films bordered close to the sex film but were intended as regular comedies or art films, and treated seriously by reviewers in the daily press, like Jan Halldoff's *Rötmånad/Dog Days* (1970), with model Christina Lindberg in a mostly nude role. These were produced by the mainstream companies (in this case, the major Svensk Filmindustri [SF]). Nonetheless, *Dog Days* cashed in on its nude female lead and was one of the top box-office films in 1970–71.

According to *Svensk filmografi 7: 1970–1979*, of the approximately forty films in question, twenty-five were produced by different companies. Many of these companies – like Minerva International Films or Opal Film – only produced one or two films during this period. However, Swedish Filmproduction Investment AB, Filminvest AB and Saga Film AB together produced nearly half of the total production of sex films in the 1970s. There is also one distribution company, GeBe Film, which produced three sex films during the period. Compared with the more mainstream output of the 1970s, which was to a large extent produced by Svensk Filmindustri, Sandrews and Europa Film, as well as the Swedish Film Institute (which had begun to produce films during this decade), the sheer number of production companies marks out the sex film as something different.

Inge Ivarson, Swedish Filmproduction Investment AB and Filminvest

Through Swedish Filmproduction and Filminvest, Inge Ivarson produced fourteen films in the 1970s. From Swedish Filmproduction, the output consisted basically of sexploitation and erotic genre films. In the early 1970s, Swedish Filmproduction Investment AB produced eight films (see Table 1), yet none of these films were hardcore (the *Language of Love* series showed hardcore imagery, but it was contained within and justified by a documentary, sex educational framework). *Swedish Nymphet* may most aptly be described as a 'nude film', the film's most basic premise being to show off Lindberg's body, but is also quite similar to American exploitation films.[32] *Skräcken har 1000 ögon/Fear has 1000 Eyes* (Wickman, 1973) is an erotic Satanist horror film, whereas *The Lustful Vicar* and *Som hon bäddar får han ligga/Do You Believe in Swedish Sin?* (Gunnar Höglund, 1970) were sex comedies – one a period piece and the other contemporary.

In 1974, Filminvest went into business with *Porr i skandalskolan/The Second Coming of Eva* – a hardcore erotic comedy – followed in the same year by *Flossie*, a softcore literary adaptation starring Marie Forså. Both these films were directed by Mac Ahlberg under the pseudonym of Bert Torn and produced by Inge Ivarson under the pseudonym of Ken Hope (*The Second Coming of Eva*) and Ivan Bernhardsson (*Flossie*). Later, the same company produced *Justine och Juliette/Justine and Juliette* (1975) and *Bel Ami* (1976) – both starring American Harry Reems – and *Molly – familjeflickan/Molly* (1977). These three were also directed by Mac Ahlberg, whereas Filminvest's other 1977 project, *Ta mej i dalen/Practice Makes Perfect*, was directed by Torgny Wickman.

It is notable that two companies headed by the same producer made a significant amount (one third) of the Swedish 1970s sex films. Nearly all of these films were directed by two directors, Torgny Wickman and Mac Ahlberg, who may be described as the auteurs of the Swedish sex film. Together with Olle Hellbom (a director of children's films) and Jan Halldoff, they are definitely the most prolific directors of the decade. Furthermore, many of Wickman's films – including *Swedish and Underage, Language of Love, The Lustful Vicar, More About the Language of Love, Kärlekens XYZ/The XYZ of Love* (1971) and *Practice Makes Perfect* – were among the top films in the Swedish box-office charts.[33] Looking at the output of the two companies, one can see that Swedish Filmproduction seems to have largely focused on films with a message. All of Torgny Wickman's Swedish Filmproduction films appear to be infused with a sense of didactic mission, such as the 'square-up' in *Swedish Nymphet*, which presents itself as informing on the subject of nymphomania. However, this just might be

Table 1: Output from Swedish Filmproduction after 1970.

Year	Title	English title	Director
1970	*Kyrkoherden*	*The Lustful Vicar*	Torgny Wickman
1970	*Som hon bäddar får han ligga*	*Do You Believe in Swedish Sin?*	Gunnar Höglund
1970	*Mera ur kärlekens språk*	*More About the Language of Love*	Torgny Wickman
1971	*Kärlekens XYZ*	*The XYZ of Love*	Torgny Wickman
1973	*Det bästa ur kärlekens språk-filmerna*	*The Best of the Language of Love Films*	Torgny Wickman (compilation)
1973	*Skräcken har 1000 ögon*	*Fear has 1000 Eyes*	Torgny Wickman
1973	*Anita – ur en tonårsflickas dagbok*	*Swedish Nymphet*	Torgny Wickman
1974	*Inkräktarna*	*Let Us Play Sex*	Torgny Wickman

Table 2: Output from Filminvest from 1974–77.

Year	Title	English title	Director
1974	*Porr i skandalskolan*	*The Second Coming of Eva*	Mac Ahlberg/Bert Torn
1974	*Flossie*	*Flossie*	Mac Ahlberg/Bert Torn
1975	*Justine och Juliette*	*Justine and Juliette*	Mac Ahlberg
1976	*Bel Ami*	*Bel Ami*	Mac Ahlberg
1977	*Molly – familjeflickan*	*Molly*	Mac Ahlberg
1977	*Ta mej i dalen*	*Practice Makes Perfect*	Torgny Wickman

an excuse to show nudity and sex. Perhaps this is only a strategy, similar to the one of the classical exploitation film, where the 'square-up' was a way of justifying the contents.[34] Other Wickman films, like *The Lustful Vicar* and *Fear has 1000 Eyes*, are clearly anti-clerical. By presenting a film as educational or as highlighting a particular social problem, Wickman's films could defend their use of nudity and sexuality as a way to plead for tolerance, and as standing against religious inhibition and ignorance. However, after 1971, such an explanation was hardly necessary from a censorship perspective. Nonetheless, although perfectly legal, audiences might have needed reassurance or an excuse for what they were watching.

Perhaps this explains Wickman's commercial success. Catering not only to prurient interest, but also to social conscience and educational interest, it may have been possible to stand in line for a ticket to one of his films without being embarrassed. Economic historian Klara Arnberg and myself have argued that during the time period (i.e. 1965–75), men's magazines (e.g. *FIB/Aktuellt* and *Lektyr*) and sex films found their own niche in the market, 'in-between' the pornographic and the mainstream. On the one hand, the films and the magazines took advantage of the new sex-liberal discourse – quite evident in Wickman's didactic films – but also of an existing, mainstream infrastructure which they could not have used if they had been purely pornographic. Some of the actresses performing in these films were also models and appeared in the men's magazines.[35]

On the other hand, the films of Filminvest which were produced at a later stage in the 1970s and, with the exception of Wickman's *Practice Makes Perfect*, never made the top box-office list, could, as I have mentioned previously, be described as an attempt at making 'quality porn'. Indeed, four of Filminvest's films – *Flossie*, *Justine and Juliette*, *Bel Ami* and *Molly* – were literary adaptations, directed by Mac Ahlberg.

Saga Film and Joe Sarno

Saga Film produced six films (five of them in the 1970s) and seems to have worked closely with production companies abroad. All of their films were directed by American directors, namely Paul D. Gerber, Charles Kaufman and Joe Sarno. Apparently, Saga Film was the most transnational of the Swedish sex film production companies, although Swedish

Filmproduction and Filminvest also collaborated with companies from other countries (most notably France). In the case of Saga Film, *Nøglehullet/The Key Hole* (Gerber, 1974) was a co-production with the Danish companies Clearlight, Centrum Filmproduktion A/S and A og S Productions, whereas the two Sarno films – *Den pornografiska jungfrun/Vampire Ecstasy* (1973) and *Vild på sex/Bibi – Confessions of a Sweet Sixteen* (1974) – were produced together with the West German company Monarex; the Kaufman film *Monas hemliga sexdrömmar/Sextacy* (1977) was made in collaboration with Duty Productions (USA) and Reinstadt Produktion (West Germany). Gerber's other film, *I lust och nöd/Private Pleasures* (1976), however, was entirely Swedish-produced, through a collaboration between Saga and Premiär Film.

Joe Sarno directed some ten films in Sweden, from *Jag – en oskuld/Inga* in 1968 to *Fäbodjäntan/Come and Blow the Horn* in 1978. These were produced by different companies and nearly always in collaboration with foreign production companies. As previously mentioned, Saga Film produced two of them; Joe Sarno Productions produced the hardcore films *Kärleksön/Love Island* (1978) and *Come and Blow the Horn* in collaboration with Swedish GeBe Film; Unicorn Enterprises made *Swedish Wildcats* (1972) and *Någon att älska/Inga Two* (1971) in collaboration with other companies.

Influence from abroad: The Danes' intelligent handling of pornography

By making my choice of films among those listed in *Svensk filmografi 7*, I have focused on films that have been regarded as Swedish enough to be included in the filmography. According to the foreword in the filmography, films included are 'with few exceptions, theatrically released films which are entirely or partly produced in Sweden'.[36] The film should be at least 2000 metres long (approximately seventy-three minutes in duration), again with some exceptions; a few films that have neither been screened nor censored in Sweden have been included due to their Swedish producers.

The most successful group of sex films were foreign, more specifically Danish. These frequently appeared on the box-office lists of the annual reports of the Swedish Film Institute. Although none of them followed up *Mazurka på sengekanten/Bedside Mazurka*'s (John Hilbard, 1970) number-one position, the *Bedside* and *Zodiac* films (see Tables 3 and 4) were all listed in the annual reports (except *Agent 69 Jensen i skorpionens tegn/Agent 69 Jensen in the Sign of the Scorpio* [Werner Hedman, 1978]).

Other foreign films, such as the West German *Geh, zieh dein Dirndl aus/Love Bavarian Style* (Rothemund, 1973) and *Alpenglühn im Dirndlrock/Alp Glow in Dirndl Skirt* (Rothemund, 1974), also made the list but none with the same success as the Danish films.

These Danish films became very influential, not least because they initially received favourable treatment by Swedish reviewers.

Bedside Mazurka is described by Stevenson as 'sex without dirt'.[37] Starring Ole Søltoft as a virginal teacher at a private school, the basic premise of the story is that he must find a

Table 3: The *Bedside* films.

Year	Title	English title	Director
1970	*Mazurka på sengekanten*	*Bedside Mazurka/Bedtime Mazurka*	John Hilbard
1971	*Tandlaege på sengekanten*	*Bedside Dentist*	John Hilbard
1972	*Rektor på sengekanten*	*Bedside Head*	John Hilbard
1972	*Motorvej på sengekanten*	*Bedside Highway*	John Hilbard
1973	*Romantik på sengekanten*	*Between the Sheets*	John Hilbard
1975	*Der må vaere en sengekant*	*Come to My Bedside*	John Hilbard
1976	*Hoppla på sengekanten*	*Jumpin' at the Bedside*	John Hilbard

Table 4: The *Zodiac* films.

Year	Title	English title	Director
1973	*I jomfruens tegn*	*In the Sign of the Virgin/Danish Pastries*	Finn Karlsson
1974	*I tyrens tegn*	*In the Sign of the Taurus*	Werner Hedman
1975	*I tvillingernes tegn*	*In the Sign of the Gemini*	Werner Hedman
1976	*I løvens tegn*	*In the Sign of the Lion*	Werner Hedman
1977	*Agent 69 Jensen i skorpionens tegn*	*Agent 69 Jensen in the Sign of the Scorpio*	Werner Hedman
1978	*Agent 69 Jensen i Skyttens tegn*	*Agent 69 Jensen in the Sign of Sagittarius*	Werner Hedman

wife in order to become headmaster. Since his students want him to get the job, they try to help him in every conceivable way. The film is based on material by the Danish author Carl Erik Soya and was a success in Denmark, but even more so in Sweden. In an article in the Swedish tabloid *Kvällsposten* regarding the commercial success of the film, it is described as 'giggle porn' [*fnissporr*].[38] Later in the same tabloid, another journalist explains how he became curious about the film and went to see it. Here, the giggle-provoking quality of the film is underlined in the introduction:

> It was not the usual Nordic solemnity between the sheets. [...] Besides, it is wrong to call Bedside Mazurka a porn film. Porn films are crowded with people without the upper body. In Bedside Mazurka, you could look the people in the eyes. Too [sic].[39]

He further contends that the film has no more to do with reality than porn films, which makes it into a 'trifle', but that this trifle is nonetheless 'good-looking' and 'softer' (than porn films, one supposes).

In the largest Swedish daily, *Dagens Nyheter*, prominent film critic Mauritz Edström, in a short but all-in-all favourable review of the same film, called it a 'comedy from the age of porn'. Although he too implies that the film is of little weight, he still concludes that 'for once it becomes not only porn but also provides a real tone of Soya's erotic cheeriness'.[40] Apparently, *Bedside Mazurka* was found to be too good to be porn, although it was close enough to that genre for critics to feel the need to distinguish it from porn by claiming that it was not porn, or at least not 'only' porn or not 'simply' porn. Considering how extremely discreet the film is in its sexual representation, the proximity of *Bedside Mazurka* to the porn genre is indeed contextual, and the need to distinguish it as better than porn or different from porn would seem moot in a contemporary context.

Not only were reviewers favourably inclined to or happily surprised by the film, *Bedside Mazurka* was also a huge commercial success in Sweden, earning the top position on the box-office chart for foreign films two years in a row. The fact that it was somehow sanctioned by critics probably played a part in the film's success. In any case, *Bedside Mazurka* became a reference point for later films, spawning a whole series of increasingly explicit *Bedside* films, eventually incorporating some hardcore material and combining non-pornographic actors with porn performers. Although the sexually explicit elements of the first film are ever so small and ever so discreet, *Bedside Mazurka* still set the standard for what in Sweden would be called Danish 'happy porn'. Altman notes that a cycle of films following a successful formula forms the basis for a new genre or subgenre,[41] which certainly occurred with the Danish *Bedside* films, and the later more explicit *Zodiac* films. In a 1975 article about the current situation for Danish film, the very first sentence says: 'Danish film – is it only happy porn and full speed at the bedside?'[42] When *I jomfruens tegn/In the Sign of the Virgin* (Finn Karlsson) was released in Sweden in 1973, a strategy of aligning it with other films was employed, with the advertisement for the film stating boldly: 'Ole "Mazurka" Söltoft in the largest, most audacious and funniest Danish sex-porn comedy'.[43] Nonetheless, when the film was reviewed, it was found lacking in comparison with the earlier prototype:

> One used to speak about Danish happy porn, how intelligent it was and with what wit the Danes handled pornography. That was when the first 'Mazurka'-film came. But those days are long gone. The latest production with Ole Söltoft hits rock bottom.[44]

In the Sign of the Virgin – perhaps more well-known as *Danish Pastries* – was the first of the *Zodiac* films. It contains hardcore scenes and combines non-performing, established Danish actors with porn performers. In contrast to the Swedish reviewer, in Jack Stevenson's opinion it has, through its many scenes with nude women, a 'vibrancy and erotic energy that scenes of actual fornication cannot equal'.[45] It is likely that the judgement of the Swedish reviewer is dependent on the inclusion of hardcore scenes rather than the whole of the film. The wit with which the Danes handled pornography had only partly to do with the humour of the 'happy porn' films, and a lot more to do with their previously discreet depiction of sex.

'An adequate declaration of contents' – *More About the Language of Love*

> As the present film can be expected to be presented as a sex educational film, the purely pornographic features may come to run counter to the current legislation as well as to the coming. Under the condition that the film is advertised as a pornographic film, the Committee has no objections to the public exhibition of these parts of the film. However, in the case that the film would be presented as an educational film concerning sexual matters, the Committee finds that the purely pornographic elements are irreconcilable with the demand for an adequate declaration of contents.[46]

This quotation is from the records of the National Board of Film Censors for the film *Mera ur kärlekens språk/More about the Language of Love* (Wickman, 1970), which went through the censorship process during the fall of 1970. Submitted to the Board only a few months before the removal of the obscenity clause in the Penal Code, *More about the Langauge of Love* was the follow-up to Wickman's hugely successful sex education film *Language of Love*. Scenes from a sex club in Copenhagen featuring live shows, as well as from the shooting of a porn film, were regarded as unquestionably pornographic by the Board. One of the problems with the film, as Elisabet Björklund points out in her study about sex education films in Sweden, was that the new law – which replaced the obscenity clause – somewhat ironically perhaps, called for a clear label of pornography, so that people might avoid it should they wish. Putting clear-cut pornography (the sequence from the porn shoot and the live-show in the sex club) in a sex education film would thus be a way of springing pornography upon unknowing spectators, according to the Advisory Council. However, as Björklund wryly observes, when the later sequels to *Language of Love* were submitted, after legalisation, this problem did not arise in any of the Board's discussions.[47]

The censorship process was prolonged for several reasons: firstly, the censors decided to cut one scene from the film and the film-makers sent in another scene for approval to be inserted in place of the missing one; secondly, it was subsequently referred to the Advisory Council to the Board, Filmgranskningsrådet; and thirdly, the Board's decision was appealed to parliament. The records regarding this are quite extensive as they contain the minutes from the Board's meetings.[48] The Board and the advisory committee concluded that the film was presented as an informational and educational film, but that the scenes which depicted the activities during the shooting of a porn film and at a sex club in Copenhagen were highly problematic in relation to current law, which, moreover, was about to change (with the removal of the obscenity clause in 1971).

Nils Bejerot, the physician who was called in as an expert, claimed that the film consisted of three components: 'honest sex education, gross pornography, and commercial speculation', which were incompatible in any 'decent way'.[49] Bejerot is interesting in this context. In Klara Arnberg and Tommy Gustafsson's study of moral panics in Sweden, he is described as a 'moral panicker', who frequently agitated against various dangers.[50] He published a book in the 1950s that warned against the dangers of comics, based to a large extent on an American book, Fredric Wertham's *Seduction of the Innocent*,[51] and in the 1960s he began his work on narcotics and drug abuse. Maybe this is why he was called in to the Board on this case, as one of the scenes that was eventually cut from the film dealt with drug use and sexuality. (Bejerot's standpoint on drugs later became influential in Sweden's zero tolerance policy.)

At a later meeting, film censor Roland Häggbom explained that the title of the film did not provide any support for a 'traditional interpretation of the concept of "sex education"'. Furthermore, he wrote that regardless of whether or not the existing law did or did not allow visual information about pornography to be spread, the consequences could be problematic.[52]

When the film premiered at cinemas, the advertisement made a great show of the battle for the rights to screen it, with the caption above the title stating 'Finally released in completely unedited shape after a decision by his Royal Majesty on November 13' in large, capital letters. This statement actually stretches the truth a little bit, since one scene in the originally submitted version of the film had been replaced. Nevertheless, the strategy of evoking a censorship process places the marketing of the film firmly within the tradition of films which flaunt their transgressive character, and thereby within the lower genres. Furthermore, it evokes the sensation of the earlier film in the series, *Language of Love*, in order to enhance interest: 'After the year-long, enormous success "Language of Love" comes More About the Language of Love.'[53]

As mentioned earlier, the problem of the genre of the *Language of Love* films is still unresolved.[54] The opinion of the Advisory Council thus seems to have prevailed, since they are usually described as pornographic films disguised as sex education. Nevertheless, they do not fit perfectly into either of those genres. In a sense, they might be described as Swedish sexploitation films, and thus as belonging to a national subcategory or a variation of the American sexploitation film, much like the marriage manual films. However, as Björklund points out, actors performed as physicians and scientists in the American sexploitation films, whereas the experts in the *Language of Love* films were real (and also somewhat well-known among the public).[55] In a review of the third film of the series, *The XYZ of Love*, one journalist wrote: 'It has been said about the earliest love films that they are stereotypical, glossy, mechanical and that they are bad porn'.[56] Yet looking at the series today, it is possible to discern a commitment to a sexual mission which may be naive, may be misguided, may be speculative, but still calls for education, tolerance and acceptance in matters of sex.[57]

Nudity, softcore, hardcore: *Swedish Nymphet, Flossie* and *Happy Family*

The three films discussed in this section represent three different kinds of sex films. One, *Swedish Nymphet*, has been described by the female lead Christina Lindberg as a 'nude film' [*nakenfilm*],[58] but can very well be regarded as a Swedish version of the American exploitation film.[59] Meanwhile, *Flossie* is softcore and *Happy Family* (Arlanch Heinz, 1976) is a hardcore narrative porn film.

The advertisement for *Swedish Nymphet* presented a drawing of the poster image: Stellan Skarsgård holding Christina Lindberg's sweater, in the process of pulling it down over her exposed breasts. No taglines, no sensational words of pornography or sex.[60] Most probably Christina Lindberg's presence both signalled what kind of a film it was, as well as worked as an attraction for the audience. Monica Tunbäck-Hanson wrote unfavourably of the film in *Göteborgsposten*, but stated that it was not a porn film: 'Now it must be said, however, that the person who goes to see Anita in order to see a porn film goes in vain. Whatever happens happens discreetly'.[61]

The narrative of *Swedish Nymphet* focuses to a large extent on Christina Lindberg, who plays Anita. Anita is a young woman in a small town whose parents seem to have preferred her younger sister to her. Growing up without love has led her to believe that she is worthless, and therefore she compulsively seeks comfort through casual sexual encounters. These encounters lead to a reputation as a prostitute, and she becomes more and more ostracized in the small-town community. Anita runs away to Stockholm, where she picks up men on Sergels torg in the centre of Stockholm. By coincidence, she meets Erik (played by Stellan Skarsgård), who is a psychology student. He lives in a cooperative with some musicians who play classical music. Erik soon diagnoses Anita as a nymphomaniac and attempts to cure her through therapy. Among the musicians and with the aid of Erik, she gets better, but relapses when Erik tells her that she must have an orgasm in order to be fully cured. When a vibrator does not help her, she leaves the cooperative and begins to perform at a sex club. In the end, Erik finds her, and, through mutual intercourse, she finally gets the orgasm that cures her nymphomania.

The film shows sexual situations and intercourse without being very explicit. Lindberg's genitals are painstakingly avoided, sometimes by obscuring them with something in the foreground, such as when she lies down naked on the floor and the angle of the shot has the leg of a young man standing in front of her so as to exactly cover her genitals. In intercourse situations, the participants are shown from the waist up or from the side so that hips are shown but no more. Lindberg's breasts are, however, generously exposed, and her nude body is also frequently shown. Descriptions of the film at svenskfilmdatabas.se and by Klubb Super8 explain that the film is typical for its time in that it attempts to make erotica more decent by emphasizing a social problem.[62] However, the social problem in the film further emphasizes Anita's misery, as well as provides her with an excuse for her licentious behaviour. On the one hand, the scenes in which she has sex with markedly older, puffier and quite contemptuous or distant men provide a kinky erotic titillation; she is also humiliated by the other people in the small town where she lives, and when she comes to Erik's collective, one of the women there gives her a black eye after Anita flirts with her boyfriend. On the other hand, she is not really bad, because she is taken over by an urge that is stronger than her – her nymphomania. The pity that is evoked for Anita is thus tinged with lust, but she is at the same time not 'really' a bad girl, more an innocent in the clutches of her sickness.

Although the film purports to be about a problem that should be met with understanding rather than condemnation, it is distinguished both by a double standard and an almost sadistic treatment of its main character, hidden under the cloak of preaching for tolerance. It simultaneously criticizes bigotry, hypocrisy and the elderly men who exploit Anita while giving an impression of revelling in her misery and her nakedness. It seems to juxtapose education, culture and tolerance with the sordid environment of Anita's background. Erik is a modern and equal young man who cooks and does the dishes, but he also utilizes the 'medical gaze' on Anita, zoning in on her problem and deciding to solve it.[63]

Flossie, on the other hand, is based on an erotic novella that was translated to Swedish in 1965. The original, *Flossie: A Venus of Fifteen* was anonymously published in England in 1897. According to Swedish publisher Carl-Michael Edenborg, *Flossie* has played a paradoxically significant role in Sweden – where many erotic literary classics are still not published – with several sequels written by a Swedish author under the pseudonym 'Jack Archer' (the male protagonist of the original novella). At least three different translations into Swedish of the original were made by different publishers over the course of only a few years, and in 1974, the film *Flossie* was directed by Mac Ahlberg, with Marie Forså in the titular role. The film is narrated by a man by the name of Jack Archer (Jack Frank), and although it is set in contemporary Stockholm rather than late nineteenth-century London, the dialogue is taken almost verbatim from the first Swedish translation.[64] Jack describes how he meets Flossie through a mutual female friend (Kim Frank), and how he is instantly attracted to her. Flossie is a virgin, yet quite experienced in a conventional manner (meaning that she has done most everything except vaginal intercourse). After an initial meeting which leads to petting and oral sex, they recount stories of their sexual adventures to each other, which are shown in flashbacks. At the end of the film, they have intercourse in a threesome with the female friend.

Like in many narrative pornographic films, the narrative in this film functions as a frame for the sexual flashbacks. The film contains no explicit hardcore imagery during intercourse. However, there is one scene in which Jack Frank's erect penis is shown. Marie Forså was never filmed in hardcore close-ups, although a stubborn rumour around her claims that she did have intercourse during the sex scenes, so the sex shown is supposedly unsimulated.

Flossie can be said to be the first of a string of productions by the Mac Ahlberg/Inge Ivarson team which were based on literary originals, used English-sounding pseudonyms for the actors, had comparatively high budgets and an ambitious musical score (in this case utilizing classical music such as by Chopin). As such, one could describe *Flossie* as 'quality porn', which was also the ambition of the producer.[65] This would be a pornographic film which purports to offer more than simply scenes of intercourse, or at least to be somewhat tasteful and elegant, which is also how it was described in adverts: an 'elegant Swedish porn film'.[66] Quality porn films generally blur the line between softcore and hardcore, with later films mixing simulated intercourse with hardcore scenes, such as in *Justine and Juliette* or *Bel Ami*. Since Forså was not the only actress who did not want to be filmed with genital close-ups, the sexual numbers alternate between softcore and hardcore depending on what the actors/performers accepted. In a later film, *Molly*, body doubles were used.

Finally, *Happy Family* is simply called 'new Swedish hardcore', and was shown at Fenix, a porn cinema in Stockholm.[67] I have not found any reviews of the film. *Happy Family* has a voice-over by Marie Forså, and begins with the female protagonist (Anita Westberg) out riding in a foggy autumn landscape. She thinks back upon how she had sex with her boyfriend in the summer, how he then had sex with her mother, and how she had sex with her mother's lesbian lover for revenge. These and subsequent events are shown in flashbacks. *Happy Family* is a regular hardcore film, with explicit sex scenes and 'money shots'. The narrative functions to frame the sexual numbers and it has some comedic elements involving the father in the family.

Conclusion

As I stated at the beginning of this chapter, these films could most simply be grouped together under the loose label of quite heterogeneous 'sex films'. All of them have been given the colour code yellow from the National Board of Film Censors, which meant they were forbidden for children under fifteen. In Sweden, however, that label has never, for several reasons, carried the connotations of the X-rated film – although *barnförbjudet* ('adults only', approximately 'forbidden for children') in certain contexts might signal pornography. All of them have sex as their focus – whether that be in an arousing, educational, scary and/or humorous fashion – and sex may be said to be their raison d'être. Still, the only films discussed here which present hardcore sex in graphic close-ups, and thus look anything like a contemporary adult production, are *Happy Family* and *In the Sign of the Virgin*. This is probably the reason that film historian Leif Furhammar describes them as 'more or less advanced pornography' in his history of Swedish film, since the rudimentary generic categorization which I made, and which he is (probably) basing his estimate on as well, includes all these diverse kinds of films. Furhammar and I might differ on a few individual titles, but the main body of the roughly forty out of 205 films listed in *Svensk filmografi* is probably the same. This is to be expected given that genre boundaries are rarely fixed but always flexible. Many genres consist of a corpus of films which a majority can agree upon and an additional number of films which may or may not belong to that genre. Still, the concurrence of Furhammar's and my own estimates indicate that these films share some kind of characteristic or quality which groups them together.

Nevertheless, these films were called various things by their contemporaries. In the advertisements for the porn cinemas, as well as the regular cinemas which intermittently exhibited these films, words like 'pornography' or 'hardcore' functioned as positive signs, telling a prospective audience that they could find what they were looking for. Furthermore, in accordance with the new law that had replaced the obscenity clause, pornography had to be labelled as such in order to provide an 'adequate declaration of content'. It was therefore necessary to be clear that sexually explicit material was to be found in the film. For the sex clubs and sex stores, this declaration was not necessary; it sufficed to announce 'film screening' – the context defined the films' content.

For the reviewers, the porn label was always negative, suggesting that the film at hand held no value other than the questionable one of providing sexual titillation and arousal for the mere sake of profit. Furthermore, since film reviewers most often liked to present themselves as experienced men (or, more rarely, women) of the world, they refused to let on that the film could be arousing to them.[68] A contempt – sometimes slight, sometimes stronger – for people who found films such as these exciting is implied in reviews and articles. In *Dagens Nyheter*, the reviewer complained about *In the Sign of the Virgin*, proclaiming: 'At the first Monday screening at Festival there was not one girl in sight. That is a good testimony to the women in Stockholm. Try to prevent your boyfriends from going there too!'[69] Otherwise, Danish 'happy porn' was in some ways an exception, but only as long as it remained on the correct territory of discreet softcore. This probably has to do with the fact that these films had high production values, quite good actors and delivered their sex stories with a good deal of light-hearted humour. Although Mauritz Edström, a heavyweight cinephile in Sweden, as well as Tore Borglund in the tabloid *Kvällsposten*, had to explain that *Bedside Mazurka* was trivial and insignificant, they still reviewed it favourably.[70]

From the mid-seventies on, there is both a development towards more hardcore material in feature films and a simultaneous development with increasing criticism of pornography and commercial sexuality. Accordingly, pornography is again more clearly delineated and limited, a process that culminates with the introduction of the VCR. As Kendrick notes in the afterword to the second edition of *The Secret Museum*, porn films began to be clearly labelled as such again, placed in a certain section of the video store, and eventually disappeared from public exhibition in cinemas (except in those sex stores that were still in business).[71]

Looking at the production of the Swedish sex film of the 1970s, one can note that, first of all, the output was a lot more diverse than might be expected; erotic genre films, sex educationals, and softcore and hardcore narrative pornography were included in the total production of 35mm films made for theatrical release. What must be kept in mind is that a lot of films were imported from abroad – both the looser sex film genre and, more specifically, hardcore pornography. For instance, American, West German and French films were screened in Swedish cinemas, but the most successful of the imported films were the Danish 'happy porn' films, which may have been regarded as sanctioned by critics given their initially good reviews. Another thing that must be kept in mind is the number of non-theatrically released films which were shown in the sex clubs and sex stores. (Some of these will be the focus of Chapter 5 in this volume.)

Accordingly, the question of format and film gauge has significance for the definition of pornographic film. This is not just because 8mm, 16mm and 35mm films were exhibited in different contexts, but also due to the fact that the films screened in regular cinemas were often distributed by larger distribution companies that would provide films to several movie theatres across the country, whereas distribution in the case of the 8mm films was not, during the years I have studied, nationally centralized but operated on a very local level. Thus, the apparatus surrounding the 35mm films was larger, but perhaps also more efficient.

In addition, the different formats of films reached different audiences, and were provided with meaning depending on other entertainment offered in the same place. The sex films were screened at regular cinemas where other film genres were represented as well, whereas the 16mm and 8mm films exhibited in the clubs were accompanied by striptease and live shows; moreover, the stores sold magazines, books and sexual paraphernalia in addition to screening films. There was an entirely different mode of spectatorship in the movie theatres, not least of which was that the movie started at a particular time, which meant that you bought your ticket and entered with other people. In addition, access to regular theatres was not informally gendered in the same manner as access to stores and clubs. Consequently, audience demographics may very well have been different, with a more mixed audience at the regular theatres, and a more homogenously male audience in the clubs and stores. Of course there was no prohibition on women entering those premises as customers – on the contrary, some clubs encouraged female presence by offering free entrance – but informal norms and codes made it more difficult for women to venture into these spaces. The various exhibition contexts for sexually explicit films were thus stratified: regular cinemas showed various kinds of films, among them sex films; porn cinemas had a non-stop programme of (often) one feature-length pornographic film and a number of shorts; clubs screened 16mm or 8mm hardcore films as part of a larger offer of sexual entertainment; and stores mainly showed 8mm films – at first in front of an audience and eventually in private booths.

Notes

1 Eric Schaefer, *Bold! Daring! Shocking! True!: A History of Exploitation Films, 1919–1959,* Durham, NC: Duke University Press, 1999, pp. 6–8.

2 Cf. Mariah Larsson, 'Making Love Detumescently: Some Preliminary Notes on the Body Language of the Penis', *Kosmorama,* no. 258 (www.kosmorama.org).

3 As described in Leif Silbersky & Carlösten Nordmark, *Såra tukt och sedlighet: en debattbok om pornografin,* Stockholm: Prisma, 1969.

4 Leif Furhammar, *Filmen i Sverige: En historia i tio kapitel,* Höganäs: Wiken, 1991, p. 312 (emphasis added).

5 Elisabet Björklund, 'The Most Delicate Subject': A History of Sex Education Films in Sweden, Ph.D. diss. Lund: Lund University, 2012, chapter 3: 'The *Language of Love* Films: Sex Education or Pornography?'

6 Klara Arnberg & Mariah Larsson, 'Benefits of the In-Between: Swedish Men's Magazines and Sex Films 1965–1975', *Sexuality & Culture,* vol. 18, no. 2, 2013.

7 Furhammar, 1991, pp. 328–29.

8 Rick Altman, *Film/Genre,* London: BFI Publishing, 1999.

9 For instance, Klubb Super8 distributes old Swedish sex films on DVD; Daniel Ekeroth wrote and compiled both *Swedish Sensationsfilms: A Clandestine History of Sex, Thrillers, and*

Kicker Cinema, New York: Bazillion Points, 2011 and (under the name Daniel Dellamorte), *Svensk sensationsfilm: en ocensurerad guide till den fördolda svenska filmhistorien, 1951–1993*, Malmö: Tamara Press, 2003. Between 1995 and 1997, the magazine *magasin defect* was published, devoting itself to cult cinema.

10 Cf. Stefano Baschiera & Francesco Di Chiara, 'Once Upon a Time in Italy: Transnational Features of Genre Production 1960s–1970s', *Film International*, vol. 8, no. 6, 2010, pp. 30–39.

11 Walter Kendrick, *The Secret Museum: Pornography in Modern Culture*, Berkeley, CA: University of California Press, 1996 [1987].

12 Kendrick, 1996.

13 Lynn Hunt, 'Introduction. Obscenity and the Origins of Modernity', in Lynn Hunt (ed.), *The Invention of Pornography: Obscenity and the Origins of Modernity, 1500–1800*, New York: Zone Books, 1996.

14 Cf. Magnus Ullén, *Bara för dig: Pornografi, konsumtion, berättande*, Stockholm: Vertigo förlag, 2009, p. 45.

15 Laura Kipnis, *Bound and Gagged: Pornography and the Politics of Fantasy in America*, New York: Grove Press, 1996, p. 141.

16 Kipnis, 1999, p. 164.

17 Cf. Lehman's claim that one should rather talk about art and non-art in relation to porn than about high and low culture. Peter Lehman, 'Introduction: "A Dirty Little Secret" – Why Teach and Study Pornography?', in Peter Lehman (ed.), *Pornography: Film and Culture*, New Brunswick, NJ: Rutgers University Press, 2006, pp. 1–24. Cf. Mariah Larsson, 'National/Transnational Genre: Pornography in Transition', in Tommy Gustafsson & Pietari Kääpä (eds), *Nordic Genre Film: Small Nation Film Cultures*, Edinburgh: Edinburgh University Press, 2015, pp. 220–21.

18 For example, Swedish Njutafilms released *Förbjudna filmer från tjugotalets Paris* in 2003, and collections of films from the 1920s, 1930s, 1940s, etc. have also been produced.

19 Cf. Linda Williams, '"White Slavery", or the Ethnography of "Sex Workers": Women in Stag Films at the Kinsey Archive', in Claire Hines & Darren Kerr (eds), *Hard to Swallow: Hard-Core Pornography On Screen*, London: Wallflower Press, 2012, pp. 81–100.

20 Until the 1960s, this is true of most countries that I know of, including the United States, the United Kingdom, the Scandinavian countries and so on.

21 Tommy Gustafsson & Mariah Larsson, 'Porren inför lagen: Två fallstudier angående den officiella attityden till offentligt visad pornografisk film 1921 och 1971', *Historisk tidskrift*, vol. 129, no. 3, 2009. See also, Tommy Gustafsson, 'The Open Secret: Illegal Screenings of Pornographic Films for Public Audiences in Sweden 1921–1943', in Elisabet Björklund & Mariah Larsson (eds), *Swedish Cinema and the Sexual Revolution: Critical Essays*, Jefferson, NC: McFarland, 2016, pp. 101–115.

22 Cf. Linda Williams' discussion of the stag film as a kind of foreplay and the potential presence of women at such screenings in Linda Williams, *Hardcore: Power, Pleasure, and the 'Frenzy of the Visible'*, Berkeley, CA & London: University of California Press, 1999 [1989], p. 74.

23 See Malte Hagener (ed.), *Geschlecht in Fesseln: Sexualität zwischen Aufklärung und Ausbeutung im Weimarer Kino 1918–1933*, München: Edition Text + Kritik, 2000. For the sex education film in Sweden, see Björklund, 2012.

24 Schaefer, 1999.

25 See Lars Gustaf Andersson, 'Peter Weiss: Underground and Resistance', in Mariah Larsson & Anders Marklund (eds), *Swedish Film: An Introduction and Reader*, Lund: Nordic Academic Press, 2010, pp. 229–38. For the quotation, see svenskfilmdatabas.se, search entry 'Enligt lag'.

26 Although the censors made no less than six cuts in *Behind the Green Door*, the other two were released uncut with a fifteen age limit.

27 Lars Åhlander (ed.), *Svensk filmografi 7: 1970–1979*, Stockholm: Norstedts/SFI, 1989.

28 Jack Stevenson, *Scandinavian Blue: The Erotic Cinema of Sweden and Denmark in the 1960s and 1970s*, Jefferson, NC: McFarland, 2010.

29 Mariah Larsson, 'Practice Makes Perfect? The Production of the Swedish Sex Film in the 1970s', *Film International*, Special issue: 'Making Movies in Europe', vol. 8, no. 6, 2010.

30 Furhammar, 1991, p. 312.

31 See the annual reports of the Swedish Film Institute: *Svenska filminstitutets verksamhetsberättelse 1969–70*, Stockholm: Swedish Film Institute, 1970; *Svenska filminstitutets verksamhetsberättelse 1970–71*, Stockholm: Swedish Film Institute, 1971; *Svenska filminstitutets verksamhetsberättelse 1971–72*, Stockholm: Swedish Film Institute, 1972; *Svenska filminstitutets verksamhetsberättelse 1972–73*, Stockholm: Swedish Film Institute, 1973; *Svenska filminstitutets verksamhetsberättelse 1973–74*, Stockholm: Swedish Film Institute, 1974; *Svenska filminstitutets verksamhetsberättelse 1974–75*, Stockholm: Swedish Film Institute, 1975; *Svenska filminstitutets verksamhetsberättelse 1975–76*, Stockholm: Swedish Film Institute, 1976.

32 Schaefer, 1999, pp. 69–73.

33 See Annual Reports, SFI.

34 Schaefer, 1999, p. 71.

35 Arnberg & Larsson, 'Benefits of the In-Between', 2013.

36 Åhlander, 1989, p. 50.

37 Stevenson, 2010, p. 160.

38 Bertil Behring, 'Mazurkan går över Sverige: Fnissporr ger bion 1 miljon', *Kvällsposten*, February 7, 1971.

39 Tore Borglund, 'Ömhet och politik hör ihop', *Kvällsposten*, April 20, 1970.

40 Mauritz Edström, 'Rolig dansk fräckis', *Dagens Nyheter*, December 27, 1970.

41 Altman, 1999, p. 61.

42 Kerstin Sedvallson, 'Inte bara gladporr i dagens danska filmer', *Dagens Nyheter*, December 18, 1975.

43 *Dagens Nyheter*, August 13, 1973.

44 Thorleif Hellbom, 'Danska gladporren en saga blott', *Dagens Nyheter*, August 14, 1973.

45 Stevenson, 2010, p. 216.

46 Censorship records for *More about the Language of Love* from the National Board of Film Censors. Registration no 109 472.

47 Björklund, 2012, p. 191.

48 For a more thorough overview of the censorship process for *More About the Language of Love*, see Björklund, 2012.

49 Minutes from the meeting held September 15, 1970. Records from the archive of the National Board of Film Censors (Statens biografbyrå). Record number 109 472.

50 Klara Arnberg & Tommy Gustafsson, *Moralpanik och lågkultur: genus- och mediehistoriska analyser*, Stockholm: Atlas, 2013.

51 Nils Bejerot, *Barn – serier – samhälle*, Stockholm: Folket i bild, 1954; Fredric Wertham, *Seduction of the Innocent*, New York: Rineheart, 1954.

52 Attachment to the minutes from the meeting held September 29, 1970. Records from the archive of the National Board of Film Censors (Statens biografbyrå). Record number 109 472.

53 Advertisement in *Dagens Nyheter*, 18 November 1970.

54 Björklund, 2012, pp. 153–200.

55 Björklund, 2012, pp. 153–200.

56 Eva Ekselius, 'Hur man botar sexångest', *Dagens Nyheter*, July 9, 1971.

57 In an interview with Maj-Briht Bergström-Walan, the sexologist who was one of the driving forces behind the films and whose participation actually implies the films' honest intentions of being sex educational, a kind of disappointment that the film had been regarded as pornographic could be understood. For instance, the fact that *Language of Love* was screened in porn cinemas in New York was to her due to a gross misunderstanding of the film's purposes. Her reaction may seem naïve, but testifies to the sense of a mission that many sex educators, sex therapists and sexologists seem to have been feeling. Maj-Briht Bergström-Walan, interviewed by Elisabet Björklund & Mariah Larsson, Stockholm, November 9, 2010.

58 Christina Lindberg, interviewed by Mariah Larsson, Malmö University, February 19, 2009.

59 Cf. Schaefer, 1999.

60 *Sydsvenska Dagbladet Snällposten*, December 24, 1973.

61 Monica Tunbäck Hansson, *Göteborgsposten*, January 22, 1974.

62 See 'Anita', http://www.svenskfilmdatabas.se/ [Accessed 22 July 2007].

63 Mary Ann Doane, *The Desire to Desire: The Woman's Film of the 1940s*, Houndmills & London: MacMillan Press, 1987, pp. 38–69. For a more detailed analysis of *Anita*, see Kevin Heffernan, 'Many of Your Finer Nudie Films: Saga Film, Swedish National Cinema, and Seventies Transnational Erotic Film', in Björklund & Larsson (eds) *Swedish Cinema and the Sexual Revolution: Critical Essays*, Jefferson, NC: McFarland, 2016, pp. 216–232.

64 Carl Michael Edenborg, 'Utgivarens förord', in *Anonym: Flossie: En sextonårig Venus. Av en som känt denna tjusande gudinna och dyrkat vid hennes helgedom*, Stockholm & Sala: Vertigo förlag, 2013, pp. 5–6.

65 Inge Ivarson, interviewed by Elisabet Björklund & Mariah Larsson, Stockholm, November 8, 2010.

66 *Kvällsposten*, January 18, 1975.

67 *Dagens Nyheter*, April 20, 1976.

68 Cf. Mariah Larsson, *Skenet som bedrog: Mai Zetterling och det svenska sextiotalet*, Lund: Sekel bokförlag, 2006, pp. 206–07.

69 Hellbom, 1973.

70 Edström, 1970; Borglund, 1970.

71 Kendrick, 1996, p. 250.

Chapter 3

Constructions of sexual space: The case of Malmö

T he city of Malmö is contradictory. Located in the south, far from the capital Stockholm, it has created an identity of its own; an identity which is both more provincial and working class than the urban finesse of Stockholm, yet much closer to continental Europe and another country's capital – Copenhagen. In Maj Sjöwall and Per Wahlöö's police procedural *Murder at the Savoy*, published in Sweden in 1970 as *Polis, polis, potatismos!*, Malmö's closeness to Copenhagen and the rest of Europe is emphasized:[1]

> With the gentle wind came fumes of the rotting garbage and seaweed that had been washed up on Ribersborg Beach and in through the mouth of the harbor into the canals.
>
> The city doesn't resemble the rest of Sweden to a very great degree, largely because of its location. Malmö is closer to Rome than to the midnight sun, and the lights of the Danish coast twinkle along the horizon. And even though many winters are slushy and windblown, summers are just as often long and warm, filled with the song of the nightingale and scents from the lush vegetation of the expansive parks.
>
> Which is exactly the way it was that fair summer evening early in July 1969. It was also quiet, calm and quite deserted. The tourists weren't noticeable to any extent – they hardly ever are. As for the roaming, unwashed hash-smokers, only the first bands had arrived, and not so many more would show up either, since most of them never get past Copenhagen.[2]

Malmö was and still is Sweden's third largest town, with a population of around 265,000 in 1971 and 320,000 in 2015. When Sjöwall and Wahlöö wrote their novel, Malmö was a prosperous town, although – as *Murder at the Savoy* points out – with large differences between social classes. Between 1971 and 1976, however, Malmö entered its long decline into post-industrialism. In 1973, Kockums was the fifth largest civilian shipyard in the world. The following year, the huge 140-metre-tall gantry crane which would become an emblem of the city was first used.[3] However, shortly thereafter, with the 1974 oil crisis, the shipyard industry in Malmö began its long and slow descent. In 1987, Kockums was closed down and in 2002, the large crane was dismantled and sold to South Korea.[4] The post-industrial recession for the city that began in 1974 continued until the late 1990s or even early 2000s.

In this chapter and the next, we shall explore Malmö as a sexual, urban space. More specifically, focus will be on a very particular kind of sexual space, namely the stores, clubs and cinemas where pornographic films were screened. As such, I will not discuss the films themselves here, nor the problems involved in researching them. Instead, they will be the subject of Chapter 5. In order to map out the exhibition contexts, I have used advertisements in the evening paper *Kvällsposten*, but also maps of Malmö, photographs of the urban environment, as well as other material, such as public inquiries and studies of the modern architectural and urban history of Malmö.

Additionally, I have conducted interviews with five men who have had various experiences of these establishments. Three of these were interviewed by me in person with a recorder. One interview was conducted over the phone, with me taking notes, and the fifth informant has been sending me e-mails in response to questions or themes suggested by me. I have striven for confidentiality, and thus the informants are called Informants U, V, X, Y and Z in this study. All of them were approximately twenty years old at some point between 1965 and 1975.

Finally, I have made use of interview material from another research project, made with sex workers in the 1970s. These interviews were performed by two sociologists during a project which resulted in two dissertations in sociology in the early 1980s.[5] I have been allowed to read the transcriptions from these interviews. Here, too, I have striven for confidentiality.

Another type of material consists of scholarly articles or reports from around the period studied here. The report *Svarta Affärer*/'Shady Business' was actually made during the mid-seventies and deals with, among other things, the sex clubs in Malmö. This report has been very informative (as has David A. Karp's article on pornographic book stores in New York from 1973).

Theoretical perspectives are mostly inspired by urban studies (mainly feminist geography and sexual space theory) and sexuality studies (in particular, the sexual script theory developed by John H. Gagnon and William Simon).[6] The first part of the chapter deals with the various exhibition contexts as part of the urban space more generally, whereas the next chapter will discuss some of these establishments in greater detail.

My claim in the introduction that the proximity of sex and sexual expressions have decreased in everyday public life in Sweden since the 1970s can be confirmed by looking at a sample of the laws regulating sex and sexual images. Already by 1971, the law replacing the obscenity law in the Swedish penal code forbade the display of sexually explicit material. This law, however, was not properly enforced in the 1970s, much to the chagrin of the women's movement.[7] Laws against child pornography came into effect in 1980, and were even further reinforced in the 1990s and 2000s, with a change in the Swedish constitution excepting child pornography from the laws regulating freedom of expression. In the early 1980s, the moral panic surrounding the VCR also resulted in a more pervasive regulation of private screenings in the home. The new law demanded that all videos have an equivalent of a publisher who was legally responsible for what was shown in the video and could be prosecuted for illegal depictions of violence [*olaga våldsskildring*], which included scenes of violence in combination with sex.[8] In 1982, a law prohibiting pornographic performance [*pornografisk föreställning*] – meaning shows with live performers – was implemented to curtail the market for prostitution in the sex clubs, where such shows were regular parts of the repertoire.[9] Between 1987 and 2004, in order to curb the spread of HIV, the 'sauna club law' regulated places where homosexuals could meet for sexual encounters, a highly controversial law, criticized for discriminating and demonizing gays. Furthermore, whether due to the law or to changing communication technologies, street prostitution in Sweden has decreased since the Sex Purchases Act in 1999.[10]

In addition to these laws, the technical development made home viewing of pornography more accessible – with VCR in the late seventies and early eighties as the first revolution, and the Internet in the late nineties as the second. The consumption patterns for pornography changed and moved from a largely public consumption to a more private one, before again defusing the boundaries between public and private through the Internet. Today, only a few sex stores remain in Malmö, and even fewer offer screenings of films to customers.[11]

Although Internet increases the availability and makes legal action more difficult, and although the acceptance for sexually explicit imagery in different visual media has in some respects increased since the 1970s, pornography and sexual expressions are from this perspective actually a lot more controlled by laws today than during the period relevant to this study. All these laws have good intentions, such as attempting to make the nation safer, increase equality between the sexes, protect children from being harmed, or contain the spread of a disease which was deemed a threat. One may very well read these laws as a reaction against a progressive dispersion of what was considered a problematic attitude to sexuality, which was regarded as exploiting and reifying human beings, profiting on loneliness and lust for sensationalism and causing drug abuse, inequality and criminality.[12] Also, these laws follow from a notion of sexuality as possibly destructive, and can thus also be read as an attempt to regulate sexuality into less destructive domains. Sweden's official view of sexuality has been criticized, most notably by anthropologist Don Kulick, who claims that 'good sex in Sweden' is not defined as procreative sex within the institution of matrimony, but as an activity to take part between equal partners in a relation characterized by love and mutual respect.[13] All sex that does not fall into this category – for example, promiscuity, certain BDSM practices, or the selling and buying of sexual services – is frowned upon.

As discussed in Chapter 1, although some during the debate on sexuality in the 1960s held that pornography would benefit from being legalized by becoming better (i.e. less vulgar and shabby), this notion changed in the 1970s as the argument moved in a different direction.[14] In hindsight, it is easy to say that those who argued for a legalization of pornography and liberalization of sexual matters in general in the 1960s were naïve and misguided.[15] Nevertheless, several factors during the 1970s combined to create what some described as the negative consequences of the legalization of pornography: increasing unemployment numbers, growing inflation, the oil crisis in 1974, and the spread of heroin in the mid-seventies.[16] In Malmö, these problems were specifically related to the city as a seaport, as Kockums, which had provided many with job opportunities, went into decline and began letting go of employees.

Moreover, the sex clubs and stores which I will discuss in this chapter were often situated in buildings and areas of urban decay, such as former workers' apartment houses, buildings which were projected to be taken down, and neighbourhoods of general crime and delinquency. That kind of urban decay is not unique to Malmö in any way – many cities in Sweden (as well as in other parts of the world) had their city centres reconstructed in the 1960s and 1970s. An important part of the social democratic welfare project had to do with the 'building away' of social problems by tearing down blocks and houses associated with slum and dirt, and erecting new apartment complexes in suburbs. Between 1965 and 1975, Miljonprogrammet, the million dwelling programme, was to result in one million new homes for the working- and lower-middle classes.[17] However, in Malmö, the process which began in the late 1950s was quite prolonged, with the last old buildings taken down in the 1980s.[18]

For instance, a very old but poor and downtrodden area called Caroli was demolished in the late 1960s, and a shopping centre with a modern apartment compound was built in its stead (Caroli City 1970–71). Jerusalemgatan, one of the oldest streets in Malmö but also known as a street used for prostitution, disappeared due to the new construction. Other spots which were taken down to make space for modern housing or city centres included Lugnet, around Södervärn and along Nobelvägen (Sofielund). In some cases, there was a protracted period of time before the new buildings were erected, and thus so-called 'bomb holes' – entire blocks which had been torn down – marked the cityscape of Malmö. I will describe Lugnet and the establishments located there in more detail further on in the next chapter.

The sex clubs Delicate and Picant advertised in *Kvällsposten* during those years, and it is likely that their activities ended when the actual facilities were taken down, especially since the attitude towards the sex business had become less benevolent in the mid-1970s. There was also a case against a landlord in Malmö who was prosecuted for procuring but acquitted on appeal. According to the prosecutor, he knowingly leased apartments to sex workers, and some of these apartments functioned as 'posing studios' [*poseringsateljéer*]. His buildings were notorious for their low standard, and although the title 'slumlord' may be correct in this case, the title 'pimp' was dismissed by the courts.[19]

From these accounts it would seem that the seventies were not a very happy decade. Although the usual narrative of Malmö in the 1970s mainly deals with the negative events – like the beginnings of the downfall of Kockums, the 'bomb holes' and increasing unemployment – it does not paint a complete picture. The seventies were also a time of radical political movements (such as the women's movement) and developments in music, including prog rock, the national progressive leftist music wave of the 1970s and, in 1971, the first Folkfesten [The People's Festival] that took place in Malmö. Folkfesten would become a recurring annual event and is still organized today. Pornography and the sex industry are linked both to this negative narrative of Malmö and to the radical political and musical developments in a puzzling paradox, with the discussion of sexual liberation continuing into the 1970s, but changing both due to new political ideas and an increasingly uncomfortable reality. An example of this could be Cornelis Vreesvijk, who played at the very first Folkfesten but also appeared in *The Lustful Vicar*. To be young and to be radical also meant to relate in some way to sexual morals, and to discard an older generation's more puritan ideals. This is important to keep in mind because later in the 1970s this notion changes. Although pornography and the women's movement in some senses shared the same focus of interest – as evidenced by Germaine Greer's presence as a member of the jury of the very first Wet Dreams festival in Amsterdam – they would very soon be on opposing sides in a struggle for the right of interpretation of female sexuality.[20] In the late 1970s and 1980s, being radical rather entailed being *against* pornography.

Nevertheless, there was a thriving sex business in Malmö. Although contributing to it, the legalization of pornography and the spread of the sex clubs and stores were by no means its only cause. Although discussed in later debates as the cause of 'secondary effects' or 'secondary impact', such as crime and lowered property values, sex stores and sex clubs in Malmö in the 1970s rather seem to have themselves been the secondary effect of changing legislation and low property values.[21] Malmö's proximity to Denmark also played a part. Pornography became a part of public, urban space throughout the 1960s and 1970s: first through the stores which displayed pornography and other sexual paraphernalia in their windows; and later during the seventies through not only stores and clubs, but also grocery stores, kiosks and tobacco stands, where pornographic magazines were openly sold. These eventually stopped displaying overtly, but the stores and clubs signalled instead their presence through curtains and black boards in front of their windows.

Exhibition contexts

There were several different screening contexts in Malmö (and elsewhere) at this time. Pornographic films were screened in regular cinemas, as well as in porn cinemas, sex clubs, sex stores and at home. Since I regard the screenings at home as private – whether they took place in solitude, with a partner, a handful of friends or at parties – they are excluded from this investigation, although it is still important to keep their existence in mind. Screenings at home were not a product of the VCR; the VCR merely made it easier to view and became more widely spread among the general population than the 8mm or Super 8 projector. Private screenings are also important because they provided one market for the sex stores, which sold and let out films for home viewing.

In the regular cinemas, films such as those discussed in Chapter 2 were screened. As I argued in that chapter, the generic belonging of these films is not obvious. Although not conforming to what is understood as pornography today, they were frequently referred to as porn films or as 'not porn'. The screenings were advertised with show times among the other advertisements and can be seen as part of the regular fare. The only porn cinema in

Malmö was Spegeln, which showed a non-stop programme of one hardcore feature film and a number of shorts. During opening hours, spectators paid the admission fee and entered for as long or as briefly as they liked.

The sex clubs screened 16mm or 8mm films. Those which attempted a more 'upscale' demeanour screened 16mm film, and advertised these as 'cinema film' or 'sound film'. One of the clubs advertised its programme using titles, which has made it possible for me to identify some of them in the database of the National Board of Film Censors. Here, the screenings were part of a larger programme of entertainment, including striptease, live shows, water shows (involving onstage bathing), lesbian shows and so on.

In the sex stores, films were screened as a strategy for attracting customers. Some advertisements advertised the fact that '[y]ou can watch the film and you can buy the film'. In the beginning, films were often screened in front of an audience, but the use of private booths eventually became standard practice. The boundary between club and store was vague. In the 1960s, stores offered membership and addresses to the clubs, acting as a kind of 'go-between' for the clandestine enterprises.[22]

In the late 1960s, a handball club started to arrange members-only parties with striptease dancers in order to attract more members. Despite an increase in membership, the National Handball Association reacted strongly and put a stop to the activities.[23] Meanwhile, some of the stores advertised film screenings as well as shows in order to attract customers.

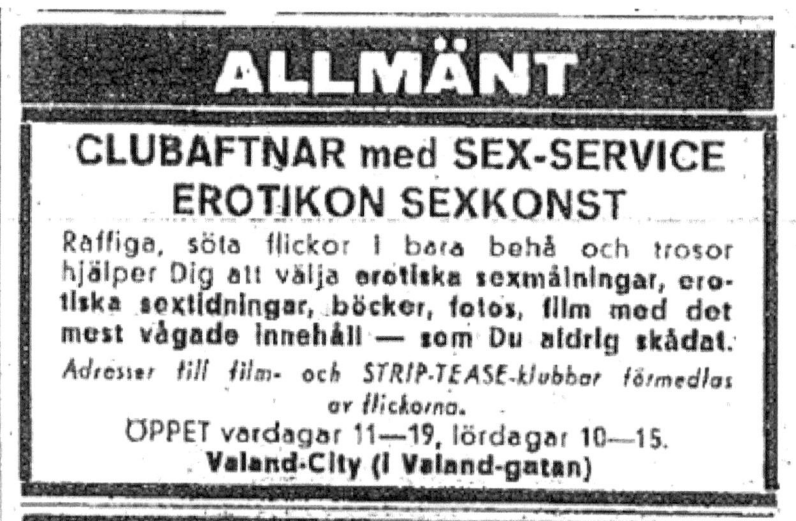

Figure 1: 'Club evenings with sex service, eroticon, sex art. Stunning, pretty girls in only bra and panties will help you select erotic sex paintings, erotic sex magazines, books, photos, film with the most daring content – like you have never seen. *Addresses to film- and striptease-clubs are provided by the girls*'. Advertisement from *Kvällsposten*, January 10, 1969.

The stores and clubs: Urban geography

According to the investigation *Svarta affärer*, there were more than thirty clubs operating in Malmö in the mid-seventies.[24] Not all of these advertised in the press (I have counted at most seventeen advertisements for both clubs and stores).[25] Judging from these adverts, the heyday for establishments dealing in sexual and pornographic entertainment was during the first few years after the removal of the obscenity paragraph from the penal code. This is also reasonable in relation to accessible historical sources. In the mid-seventies, the Malmö police department, in collaboration with the social authorities, took action against the clubs and closed several of them down. Since, as the police claimed, there was prostitution on the premises, the owners were indicted for procuring.[26] Between 1971 and 1974, adverts are plentiful and increasingly flamboyant, whereas in the fall of 1977, only three establishments advertised in the local tabloid newspaper. These three advertisements were unobtrusive and claimed nothing but film screenings as entertainment. Prostitution was regarded as connected to the performances onstage, rather than to the screenings. In the early 1980s, a new law – mentioned above – was passed, prohibiting 'pornographic performances', by which was meant shows with live performers. The intention of this law was to curb prostitution, but it also meant that, in combination with the spread of the VCR, those establishments that provided sexual entertainment had lost their reason for existence, so to speak, as well as a large share of their clientele. In the 1980s, almost all sex stores, clubs and porn theatres closed down in Sweden. Today, only a few clubs exist in Stockholm and Gothenburg. In addition, there is a small chain of strip clubs called McDragans, with four premises located both in the countryside and small towns.[27] In Malmö, only a few stores remain, with Grottan ('The Cave') as the oldest, opened some time in the late 1960s.

Additionally, there was much diversity among the clubs. For instance, the opening hours differed to a large extent. In the fall of 1972, the clubs which stayed open the longest (Arabia Sex Night Club, Club Stick Inn, Kakadu Night Club, Sex Night Club Venus, Sex Night Club Picant and Delicate) were open until 3 a.m. Others closed a lot earlier, like Club Adam (8 p.m.), but most closed around midnight (varying from 10.30 p.m. to 1 a.m.).[28] Most likely, the establishments attracted different customer groups: those open late at night were aimed at businessmen and tourists, whereas the earlier ones were places where you could drop in on your way from work (at least judging from the adverts). One of my informants described how he would go out on Fridays hoping to meet a woman, and when that failed he would drop into one of the stores he passed on his way home.[29] Apart from Venus and Picant, which, judging by the adverts, were the most extravagant and opened at 6 p.m. and 5 p.m. respectively, all opened around noon. None of the places were licensed to serve alcohol, although some of them did so under the counter.[30]

Furthermore, the establishments were – by coincidence or not – situated in clusters. In 1972, for instance, a large number were located in the area around Möllevångstorget Square, two (Delicate and Picant) on Kaptensgatan in the Lugnet area, two in the finer area of the

Old Town (Venus on Snapperupsgatan and Pigalle on Mäster Johansgatan), and another two further off (Grottan on Östra Förstadsgatan and Stick Inn on Vattenverksvägen) in the north-eastern part of town. As you only had to report your activities once you had opened such an establishment (later in the 1970s, a permit was required), there was nothing (except the price of the rent) to prevent new clubs and stores opening in any area. Interestingly, Rörsjöstaden – the area where a lot of the street prostitution (on Kungsgatan) and posing studios were located – only had clubs or stores around the perimeter of the neighbourhood.[31] Since, according to the police investigation, there was prostitution in the clubs as well, there was actually prostitution going on in most of Malmö at the time, albeit in different forms.

What the adverts and the maps – in combination with the urban history of Malmö's prostitution streets – thus outline is a city more or less steeped in sex. From the railway station in the northern part of the city to Södervärn in the southern part, and from Triangeln to Kirseberg, at the appropriate time of day you would never have to walk for more than ten or fifteen minutes to either encounter a sex club, a sex store or a prostitution street. It may very well have been possible to walk through Malmö choosing not to notice these establishments and milieus, but I would contend that it is not an exaggeration to say that a commercial sexuality characterized the public, urban space of Malmö during the first half of the 1970s.

Public space and the geography of fear

Public spaces are those which are accessible to everyone, like town squares, streets and pavements, and open harbours. Most of the outdoor urban space which is not part of someone's home or office is public space. It is where anyone can go without paying for entrance or a particular permit. Public space is abstract as well as material; it is a concept which is intimately connected to the notion of democracy, but it also tangibly consists of the very streets, pavements, squares and parks of a city, town or village. The city is said to belong to the citizens,[32] and urbanity and cityscapes are often ideally associated with not only its streets and buildings, but also with the people populating its public spaces.[33] This is why we say, for instance, that downtown Los Angeles during the 1980s and 1990s was a 'dead' downtown, because no people were seen in the streets (except for the homeless).[34] Nevertheless, the trend for a long period during the post-war years was that people moved out of the city centres to the suburbs, leaving the centres scarcely inhabited, unrenovated and with relatively cheap rents. The gentrification of city centres – or perhaps in some cases, the regentrification of city centres – with escalating real estate prices, careful renovation and couples continuing to live downtown even after they have children is quite a recent phenomenon. However, in the 1970s, this process had not yet begun in earnest.

To reiterate: ideally, the city is populated with people of all kinds – young, old, men, women, people of various ethnicities, religious confessions and sexualities. Access to public space is not only regarded as a vital component in a democratic society, but also as what creates a sense of 'life' in the urban environment.[35]

In reality, however, public space is regulated by informal codes and norms. One of the factors that regulate people's movement in public space is described by some scholars as the 'geography of fear'.[36] In this analysis, women are careful not to go into areas which they perceive as unsafe; yet gays, elderly persons and people of a minority ethnic or religious belonging, for instance, may also feel that they need to tread cautiously in what might be a dangerous public space, with gay bashers, bag snatchers and racist hate groups making the streets unsafe for people who are marked as different either in strength and ability to defend themselves, or in a way that may be construed as provocative. Thus, in the concept of public space, there is a residue of the Greek notion of *demos* – the people – which in ancient Greece meant the free, grown men of the state. Grown, (seemingly) heterosexual men of the majority ethnic and religious belonging are, from this perspective, the ones whose right to public space is rarely questioned. However, space is diverse and certain parts of a city may primarily belong to gays (like the Castro District in San Francisco, Church and Wellesly in Toronto, and 'Rundan' in Gothenburg from the 1920s to the 1960s), and others to parents and children (like playgrounds).[37] A recent study of veiled, Muslim women in Malmö showed that, due to harassment, they did not feel that large parts of the city were safe for them.[38] Interestingly, although the suburban area of Rosengård is often depicted in press and media as a dangerous place to live due to ethnic segregation, high unemployment and social unrest, this is where these women felt the safest (being, for them, 'home', their own neighbourhood), whereas Möllevångstorget (the city square closest to Rosengård, also with a somewhat bad reputation in press and media, and with an ethnically mixed population) was felt to be semi-safe. Consequently, and in contradiction to how other Malmöites may feel, the further west/north-west in the city, the more dangerous the city was perceived.

Additionally, there is a temporal dimension to space, which means that some areas are considered safe in the daytime but not after dark. For instance, parks, alleyways, bicycle routes and tunnels might be perceived as perfectly safe in the daytime, but are avoided at night. Within feminist geography, and inspired by Henri Lefebvre's theories on space, Swedish urban scholar Carina Listerborn proposes three levels of fear: the first is the fear of space, which is a subjective representation of space and influenced by rumours, built environments, previous experiences and personal relationships – that is, discourses which shape our thinking; secondly, there is the fear of what the space represents (e.g. the social relations of power manifested in the urban landscape, or 'the mobilization of representations of women as passive victims and men as active aggressors');[39] and thirdly, there is the direct experience of fear and space.[40] The first two are of especial interest here, as the sex stores and sex clubs may both have been surrounded by rumours and other discourses which shaped women's perception of them, as well as quite blatantly displayed material which could easily be interpreted as conveying men as aggressors and women as victims.

As Jane Juffer argues in her study *At Home with Pornography: Women, Sex and Everyday Life* (1998), access is important in relation to the consumption of pornography. The

American zoning laws – which regulate where sites for adult entertainment can be located – most often place such establishments in areas perceived of as unsafe by women.[41] Although there were no such zoning laws in Malmö in the 1970s, many of the neighbourhoods where the sex stores were located were already in disrepute and may not have been perceived of as safe. Together with the traditional division of space into a public sphere belonging to men and a private sphere belonging to women, zoning laws constrict women's consumption of pornography and delimit it to the home.[42] This gendering of the public and private spheres can be compared with the movements of homosexual men and women in Gothenburg between 1950 and 1980. Homosexual men more frequently met outdoors, in public spaces, whereas homosexual women moved in the public space mostly for transportation.[43]

In a study by Baptiste Coulmont and Phil Hubbard, the need to protect minors or children is claimed to be the first and foremost argument in the regulation of sex commerce in Great Britain and France from the 1970s onward.[44] Preventing shops from opening in the vicinity of schools, for instance, or in residential areas where families live, or the obligation of the shops to put up a sign stating the age limit to enter is made on the basis that society needs to protect its young.[45]

Although children were clearly important in the national regulation of commercial sex (as the law on child pornography in 1980 demonstrates), it seems that in Sweden it was more a question of protecting children from being hurt in the process of the production of pornography.[46] The possible dangers of children consuming or even simply seeing pornographic material does not really seem to have been an issue. On the contrary, one assumption of the late 1960s was that children were not harmed by seeing images of sexual activity. In the inquiry into film censorship, the inquirers stated for instance that:

> The inquiry finds itself able to, from the present material, draw the conclusion that in the matter of the large majority of children it is unlikely that they would come to harm by seeing depictions of sexuality in regular narrative films or pornographic films.[47]

Although, as the inquirers claimed, it may not be suitable for children to have unlimited access to films which contained very explicit, and perhaps even sadistic, depictions of sexuality, it may also be that sexual depictions could have favourable effects on the individual.[48]

In regards to being exposed to sexual material, children do not appear to have been the main focus for protection against harm in Sweden. This may seem paradoxical, since they have been the reason for protective measures in several other instances, like the establishing of a film censorship institution in 1911, or when the debate on 'video violence' raged in the early 1980s.[49] Instead, the reason for regulation of shops and clubs was prostitution, and rather the protection of women, although one significant point was that some of the sex workers were minors. The law against the display of overly explicit sexual material seems to align itself with the notion that, as Coulmont and Hubbard write, 'a consumer's right to access pornography should not be allowed to impinge on the lives of those who do not wish to'.[50] During the seventies, the women's movement complained that the law was not properly enforced, and sex shops in several countries were condemned 'with "Take back the night" demonstrations ('La nuit est à nous' in France) implicating sex shops in [the] wider process of sexual objectification that limited women's rights to public space'.[51]

Similarly, in Sweden, sexual imagery and merchandise for consumption in the public space were regarded as contributing to an objectification of women which privileged not only a male gaze, but a male proprietorship of and right to women in general. Accordingly, pornography and prostitution were logically connected to rape, and thereby regulated female access to public space.[52] All three conveyed the message that women's bodies were available to an uncontrollable male sexuality unless women conformed to certain norms regarding their own behaviour.[53] In her reaction to the sex crime inquiry, Maria-Pia Boëthius – with a high degree of empathy – describes the sense of fear governing women's lives:

> In fact, we women walk around all the time and are afraid of being raped. It sounds exaggerated – but the truth is that the thought exists in the back of our heads all the time. […] Our freedom as women, as half of the population, is limited. We do not live in a free society where we can freely socialize with men how and when we like. We must all the time keep in mind that there is a number of situations in which we cannot place ourselves with men because we may run the risk of being raped. And if we do get raped in those situations, society has no understanding for us. The blame is ours.[54]

Boëthius' description of the constricted freedom of women in society concurs with descriptions within theories of the geography of fear. Thus, movement is regulated by fear of rape and, in accordance with radical feminist theories about the 'war on women', rape is the number-one oppressive mechanism which constricts women.[55] Since rape is an expression of men's 'right' to women, in that line of reasoning, pornography and prostitution belong to the same logic of ownership, denial of female agency and subjectivity, and male privilege. The dictum 'porn is the theory, rape is the practice' quite aptly captures this idea: porn teaches men that women are sexually available and that 'no' means 'yes'. It is no coincidence, then, that the sex clubs and stores, as well as porn cinemas, were regarded as spaces for male dominance, oppression of women and conveyors of the message of the commercial availability of the female body.[56]

Nevertheless, from my studies, it seems as if this public, sexual space was not uniform, but actually quite complex. Although most of my informants tend to describe these places in negative terms as 'shabby', 'run-down', 'smelly' or 'seedy', and thus disassociating themselves from them, their own relationships to and uses of these places varied. In all of these establishments, pornography in different forms was on display – as merchandise or as entertainment – yet the function of it may have differed. The desired object may have been the female body, but this is not necessarily true in each case. On the one hand, the stores, clubs and the porn cinema Spegeln seem to present a massive male, sexual hegemony. On the other hand, it needs to be noted that some of these places were owned or run by women or couples. The women who worked in these clubs seem to have found them less unsafe than working on the street or in posing studios.

'Public privacy' or public, sexual space in the stores

Although sometimes demanding a fee for entering or membership status, the sex stores and sex clubs can, through their mere existence and their signs and window displays, easily be regarded as public places of male sexual privilege. Moreover, with prostitution, the screenings of pornographic films, the sexual entertainment of striptease and live shows, and a nearly exclusively male clientele (all my informants seem to be an agreement that women were rarely seen as customers, only as workers in the stores and clubs), their permeating of the cityscape of Malmö (and other cities) can be described as a male domination of public, sexual space. This is also how the clubs are perceived in the investigation *Svarta affärer*, although the framework is not so much feminist as a Marxist and sociological one, of the aforementioned commercialization of interpersonal relations.[57] The traditional feminist analysis of public space and male domination of space also seem to underline such an understanding.

Nevertheless, some kind of paradox is at work. In an American study from 1973, sociologist David A. Karp discusses the need for 'public privacy' when consuming sexual material.[58] Karp notes several strategies of customers, as well as of those pornographic bookstores included in the study. For instance, customers tend to hang around outside of the stores, seemingly nonchalant, before they enter. The stores provide shelter from the eyes of the street by having the windows covered in some way (often by black paint), and offer discretion through the brown paper bags in which the purchased material can be hidden.[59]

Furthermore, as Karp states, customers within the stores seem suspicious of others and tend to avoid eye contact. The interior geography of the stores facilitates such avoidance. Although Karp does not go into detail on the layout of the stores, sex stores have been described by other researchers as labyrinthine, and I have discussed elsewhere the difference between visibility and invisibility in sex stores targeting a male, female or mixed clientele.[60] Karp, however, notes that the film booths provide a higher degree of privacy, where the general norms and codes of the stores can be transgressed. For instance, it is possible to masturbate in the booths but not in the rest of the store. Karp sums up: 'Customers in pornographic bookstores protect themselves both from outsiders (persons not similarly engaged in the deviant activity) and from fellow participants.'[61] Written in the early 1970s, the prominence of the word 'deviant' in the article to some extent indicates that the act of entering a sex store and consuming sexual material was not seen as acceptable or 'normal' behaviour in the early 1970s. Although the study is made in an American context, my contention is that the same kind of puritanical view of normality was at work in Sweden as well, not least because the male-to-male sexual acts which could take place in these contexts (and which will be discussed further on in this chapter) could be defined as homosexuality, which was classified as a disease in Sweden until 1979.

Thus, it is possible to argue that even though pornography was legal, and sex stores were both legal and tolerated in Sweden at the time, a kind of social code or social norm impeded the ease with which to consume this material in these contexts. It is very likely that the social norms varied from different social groups. Among the young, the radicals or university students, pornography could be regarded as fun and daring, challenging the norms of bourgeois society, especially in the early 1970s, before the impact of the women's movement.[62] The consumption of sexual entertainment among businessmen in the clubs, meanwhile, could be seen as a pastime among others. However, the idea of pornography as challenging bourgeois norms quite necessarily stems from the notion that there is something illicit about it. Moreover, businessmen were, at this point in time, nearly exclusively male, thus keeping the visiting of sex clubs a matter between men.[63]

In later studies, the stores – and especially their film booths – are emphasized as places for possible sexual encounters between men.[64] The labyrinthine constructions of the interior space of these stores function as a game board or a stage for 'a drama of perception and misapprehension, exhibition and hiding, recognition and denial', where men can initiate contact and accept or decline an invitation to have sex.[65] That the results of these American studies can be transposed to a Swedish or Scandinavian context is evident by Swedish studies such as Benny Henriksson's *Risk Factor Love* (1995), in which video clubs are discussed as meeting places for men who have sex with men,[66] as well as Henriksson and Månsson's study 'Sexual Negotiations' (1995), and Margareta Lindholm's and Arne Nilsson's studies of the movements and behaviour of homosexual men and women in Gothenburg between 1950 and 1980.[67] Although I have no definite proof that this pattern of behaviour was going on, there is enough circumstantial evidence to indicate that this did happen.

In any case, some kind of guilt and shame regarding the stores seem to play into the codes and norms of their usage, and the consumption of sexual material. On the one hand, this is due to sexual puritanism and standard moral norms for behaviour; on the other, the possible function of these places of consumption as sites for sexual encounters between men also restricted and regulated movement in and around the stores. A complaint from one of my informants, who claimed that he very rarely ventured into the stores, was that there was a lot of 'flashing and faggoting' going on.[68] Another one of my informants used these places as sites for exploring his own sexual identity, eventually coming out as gay.[69]

The material on display, sale and exhibition in these stores had varying content. On the one hand, a lot of it was commonly heterosexual material, depicting sexual intercourse between men and women; on the other, the stores also offered homosexual porn. One of the stores, Gentlemen's Corner, had special nights designated to homosexual men – interestingly labelled 'h-sexual', an abbreviation that could just as well mean heterosexual. Furthermore, some of the porn was bestiality porn, child porn or S&M porn. The 'polymorphously perverse'[70] of which Freud speaks seems to have been at large in the 1970s sex stores, even to a greater extent than today, since some of these subcategories of porn have all but disappeared from public view.[71] However, most of the material in the stores was heterosexual. One could argue that the heterosexuality of the stores functioned as a front for male-to-male activities,

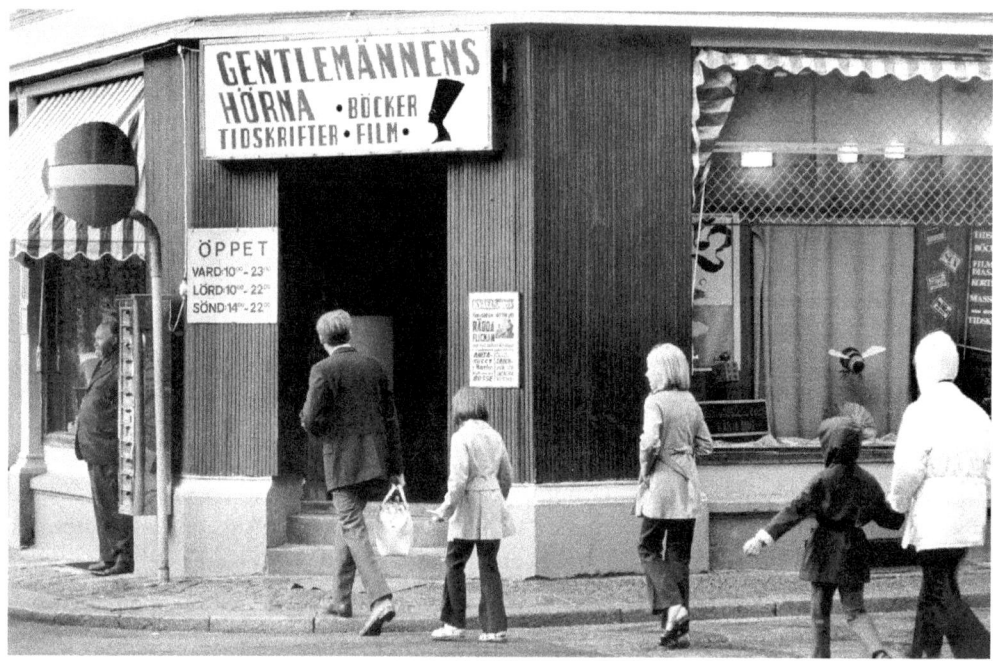

Figure 2: Gentlemännens hörna/Gentlemen's Corner. Image by Torbjörn Karlsson, *Bilder i Syd.*

or, as John Champagne puts it: 'The predominance of heterosexual films acts as a kind of institutional denial of the homoerotics of the space of the arcade'.[72]

This is not to say that all activities in all the stores were homosexual. Rather, it seems that there was a sharp dividing line between the homosexual activities and the heterosexual ones. Another one of my informants states that he never saw any kind of homosexual activity or homosexual pornography during his visits to stores, and that although there were 'older men who prowled around public toilets', in general, people were so unaware of homosexuality during this time that an acquaintance of his who was active within the left movement believed them to be from the secret police.[73]

A sharp dividing line also existed in terms of the geography of the sex workers. As stated earlier, many of the sex clubs also functioned as brothels, but outside of the clubs, Kungsgatan in Rörsjöstaden was the main venue for female-to-male prostitution. Men, on the other hand, offered sexual services on Schougens bro, a bridge crossing the canal further north, and its surroundings. These sites are not far away from each other (a five- to ten-minute walk), but were clearly designated for female-to-male and male-to-male prostitution respectively.

Nevertheless, although it may not be possible to establish the extent to which people sought out the stores for male-to-male sexual encounters or to consume homosexual pornography, the occurrence of male-to-male sex brings into question the notion of women as the sole object of desire and consumption in the stores. According to Champagne, even in those cases when heterosexual porn is consumed, the customers may still be looking for sexual encounters with other men.[74] This not only questions the notion of women as objects of desire and consumption – entailing the objectification of female bodies, the exploitation of women and so on – but also disrupts the perceived rigidity of heteronormativity, creating a fluidity or spectrum between heterosexuality and homosexuality. Champagne warns against taking this as a sign of the subversive character of the sex store, and underlines that they are still capitalist, commercial enterprises and, as such, part of the heteronormative dominant ideology. However, even within the capitalist system, people can 'thwart, if only provisionally, the "power" and violence of heteronormativity'.[75] The space of the sex store – a space for 'deviance' regardless of whether this deviance is excessive sexuality, masturbation or male-to-male sex – in such a reading seems more like a space on the margins of normality, in spite of its frequent occurrence in the cityscape.

The clubs

If the stores dissolved the perceived heterosexual logic of sexual entertainment and pornography to some extent, the clubs more straightforwardly seem to have offered a heterosexual, visual spectacle of the female body, of male and female bodies engaged in sexual acts, as well as 'girl-on-girl numbers' (so-called lesbian shows, staged, like in pornography, for the male, heterosexual gaze). According to the police and the social authorities, the sexual entertainment in the clubs functioned as a 'front' for prostitution.[76] The owners of eight clubs were indicted and convicted for procuring.[77] If the actual sex acts going on in the stores were between men or done on one's own, the actual sex acts in the clubs were between men and women (except some of those being performed onstage). According to the investigation *Svarta affärer*, the interiors of the clubs were:

> [...] quite similar, with some variations regarding size and hygiene. Most often there was a bar, some tables and chairs. In one end of the room there was some kind of stage construction. For film exhibition purposes, there was a screen behind the stage. In one corner there would be a small space for the projector and for a gramophone and record player. Also, the clubs had in common that they wanted to give customers an impression of luxury by for instance velvet tapestry and wall-to-wall carpeting.[78]

Some of the female sex workers in Malmö worked in the clubs before these were closed down by the police in 1976. They were paid by the owners to dance and strip onstage. However, they also sold sex on the premises. The women who were interviewed in the material from the 1970s had worked at several of the clubs that I have come across during my research, including Picant (sometimes called Sex Night Club Picant), Röda Rubinen, Klubb 16, Venus, Sexgrottan (sometimes called Grottan) and Royal. Some of those who had experience from the clubs seem to have preferred working in the clubs because it was 'well, not like a family but a sense of community', 'it was good and it was fun, you know. And you made good money'; or, as one woman said, 'I think it is weird that they have closed them down. It was better to work at clubs. You earned more than on the street'.[79] Also, in relation to a sense of being safe or unsafe, the clubs were preferred:

> It was OK, it was kind of safer in a way. And you didn't have to be cold in the winter. And if someone was making trouble, you only had to ring a bell and someone showed up to help you. There was like a bell, you know.

Nevertheless, some described the dancing as problematic. One woman stated surprise over the fact that she had danced in spite of being so shy: 'I can't really understand how I dared. I know how scared I am to perform or even talk if there are more than five people present. But I did it. And I didn't drink before or anything'. For another worker, it was the opposite way around:

> I am shy. I felt like a fool. I had to drink before so I became just enough drunk. So that I could do it. Otherwise I wouldn't have been able to. I had stage fright. I'll never forget the first time. I just stood up. I couldn't move. They had to come and bring me off the stage. Gave me some stiff drinks. Then it went as well as anything.

One of the sex workers claimed that the club made her feel locked in:

> At a club you are closed in, you know you have to work. To sit for thirteen hours. And not knowing who may turn up. Whoever, completely different types and no class, nothing. And always problems with the girls. […] You are not allowed to do this or that. And sometimes to sit for thirteen hours in dark rooms, it is no fun. It affects you psychologically.[80]

That going to the clubs was not a completely accepted practice is evidenced by this story:

> I remember once when I was working at Sexgrottan here in Malmö. I was dancing and a friend's father came in. I thought I was going to sink through the floor. He recognized me. But later I understood that he was going to keep quiet. He had no reason to tell anyone that he went to such places.[81]

A special feature in the men's magazine *FiB/Aktuellt* presented 'Sweden's most scantily clad girls', which included the performers at the clubs in Malmö, Stockholm and Gothenburg.[82] Less upscale than its American cousin *Playboy*, *FiB/Aktuellt*'s usual fare consisted of features on sports, criminality, and 'true stories' of rape and prostitution. Many issues had some sort of report on sex clubs and brothels in Sweden and abroad. In a typically ambiguous oscillation between fascination and moralizing, the article described the performers and their shows. According to *FiB/Aktuellt*, the specialty in Malmö is the water show.[83] At Picant (see Chapter 4), the owner herself, Ramona, 'offers the sexiest strip of the evening'. Sexyland is described as 'Malmö's smallest sex club'.[84] At most of the establishments, porn films are used as programme fillers, screened between performances on the stage. Underlined in the article is the availability of the performers. This is done implicitly, by making note of the fact that the performers may go out amongst the guests either as part of the performance or between performances, that the audience is invited to partake in the water shows; and that during one type of strip called 'contact strip' the performers ask members of the audience to touch them.[85] All these interactions with the audience, made on the presumed initiative of the female performers, function to dissolve the boundary between audience and performer. Accordingly, judging from the feature, it seems that a standard norm for bodily contact, intrinsic to the clubs and transgressing those norms existing outside of them, is set by the performers themselves (although most likely suggested, encouraged and applauded by the owners). Although social codes generally regulate and even forbid the touching of unknown people, the performing women in the clubs made touching an accepted part of the venue's code.

There may be many reasons to consume sexually explicit material and sexual entertainment – curiosity, tradition, a sense of the bizarre, a need for confirmation of sexuality and one's own sense of self, etc. – but one reason has to do with the physical reactions to the visual spectacle of sex. Visual representations of sex or sexually explicit (moving) images seem to draw an almost reflex reaction from the observing body, which might very well be one cause of its low status as a 'body genre'.[86]

Although a common conception of pornography is that it functions as masturbation fodder, it and its performance relatives (i.e. the striptease and the live show) may also be used to create an atmosphere of sex, sexual excitation and a relief from inhibition, thus facilitating and creating a demand for the sexual services provided on the same premises (albeit 'backstage').[87] As such, it may be seen as having a similar function as the stag films shown at brothels in the 1920s. As I discussed earlier in this chapter, prostitution per se was not illegal in Sweden at the time. Procuring and pimping, however, was forbidden by law. It was (and still is) illegal to obtain money from or to be provided for by a prostitute, and it is also forbidden to rent out apartments or other facilities for prostitution. Thus it must have involved a certain risk to allow such activities on the premises, a risk that nevertheless was regarded as worth taking. Club owners kept small rooms at the back or in another part of the building where women could provide customers with sexual services.[88]

Sexual scripts in the stores

As mentioned earlier, David A. Karp's study from 1973 described the behaviour of the clients of the pornographic bookstores as 'deviant'. The 'public privacy' needed for the consumption of sexual material led to a number of different strategies in the patterns of behaviour. Some strategies were developed by customers (e.g. lingering outside the store) and others by the stores themselves, such as painted or covered windows (or window displays with a backdrop behind the displayed commodities), and brown paper bags for the purchased goods.[89] As Coulmont and Hubbard point out, however, the strategies to 'hide the stores' paraphernalia and restrict it to the private realm, [...] conversely lent the stores themselves heightened visibility as they were the only ones without real windows', thus as clearly signifying of porn as porn itself.[90] Inside the stores, eye contact is avoided and there is a sense of mistrust towards other customers. Karp summarizes: '[Customers in pornographic bookstores] are involved in a highly structured social situation, where privacy norms are highly standardized and readily understood'.[91]

In two later articles, social norms guiding behaviour in sex stores are discussed as well. Richard Tewksbury, in an article from 1990, describes clearly assigned roles for clients in a store with booths in an arcade. In his description, the behaviour is almost ritualized in its structure. Tewksbury claims that different 'types' – or roles – of sex store customers have different motives for their visits, and express them in different ways. Except those that Tewksbury calls 'naïve' – basically those clients who do not know the codes – there are customers who only want to watch porn, those who want to masturbate (and perhaps be discovered, caught in the act) and those who want to have sex with other men in the store. Champagne argues convincingly for an abandonment of film analysis in favour for analysis of the context of the peep show arcade, because, he claims, the film screenings are not the most important activity going on there. Already in 1973, Karp noted that these places constituted a space for transgression of the norms of the store. Yet Champagne – like Tewksbury – highlights another aspect of them: by creating hiding places from surveillance, the labyrinthine construction of the arcades offers a space in which men can contact each other and accept or reject invitations for sex.[92]

The 'highly structured social situation', 'the types' and the 'drama of perception and misapprehension' can be understood through John Simon and William Gagnon's theoretical concept of sexual scripts.[93] 'Script' in this case functions as a metaphor for how sexual behaviour is socially produced, and since Karp, Tewksbury and Champagne either explicitly draw on Erving Goffman's theatrical metaphors of social behaviour,[94] or themselves use metaphors from the world of theatre and performance, it may seem apt to use it in this context too. Considering the 'highly structured social situation' of the sex stores, one could claim that there is a cultural scenario in which these spaces are charged with meaning, a meaning that has something to do with the 'deviance' of visiting them, but also with the fact that they are sexual spaces; in comparison with parks, men's toilets and other public spaces, the sexual intent of the visit can hardly be disputed. Regardless of whether a client is there to consume pornographic material, masturbate, meet someone or all of these things, the visit undoubtedly has something to do with sex. Furthermore, the general social norm guiding sexual behaviour does not usually comprise visits to sex stores. Consequently, the entering into of such places is associated with guilt and shame, and thus discretion is provided by the customers as well as by the stores themselves.

The forbidden nature of the stores may of course also contribute to the erotic charge. Therefore, these spaces become refuges – or 'erotic oases' – for sexual contacts and, paradoxically, exhibitionism.[95] One can imagine a certain tacit agreement between the clients which has to do with being accomplices in an illicit venture, and that whatever happens in the store stays between the clients, much like the experience of the woman, quoted earlier in this chapter, whose friend's father came in while she was dancing onstage in one of the establishments. The situational need for discretion and simultaneous erotic charge has led to the development of a strongly coded interpersonal script. As Simon and Gagnon explain: 'The concept of scripting, then, can take on a very literal meaning: not the creation of and performance of a role but the creation and staging of a drama'.[96] Accordingly, sex stores as settings of sexual activities of any kind can be regarded as spaces for the staging of a sexual drama; a frame for what Simon and Gagnon, drawing upon psychoanalytical theorists Jean Laplanche and Jean-Bertrand Pontalis, call the '*mise-en-scene* of desire', providing a stage as well as a set of codes and rules within which each actor is allowed to improvise.[97]

My informants' observations correspond with the studies that I have referred to here, namely Karp's, Tewksbury's and Champagne's. They also correspond with a study made by ethnologist Dana Berkowitz on gender behaviour in sex stores in the United States during the early 2000s, although her study mainly concerns itself with how women and men respectively behave in stores.[98] Interestingly, observations made quite recently (and more than twenty-five years after the time frame of my project) can provide insight into how these sexual scripts function. According to Berkowitz, when entering sex stores alone, men are quiet and discreet, whereas women are loud and unabashed.[99] From the theoretical perspective laid out here, it seems that the sexual scripts – and thus the norms and codes for how to behave in a sex store – are gendered; that the loud and unabashed feminine script is shaped by the fact that the sex store is a space which has recently been conquered by female consumers, while the masculine script dates back as far as to when such establishments – as well as some of the activities taking place there – were illegal and/or classified as deviant or diseased.

As Tewksbury notes, some visitors to the stores are 'naïve', or more or less unaware of the sex store script. This corresponds to my informants as well, whose familiarity with the script ranged from being more or less unaware, to a certain hesitance, to absolute confidence.[100] Compared with other spaces of consumption, it seems that entering a store or a club differed to some degree from entering any other kind of store or a restaurant, for instance. Judging from my informants, entering a store was more often done on one's own, whereas entering a club may very well have been done together with others, thus easing the entering into of an area with a different kind of script by having others to compare your own behaviour with. One of my informants expressed a remembered anxiety that he would enter into a facility and be accosted by 'some woman' who would suddenly charge him (a lot of) money.[101] Most likely, such an anxiety would be alleviated by entering with a friend or a group of friends. Nevertheless, although not very concretized, this informant's anxiety also underlines the notion of prostitution going on in the clubs. In addition, it points to a sense of some other kind of logic governing behaviour within such places, i.e. the script of the store or the club. Both men and women who had never entered into such establishments may still have formed more or less vague ideas of what they were like.

Notes

1 Maj Sjöwall & Per Wahlöö, *Polis polis potatismos*, Stockholm: Norstedts, 1970.

2 Maj Sjöwall & Per Wahlöö, *Murder at the Savoy*, New York: Vintage Books, 2009, p. 3.

3 Oscar Bjurling, Rolf Ohlsson, Bo Malmsten, P. D. Lindeberg & Lars Hamberg (eds), *Malmö stads historia. D. 7, 1939–1990*, Malmö: Malmö stad, 1994, pp. 110–12; Tyke L. Tykesson & Björn Magnusson Staaf, *Malmö i skimmer och skugga: stadsbyggnad & arkitektur 1945–2005*, Malmö: Architectus Verborum in collaboration with Malmö Stadsbyggnadskontor, 2009, p. 123.

4 Cf. Bjurling et al., *Malmö stads historia. D. 7, 1939–1990*, pp. 146–51.

5 This material will henceforth be referred to as 'sex worker interviews from the 1970s'. The two dissertations were written by Sven-Axel Månsson, *Könshandelns främjare och profitörer: om förhållandet mellan hallick och prostituerad,* Lund: Doxa, 1981, and Stig Larsson, *Könshandeln: om prostituerades villkor,* Stockholm: Skeab förlag, 1983. Månsson's dissertation deals with the pimps in Malmö and Larsson's with the conditions for the sex workers. (Månsson and Larsson had previously written the report *Svarta affärer*/'Shady Business', which I refer to frequently throughout this book.)

6 John H. Gagnon & William Simon, *Sexual Conduct: The Social Sources of Human Sexuality,* Chicago, IL: Aldine Pub. Co., 2005 [1973].

7 Cf. Klara Arnberg, *Motsättningarnas marknad: den pornografiska pressens kommersiella genombrott och regleringen av pornografi i Sverige 1950–1980,* Lund: Sekel bokförlag, 2010; Ebba Witt-Brattström, *Å alla kära systrar!: historien om mitt sjuttiotal,* Stockholm: Norstedt, 2010.

8 Cf. Jan Holmberg, 'Censorship in Sweden', in Mariah Larsson & Anders Marklund (eds), *Swedish Film: An Introduction and Reader,* Lund: Nordic Academic Press, 2010. See also various Swedish sources like Mariah Larsson, '"Vem behöver *den här* yttrandefriheten?" Om filmcensur och rörliga bilders farlighet', in Sara Johnsdotter & Aje Carlbom (eds), *Goda Sanningar? Debattklimatet och den kritiska forskningens villkor,* Lund: Nordic Academic Press, 2010; Ulf Dalquist, *Större våld än nöden kräver? Medievåldsdebatten i Sverige 1980–1995,* Ph.D. diss. Lund Univeristy, Umeå: Borea, 1998; Olle Sjögren, *Inte riktigt lagom? Om 'extremvåld', filmcensur och subkultur,* Uppsala: Filmförlaget, 1993.

9 The law did not include pornographic film screenings. See SOU 2001:14, 1998 års Sexualbrottskommitté, *Sexualbrotten: Ett ökat skydd för den sexuella integriteten och angränsande frågor,* Stockholm, 2001, pp. 372–74.

10 Charlotta Holmström & May-Len Skilbrei, 'Prostitution in the Nordic Countries', (Conference report, Stockholm, October 16–17, 2008), Copenhagen: Nordic Council of Ministers, 2009, p. 15.

11 These are Grottan – which actually is the oldest still surviving sex store in Malmö, started sometime around 1969 – Taboo and Justine & Juliette. Justine & Juliette is the most recent, offering not only products (with a focus on BDSM), but also lectures on how to improve your sex life. During my research, Film&Video on Bergsgatan was still open but has since closed down, and for a time there was a sister store to Taboo, catering to couples and women, called Me to You.

12 Cf. SOU 2001:14, 2001, pp. 380–95; Sven-Axel Månsson & Stig Larsson, *Svarta affärer: utredning om vissa klubbars och näringsställens sociala betydelse och struktur*, Malmö: Socialförvaltningen, 1976.

13 Cf. Don Kulick, 'Four Hundred Thousand Swedish Perverts', *GLQ: A Journal of Lesbian and Gay Studies,* vol. 11, no. 2, 2005, p. 208.

14 Cf. Leif Silbersky & Carlösten Nordmark, *Såra tukt och sedlighet: en debattbok om pornografin,* Stockholm: Prisma, 1969; Lena Lennerhed, *Frihet att njuta: Sexualdebatten i Sverige på 1960-talet,* Stockholm: Norstedts, 1994; Mariah Larsson, 'Drömmen om den goda pornografin: Om sextio- och sjuttiotalsfilmen och gränsen mellan konst och pornografi', *Tidskrift för genusvetenskap,* nos 1–2, 2007.

15 Cf. Larsson, 'Drömmen om den goda pornografin', 2007.

16 Cf. Bjurling et al., *Malmö stads historia 7: 1939–1990*, pp. 146–51; Bengt Svensson, *Heroinmissbruk*, Lund: Studentlitteratur, 2005, p. 19.

17 See Karl-Olov Arnstberg, *Miljonprogrammet*, Stockholm: Carlsson, 2000.

18 Tykesson & Magnusson Staaf, 2009.

19 Cf. 'Kopplerimålet: Drar sig ur de påstådda samlagen?' *Kvällsposten*, October 26, 1977; 'Unikt beslut i kopplerimålet: Lyckta dörrar', *Kvällsposten*, October 29, 1977; Månsson & Larsson 1976, pp. 112–13.

20 Cf. Mariah Larsson, 'Contested Pleasures', in Mariah Larsson & Anders Marklund (eds), *Swedish Film: An Introduction and Reader*, Lund: Nordic Academic Press, 2010; Elena Gorfinkel, 'Wet Dreams: Erotic Film Festivals of the Early 1970s and the Utopian Sexual Public Sphere', *Framework: The Journal of Cinema and Media,* vol. 47, no. 2, 2006; Carrie Pitzulo, 'The Battle in Every Man's Bed: *Playboy* and the Fiery Feminists', *Journal of the History of Sexuality*, vol. 17, no. 2, 2008.

21 For one discussion on the evidentiary link between adult businesses and 'secondary effects', see Marilyn Adler Papayanis, 'Sex and the Revanchist City: Zoning Out Pornography in New York', *Environment and Planning D: Society and Space,* vol. 18, 2000.

22 *Kvällsposten*, January 10, 1969.

23 Articles in *Kvällsposten*; Informant X.

24 Månsson & Larsson, 1976, p. 74.

25 It may also be that Månsson & Larsson (1976) count the clubs over the course of some years. Many clubs closed down and new ones were started.

26 Månsson & Larsson, 1976, p. 76.

27 See http://mcdragans.se/ [Accessed September 21, 2015].

28 *Kvällsposten*, October 1972.

29 Informant Y.

30 Månsson & Larsson, 1976, pp. 60 & 111–12.
31 Information about street prostitution and 'posing' from Månsson & Larsson, 1976, p. 100.
32 Henri Lefebvre, *The Production of Space*, Malden, MA: Blackwell, 2005 [1991].
33 Jane Jacobs, *The Death and Life of Great American Cities*, London: Pimlico, 2000 [1962].
34 Norman Klein, *The History of Forgetting: Los Angeles and the Erasure of Memory*, London: Verso, 1997.
35 Jacobs, 2000.
36 Gill Valentine, 'The Geography of Women's Fear', *Area 21*, 1989; Carina Listerborn, 'Understanding the geography of women's fear: Toward a reconceptualization of fear and space', in Liz Bondi (ed.), *Subjectivities, Knowledges, and Feminist Geographies*, Lanham, MD: Rowman & Littlefield, 2002.
37 'Rundan' in Gothenburg has been mapped out and studied by Arne Nilsson, *Såna och riktiga karlar: om manlig homosexualitet i Göteborg decennierna kring andra världskriget*, Göteborg: Anamma, 1998; and Margareta Lindholm & Arne Nilsson, *En annan stad: manligt och kvinnligt homoliv 1950–1980*, Göteborg: AlfabetaAnamma, 2002.
38 Carina Listerborn, 'Våld i staden', in Göran Graninger & Christer Knuthammar (eds), *Makten över rummet: tankar om den hållbara staden*, Linköping: Linköping University Electronic Press, 2010.
39 Quoted in Listerborn, 'Understanding the geography of women's fear', 2002, p. 42.
40 Listerborn, 'Understanding the geography of women's fear', 2002, p. 42.
41 Jane Juffer, *At Home with Pornography: Women, Sex, and Everyday Life*, New York: New York University Press, 1998, pp. 32–68.
42 Juffer, 1998.
43 Lindholm & Nilsson, 2002.
44 Baptiste Coulmont & Phil Hubbard, 'Consuming Sex: Socio-legal Shifts in the Space and Place of Sex-shops', *Journal of Law and Society*, vol. 37, no. 1, 2010.
45 Coulmont & Hubbard, 'Consuming Sex', 2010, pp. 197–98.
46 Since then, the sexualization of children has also become an issue in discussions of child pornography.
47 SOU 1969:14, p. 47.
48 SOU 1969:14, p. 48.
49 Klara Arnberg & Tommy Gustafsson, *Moralpanik och lågkultur: genus- och mediehistoriska analyser 1900–2012*, Stockholm: Atlas, 2013.
50 Coulmont & Hubbard, 2010, p. 196.
51 Coulmont & Hubbard, 2010, p. 196.
52 Maria-Pia Boëthius, *Skylla sig själv: en bok om våldtäkt*, Stockholm: Liberförlag, 1976, pp. 17, 41, 77 & 91.
53 Boëthius, 1976, pp. 91–93.
54 Boëthius, 1976, pp. 72–73 (my translation).
55 Cf. Susan Brownmiller, *Against Our Will: Men, Women and Rape*, New York: Fawcett Books, 1993 [1975]; Listerborn, 2002.
56 For instance, see the discussion of the connection between pornography and prostitution in Månsson, 1981, pp. 102–09.

57   Månsson & Larsson, 1976, p. 14.

58   David A. Karp, 'Hiding in Pornographic Bookstores: A Reconsideration of the Nature of Urban Anonymity', *Journal of Contemporary Ethnography*, no. 1, 1973, p. 433.

59   Karp, 'Hiding in Pornographic Bookstores', 1973, pp. 437–39.

60   Cf. John Champagne, '"Stop Reading Films!" Film Studies, Close Analysis, and Gay Pornography', *Cinema Journal*, vol. 36, no. 4, 1997; Mariah Larsson, 'Svarta affärer som blev vita: Om sexbutiker som sexuella rum då och nu', in Lars Plantin & Sven-Axel Månsson (eds), *Sexualitetsstudier*, Stockholm: Liber, 2012, pp. 125–139.

61   Karp, 'Hiding in Pornographic Bookstores', 1973, p. 445.

62   Informant Z.

63   Compare with the exclusively male stag parties and other 'male-only' contexts in which pornographic films were screened before the 1960s. Cf. Linda Williams, *Hardcore: Power, Pleasure, and the 'Frenzy of the Visible'*, Berkeley, CA & London: University of California Press, 1999 [1989].

64   Richard Tewksbury, 'Patrons of Porn: Research Notes on the Clientele of Adult Bookstores', *Deviant Behavior*, no. 11, 1990; Champagne, "Stop Reading Films!", 1997.

65   Champagne, "Stop Reading Films!", 1997, p. 86.

66   Benny Henriksson, *Risk Factor Love: Homosexuality, Sexual Interaction and HIV Prevention*, Göteborg: Institutionen för socialt arbete, 1995.

67   Benny Henriksson & Sven-Axel Månsson, 'Sexual Negotiations: An Ethnographic Study of Men Who Have Sex with Men', *Culture and Sexual Risk: Anthropological Perspectives of AIDS*, Amsterdam: Gordon and Breach Publisher, 1995; Lindholm & Nilsson, 2002.

68   Informant Y.

69   Informant V.

70   Champagne, "Stop Reading Films!", 1997, p. 84.

71   In journalist Göran Skytte's *Porrens profitörer*, he makes a special note of child pornography, using it to show how inherently bad the porn stores and their owners are. Cf. Göran Skytte, *Porrens profitörer: två reportage om porr- och kontaktbranschen*, Stockholm: Ordfront, 1979.

72   Champagne, "Stop Reading Films!", 1997, p. 86.

73   Informant Z.

74   Champagne, "Stop Reading Films!", 1997.

75   Champagne, "Stop Reading Films!", 1997, p. 92.

76   Månsson & Larsson, 1976.

77   Månsson & Larsson, 1976, pp. 76 & 104.

78   Månsson & Larsson, 1976, p. 80 (my translation).

79   From the sex worker interviews from the 1970s.

80   From the sex worker interviews from the 1970s.

81   From the sex worker interviews from the 1970s.

82   *FiB/Aktuellt*, no. 39, 1975, pp. 26–33.

83   *FiB/Aktuellt*, no. 39, 1975, p. 30.

84   *FiB/Aktuellt*, no. 39, 1975, p. 30.

85   *FiB/Aktuellt*, no. 39, 1975, p. 30.

86 Linda Williams, 'Film Bodies: Gender, Genre, and Excess', *Film Quarterly*, vol. 44, no. 4, 1991.

87 Månsson & Larsson, 1976.

88 Månsson & Larsson, 1976.

89 Karp, 'Hiding in Pornographic Bookstores', 1973.

90 Coulmont & Hubbard, 'Consuming Sex', 2010, p. 195.

91 Karp, 'Hiding in Pornographic Bookstores', 1973, p. 445.

92 Champagne, "Stop Reading Films!", 1997, p. 86.

93 Gagnon & Simon, 2005.

94 Erving Goffman, *The Presentation of Self in Everyday Life*, Edinburgh: Edinburgh University Social Sciences Research Centre, 1956.

95 Henriksson, 1995.

96 Simon & Gagnon, 'Sexual Scripts', 1986.

97 Simon & Gagnon, 'Sexual Scripts', 1986, p. 110 (original emphasis), quoting Jean Laplanche & Jean-Bertrand Pontalis, *The Language of Psychoanalysis*, New York: Norton, 1974.

98 Dana Berkowitz, 'Consuming Eroticism: Gender Performances and Presentations in Pornographic Establishments', *Journal of Contemporary Ethnography*, vol. 35, no. 5, 2006.

99 Berkowitz, 'Consuming Eroticism', 2006.

100 Tewksbury, 'Patrons of Porn', 1990.

101 Informant Y.

Chapter 4

Exhibition venues in Malmö

The urban space of Malmö in the first half of the 1970s was not only dominated by the shipyard industry, but also by what can be described as a flourishing sex store and sex club business. The decline of Kockums from 1974 until its closure in the 1980s coincides with a slightly delayed decline in the sex business, with the police and social authorities investigating and raiding the sex clubs in 1975 and 1976.[1] The stores and clubs were most often located in the 'bad' parts of town: areas of urban decline, workers' apartment buildings, poor neighbourhoods and buildings contracted to be taken down. But it was not just neighbourhoods themselves but also the material on display that contributed to a gendered space in Malmö, where both the fear of space – the representation of space which is influenced by rumours, built environments, previous experiences and personal relationships – and the fear of what the space represents – the social relations of power manifested in the urban landscape – regulated men's and women's movement.[2] Considering Jane Juffer's claim that access is dependent on whether a space is perceived of as safe (or even, for that matter, perceived of as targeting your particular group identity), it is not unlikely that women avoided these sites – except, of course, if they worked in them, or if they went in the company of a boyfriend. The association of the clubs with prostitution and the pornographic entertainment consumed in such places might have influenced discourses about this type of place in general; that is, sex clubs and stores became associated with male sexual excitation and women as the available object of male desire. Thus, as confirmed by my informants, the male domination of these places can also be explained by the discourses surrounding them, thereby adding to the notion that the merchandise and entertainment that were presented targeted a male clientele.

Elsie och Hasse, Delicate and Sex Night Club Picant

In 1959, a prospective study suggested that the area called Lugnet ('The Calm') – situated between Drottninggatan in the north and Föreningsgatan in the south, and Amiralsgatan in the east and Södra Förstadsgatan in the west – could provide a new district for commerce in the city. In 1961, demolition of existing buildings was commenced. It would, however, take many years before the demolition was completed, since property owners refused to sell and some of the people living there refused to move. During the late 1960s and early 1970s, several different plans for the neighbourhood were presented and discarded. In 1975, the area looked more like a wasteland than a part of a city.

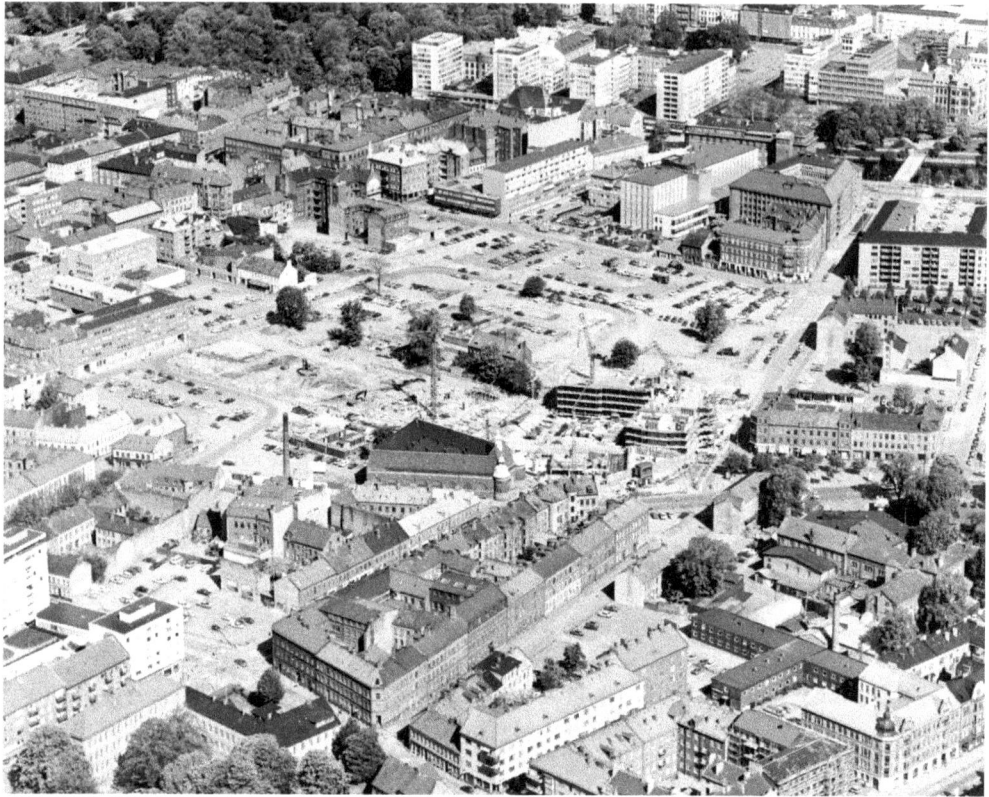

Figure 1: 'Bomb holes' – Lugnet in the summer of 1977. *Bilder i syd.*

It was not until 1977 that the construction of the new buildings was launched.[3] At least three different stores and clubs were located here in the early 1970s. Where Malmö Konserthus (the Concert Hall) now stands, there was an early enterprising store called Elsie och Hasse (Elsie and Hasse).

According to one of my informants, Elsie used to sit naked in the store window, which sometimes caused drivers in the intersection of Föreningsgatan and Amiralsgatan to idle in their cars even after the traffic lights had changed to green.[4] This anecdote is, however, unconfirmed. In this advert (Figure 2), Elsie och Hasse announce that they are starting a sex club with live shows, but they were already established at this point in time as a store.

Two other spots were located on Kaptensgatan: Delicate (number 21) and Sex Night Club Picant (number 17). Another one of my informants remembered a store on Kaptensgatan:

In one of the buildings there was a magazine store which early changed its direction and became one where porn magazines were sold. Before, these were called "men's magazines"

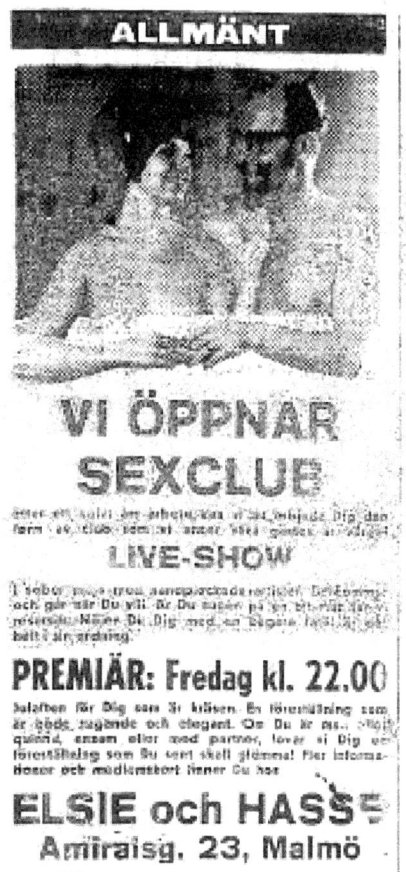

Figure 2: 'We are opening a sex club.' Advertisement from *Kvällsposten*, February 1971.

and were sold in kiosks to older bachelors and young boys. Piff and Paff and Raff etc. from H:son's empire. Now it had become an industry with more graphic images and this store displayed its entire window full of porn magazines.[5]

My impression is that this description is from the 1960s, but I am unsure as to whether I have seen the advert for this place (if there ever was one), and not all stores and clubs advertised. 'H:son's empire' refers to the Swedish porn publisher Curth Hson, who produced several different magazines. Nevertheless, the place described might be Delicate – a plainly advertised establishment which in the 1970s offered sexual entertainment. Delicate is one of those cases where the line between club and store is vague, since they also had films for rent and sold a catalogue of personal adverts.

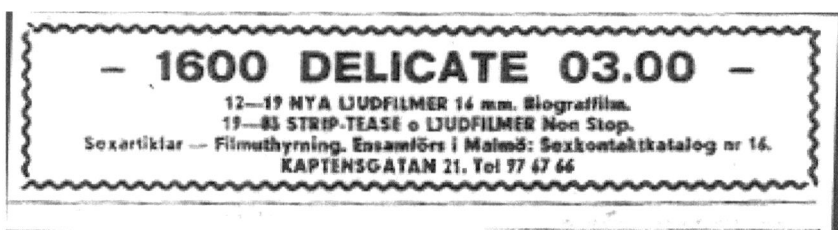

Figure 3: Advertisement for Delicate, Kaptensgatan 21. *Kvällsposten* January 22, 1973.

It may also be – and it is perhaps more likely – that Delicate is the other establishment that the informant remembers from Kaptensgatan:

The other establishment was a club, or whatever it may be called. It was located at a corner with the entrance at the intersection. The windows were covered and there were quite large signs explaining what kinds of shows took place. The door was also covered by curtains. It was a kind of coded offers that many other similar places also used – eventually more and more of these places were opened. Bath tub show, banana show, contact strip – similar phrasings which at least did not hide what was going on. […] I never entered, even though I want to remember that I passed the place every now and then: there was a temptation in what one imagined was happening in there. […] It did not even have a cheap elegance – it was very crude and I cannot even imagine that it would entice any woman to enter.[6]

Delicate offered film screenings between noon and 7 p.m.; 16mm 'cinema film' from 7 p.m. until closing (3 a.m.); and striptease shows and more film screenings non-stop.

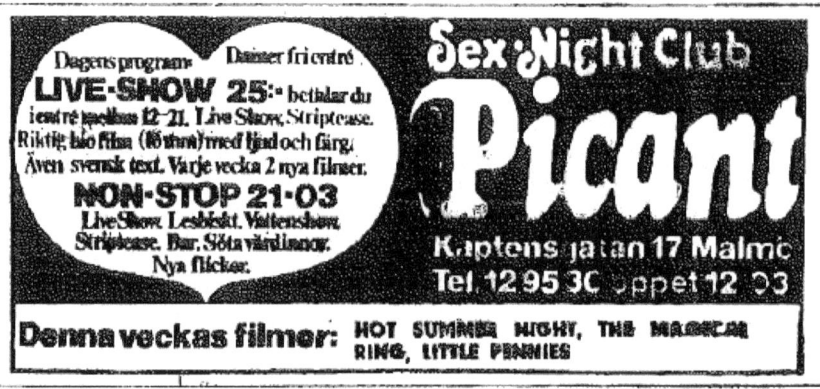

Figure 4: Sex Night Club Picant, Kaptensgatan 17. *Kvällsposten* January 21, 1975.

Moreover, Sex Night Club Picant began advertising in 1972. More flamboyantly presented, Picant offered free entrance for ladies. Picant also offered 16mm film screenings or what they called 'real cinema film'.

At some point in 1975, both Delicate and Picant stopped placing advertisements. As can be seen in the photograph above, which was taken in 1977, an entire block on Kaptensgatan is missing and this is where Delicate and Picant were located. It was, of course, cheap to rent facilities in buildings that were projected to be taken down, and it is not unlikely that club owners intended to cash in on the legalization of pornography as quickly as possible, since there was no way of knowing when business might end.

Exhibiting in booths or cabins

One of my informants described an establishment which I have not found advertisements for. It was located on the west side of Engelbrektsgatan and, according to his description, its demeanor was very discreet, with boarded-up windows and a simple sign. Further north, Engelbrektsgatan became Gråbrödersgatan, where Gentlemen's Corner – which sometimes was called 'Gentlemen's Corner' (in English) and other times 'Gentlemännens Hörna' (in Swedish) – had its premises at number 12. In comparison with Lugnet and other parts of Malmö, a large share of both the milieu and the buildings in this area, – Gamla väster ('Old West') – have been preserved, although there were unfulfilled plans in the early 1970s to establish a bus route through Engelbrektsgatan/Gråbrödersgatan. Nevertheless, a number of buildings were taken down and Engelbrektsgatan/ Gråbrödersgatan does not look the same today as it did in the 1970s. Most likely, the establishment described by my informant was located in one of those buildings that were taken down:

> Entering into the "cinema" for the first time, demanded a certain measure of willpower – what could reveal itself in there was hard to predict. A simple door, with a dark and empty hallway. The first things that hit the visitor were a damp chill, a smell of mildew and rotten wood or wet cardboard. Radiators spread some unhealthy warmth, but could not stop the cold or the well-founded sense of condemned building. I suspect the building did not have a proper foundation or perhaps more likely that there were some potato cellars which were in decay and dripping with moisture.

The screening booths were in the attic on the second floor. As a customer, you chose a film in the room on the first floor, where covers of 8mm films were placed on narrow shelves. Each cover had a number, and when you had made your selection, you presented the number to the proprietor, paid the fee and were taken upstairs where you were directed to a cabin. The proprietor loaded the projector, started the film and then left. According to the informant, there were maybe five or six cabins of varying sizes in the attic, but he rarely saw any other customers and never any women:

> There was something embarrassing, shameful, and shabby about the business that in itself contrasted with the quite emancipated atmosphere of the Danish porn films which signaled open-minded and shameless female students, the liberation of woman, and sexuality as a life-confirming, pleasure-filled party, which you did not have to be secretive about. [...] Reality on Engelbrektsgatan was quite different.

Interestingly, these films were not shown on 'loops', but loaded by hand by the proprietor.[7] You paid to see one film. My impression is that this was the common way of screening 8mm films in Malmö, but I do not have much to support it, except the fact that screenings in modern-day Grottan are conducted in much the same way (i.e. you pick a film, present the number to and pay the proprietor, who loads the selected DVD into a DVD-player). There might of course have been arcades with peep show booths in some establishments, but I have not come across this.

There are several differences between the private screenings in the peep show arcades and the cabins or booths where you pay for an entire film. First, there is no 'tease' built into the screening situation; the peep show loop ends when time allowed by the payment is at an end, 'violently severing the visual flow to demand the insertion of another quarter'.[8] In contrast, in the scenario described by my informant, you pay to see an entire film without no pause. Second, the privacy of the viewing situation is breached by the fact that you need to interact with the proprietor in order to get to see your selected film. Using numbers instead of titles minimizes the embarrassment of the situation, but the proprietor still knows which film you have chosen and has to load it into the projector. Third, there is more of a choice in picking a film from a collection rather than seeing what is on offer in the peep show booth, but this choice also entails a disclosure of what you want to watch. Finally, the apparatus is not as intrusive: the projector is located on a shelf in the door of the cabin and you see the film in front of you on the wall rather than through a machine.[9]

The films my informant describes were to a large extent from the Danish company Color Climax Corporation, founded and led by the Theander brothers. Color Climax was the largest of the 8mm companies and will be discussed further in the next chapter.

Regular cinemas and Malmö's porn cinema – Spegeln

Interestingly, and maybe consistently, one of the cinemas showing sex films, Plaza, later became the facility where the sex shop Taboo is now to be found.[10] The regular cinemas that sometimes screened sex films differed to a large degree from the ones that only screened pornography. There is an important contextual difference between the experience of 'going to the movies' to see a particular film at a certain hour and discreetly sneaking into a non-stop theater during opening hours. Films such as the Danish *Bedside* comedies, the *Language of Love* films, as well as a number of other films such as the German *Lederhosen* films, Ole Ege's *Bordellet/Bordello* (1972) and sex documentaries, were screened at the regular cinemas. Even a softcore film such as *Flossie* and the eventually more hardcore Danish *gladporr* films (including both the *Bedside* and *Zodiac* films) were screened in regular cinemas (see Chapter 2). Of course, a person could always buy their ticket and enter after the film had begun, but otherwise it is likely that people came to the cinema right before the start of the film.

Consequently, attending such a screening involved the risk of being recognized – a risk that seems to have been carefully avoided when it came to some of the other types of consumption of sexual entertainment. As noted in Chapter 2, of the Swedish sex films shown in regular theaters, those by Torgny Wickman were the most successful. It is noteworthy that the ones I have described as 'quality porn' – the Mac Ahlberg/Inge Ivarson films – did not have such a big audience, which might have to do with the fact that they are not so easily described as something other or something different from (softcore or hardcore) pornography. The Danish *gladporr* films benefited not only from their general high production values and the mixture of performing and non-performing actors (which occurred in the Swedish films as well), but also from the favorable critical reception of the first few films, which influenced the perception of them as something other, something more, something *better* than just simply pornography. Despite coming from an American context, Linda Williams' memories of seeing *Deep Throat* illustrates to some extent what I mean:

> It was not a film that one went to casually like other movies, though it did try to present itself as if it were just another movie. I was an avid movie fan at the time, but the only time I ever drove forty miles to the metropolis of Denver and paid more than three dollars to see a movie was when my partner and I, another couple, and one other male friend went to Kitty's Theater on Colfax Avenue to see Deep Throat. In this era, before very many feminists had decided that pornography was a primary cause of the objectification of women, my friends and I dared ourselves to watch and thus, by implication, to watch ourselves watch.[11]

In other words, there could be something of a challenge, a dare, to go and see such a film. People I have informally spoken to about this era also recount the sense of stretching a limit; of a certain transgression which was exciting in itself, of being daring but also embarrassed at not only seeing such films, but oftentimes seeing them with a group of friends in a mixed audience. In the case of *Deep Throat* in the United States, there was also the fact that it was such a notorious and famous film which just about 'everyone' went to see, at least if you wanted to know what was going on. The buzz surrounding the film made it into what every Hollywood blockbuster producer dreams of: a 'must-see', a special event that you would drive far and pay more to witness. In Sweden, *Deep Throat* did not have the same function. It was an influence on the feature-length pornographic film, but it did not make pornography mainstream or create a 'porn chic' moment. Rather, pornography became normalized by for, instance, the Danish *Bedside* films, which, although not hardcore – or hardly even softcore – to begin with, had the redeeming value of humour:

> Putting aside the many analyses that have been subsequently spun around this film [*Deep Throat*], my own included, what I remember most about this screening was what most people remember about pornography when they first see it in a social group: how much we laughed. It would be a mistake to underestimate the function of this film's sophomoric brand of humor in making feature-length, publicly screened pornography palatable to its initial audience. The film reassured us with the option of laughing rather than panting; or, if we did pant, the laughter helped disguise it.[12]

By calling the Danish films 'giggle porn' [*fnissporr*], it is very likely that a similar effect with regards to these films took place in Scandinavia. These were films which you could

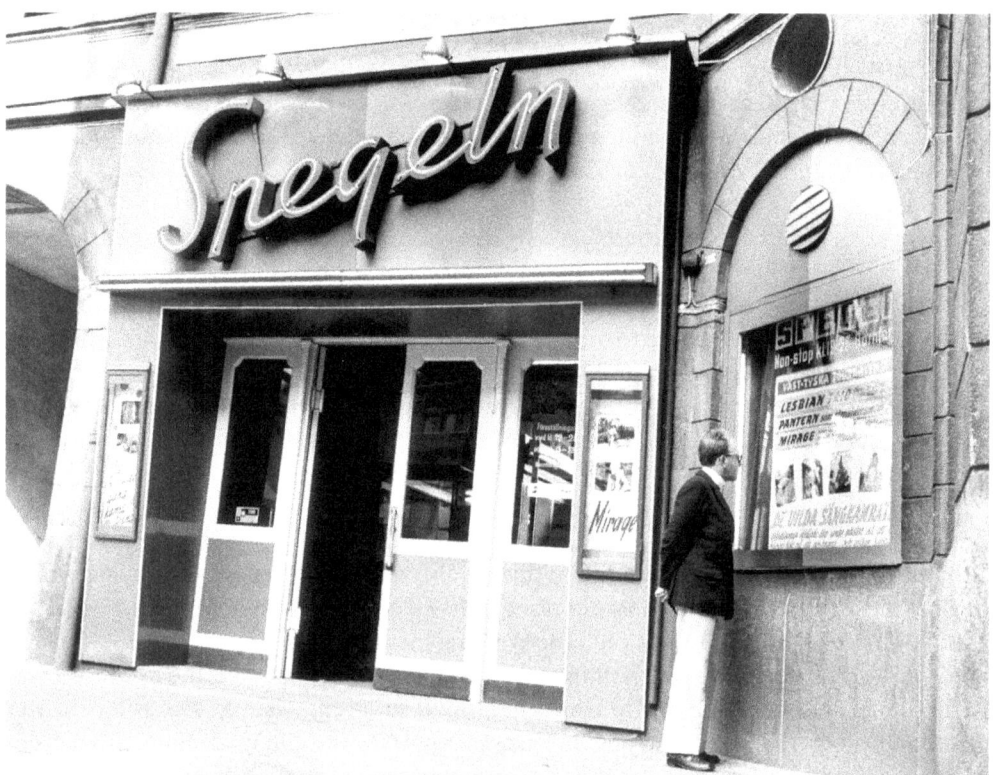

Figure 5: Spegeln in 1971. Image by Lasse Svensson, *Bilder i Syd.*

legitimately go to see, yet at the same time you might have a sense of doing something transgressive and daring; they could perhaps be described as safely illicit. As I pointed out in the previous chapter, popularity for the *Bedside* and *Zodiac* films waned as the two series continued and the genre became hardcore, but they did attract audiences throughout. In Sweden, the only sex film director whose audience numbers came even remotely close to the Danish films was Wickman. In the precarious balance between attracting and repelling spectators with all-too graphic images, Wickman apparently had a sense for equilibrium.

Nonetheless, in the discussion of the films – the discursive shaping of the genre – an important distinction took place, as well. When the National Board of Film Censors discussed Wickman's *More about the Language of Love* in terms of 'declaration of contents',[13] they were in a sense constructing a particular space for the film. An educational film – when advertised as such – constructs a very different space and audience from a pornographic one. Since *More about the Language of Love* straddled both genres, it constructed an ambiguous public viewing space, where spectators may go both in order to enlighten themselves in sexual matters and in order to find prurient images.

At the non-stop cinema of Spegeln, however, there were no such ambiguities. Spegeln was one of Malmö's longest-running cinemas, being open from 1914 to 1998. In 1943, it was named Spegeln and started screening films non-stop.

In the beginning, these films were animated films, newsreels, documentaries and shorts. In the 1960s, nudist films and other exploitation fare began to be screened during the summer and eventually Spegeln became purely a porn cinema.[14]

Although you might go there as part of the behaviour of a young, urban, radical and intellectual group (as one of my informants testifies), the purpose of the exhibition context was apparent. Located on Södra Förstadsgatan, it seemed 'shabby, aimed at dirty old men and others with whom we felt no kinship for natural reasons'.[15]

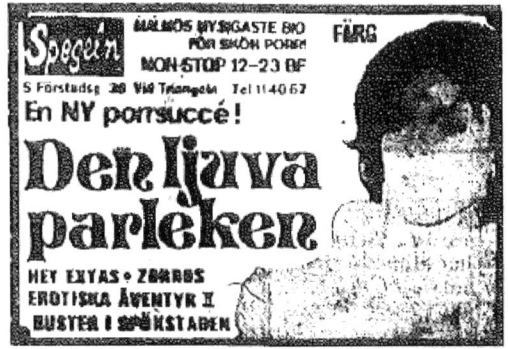 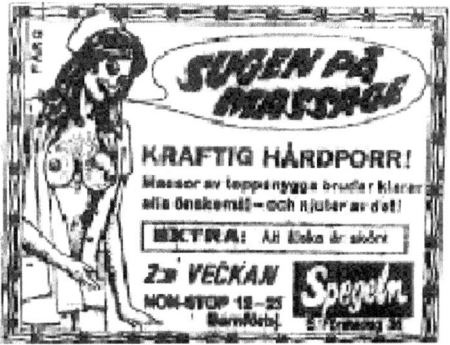

Figure 6: Advertisement for Spegeln from January 18, 1975 and January 17, 1977.

You could enter at any time during opening hours (between noon and 11 p.m.), so you could linger on the sidewalk and enter at a convenient moment. My informant describes a visit together with a girlfriend in 1977:

> The interior was, if I am not adding to my memory, spectacularly stripped; like a stable, rather, with wooden benches in booths I think, like in an old church. Unpainted and rough with a box office (was there a woman behind the counter?) that also emitted destitution, like the dance parks in the 1950s but without even minimal joy. I believe it was quite dark in the room and that it was irregular that a woman came in – it may have spread some delight but also a large share of shameful embarrassment. It lit up when they changed the reel and I remember that as a long and awkward pause.

According to my informant, the film screened at this particular occasion was made by the American underground magazine *Screw* and its publisher, Al Goldstein. *SOS: Screw on Screen* (Jim Buckley, 1975) was something of a countercultural underground pornographic film with the tagline: 'The magazine you swore you'd never read... becomes the film you can't miss'. According to the one user review on imdb.com, it is vulgar rather than funny, and all in all quite tasteless. During the screening, the girlfriend laughed out loud, disrupting the atmosphere. As in the description of the place on Engelbrektsgatan, my informant again underlines the contrast between a shameful masturbation culture and the countercultural enthusiasm that at least in theory regarded sex as a revolt against the oppression of society.

Zoning out pornography?

Using Henri Lefebvre's notions of representations of space and representational space, Marilyn Adler Papayanis analyzed the zoning laws of New York that were reinforced by former mayor Rudy Giuliani in the 1990s in order to clean out the sex businesses on Times Square and its surroundings.[16] Papayanis argues that by zoning out pornography, the neighbourhood was domesticated into a space of capital and social reproduction: 'Representations of space ensure the production of social spaces compatible with the needs of capital and hegemonic values', thus normalizing the bourgeois value system in a process that is often described as gentrification.[17] In the process, what Lefebvre calls 'lived space' – an 'alternative geography in the interstices of the power-knowledge grid',[18] which is 'linked to the clandestine or underground side of social life'[19] – is eradicated in what Papayanis calls the 'revanchist city', a process that can be described as some kind of revenge of the middle class. Connecting the gentrification of Times Square with the development after the 1989 economic crisis, and thereby regarding pornography as a scapegoat for other social problems, Papayanis' analysis is indeed insightful. Other scholars have criticized gentrification for mainstreaming adult entertainment, removing those versions which are too deviant, too transgressive and too flamboyant.[20]

In Malmö, the police raids and ensuing court procedures in the mid-seventies – which to some extent eliminated the clubs, but also made the stores more careful in what activities were offered and how they were advertised – follows the oil crisis and the decline of the shipyard Kockums. It might therefore be possible to interpret the events as a similar kind of 'scapegoating' as Papayanis sees as happening in New York. Nevertheless, what can be analysed in a nineties American context as a revanchist process by the middle class to eradicate lived space and reinforce traditional, bourgeois norms and values is not immediately transposable to a seventies Swedish context. 'Lived space' in this case would instead be referred to as 'social vulnerability' by social welfare officers. In addition, the process of gentrification did not follow the clean-up of Malmö's 'sex swamp', but would take a longer time in coming. Around the turn of the millennium, Malmö can be said to enter into gentrification through events such as the starting of Malmö University in 1998, the inauguration of the bridge between Malmö and Copenhagen in 2000, the Housing Exhibition in 2001, and the construction of the prestigious high-rise building, Turning Torso (2001–2005).

The criticism of the pornographic environment comes – at least explicitly – from a leftist/socialist perspective, which focuses on exploitation and misery rather than moral norms and deviance from such norms. Although this may still be a middle-class criticism cloaked in Marxist rhetoric, it is important to keep in mind that the national context complicates an easy translation of Papayanis' analysis, and that Malmö is a far cry from New York in matters of size and global cultural significance. Nonetheless, it would not be too far-fetched to say that the difference between the environments – New York and Malmö – is not so great, and neither are the actual attempts to eliminate the sex business so different. Juxtaposing the two cases, however, one can see that the discourses surrounding the 'cleaning up' vary greatly.

In this context, the films that were screened, rented out or sold seem to be of little significance. Nevertheless, one of my informants kept emphasizing the contrast between the contents of the films – countercultural, sexually emancipated, explicitly and joyously depicting sexual acts – with the drab reality and shameful presence of the men in the audience or as customers. On the one hand, it would be easy to dismiss the films and focus on the actual sexual activities going on (as the social workers and the police did); on the other hand, the films frequently make their presence known. Not only are they one of the reasons to gather or to seek out a private booth, they contribute to the construction of sexual space in the stores as well as the clubs. Although other performances in the clubs – like the live shows – functioned as sexually enticing and relieving of inhibition, the films themselves also performed on the audience. In addition, they created atmosphere. They may have also created an image of a utopian sexual space – one which is not shared with sex workers and masturbating men.

Notes

1   Oscar Bjurling, Rolf Ohlsson, Bo Malmsten, P. D. Lindeberg & Lars Hamberg (eds), *Malmö stads historia. D. 7, 1939–1990*, Malmö: Malmö stad, 1994.

2   Carina Listerborn, 'Understanding the geography of women's fear: Toward a reconceptualization of fear and space', in Liz Bondi (ed.), *Subjectivities, Knowledges, and Feminist Geographies,* Lanham, MD: Rowman & Littlefield, 2002.

3   Tyke L. Tykesson & Björn Magnusson Staaf, *Malmö i skimmer och skugga: stadsbyggnad & arkitektur 1945–2005,* Malmö: Architectus Verborum in collaboration with Malmö Stadsbyggnadskontor, 2009, pp. 177–182.

4   Informant X.

5   Informant Z.

6   Informant Z.

7   Amy Herzog explains that the peep show booth most often showed 8mm film and you got to see a couple of minutes for every twenty-five cents that you deposited into the machine. Cf. Amy Herzog, 'In the Flesh: Space and Embodiment in the Pornographic Peep Show Arcade', *Velvet Light Trap*, no. 62, Fall 2008, p. 33.

8   Herzog, 'In the Flesh', 2008, p. 35.

9   Informant Z.

10 Södra Förstadsgatan 81. See Uffe Stauslund, *Bio i Malmö: Malmös biografer genom tiderna,* Malmö: Corona förlag, 2001, p. 63.

11 Linda Williams, *Screening Sex,* Durham: Duke University Press, 2008, p. 125.

12 Williams, 2008, p. 131.

13 Censorship records from the National Board of Film Censors. See previous chapter for entire quotation.

14 Stauslund, 2001, pp. 86–90. I suspect the development into a porn cinema happened during the 1960s, but I have not been able to confirm this.

15 Informant Z.

16 Marilyn Adler Papayanis, 'Sex and the Revanchist City: Zoning Out Pornography in New York', *Environment and Planning D: Society and Space,* vol. 18, 2000.

17 Papayanis, 'Sex and the Revanchist City', 2000, p. 352.

18 Papayanis, 'Sex and the Revanchist City', 2000, p. 351.

19 Papayanis, 'Sex and the Revanchist City', 2000, p. 351, quotation from Lefebvre 1991, p. 33.

20 Phil Hubbard, Roger Matthews, Jane Scoular & Laura Agustín, 'Away from Prying Eyes? The Urban Geographies of "Adult Entertainment"', *Progress in Human Geography,* vol. 32, no. 3, 2008.

Chapter 5

Size does matter: The substandard pornographic films of the 1970s

O n the back cover of the Expo film *Teenage Sex Game*, exhibited in Malmö in the early fall of 1973, the description (in English, French and German) reads:

Two young couples are spending the evening together. The atmosphere is gay and one gets the impression that the evening will not finish as soberly as it started. A progressive form of 'blind man's buff' breaks down any inhibitions that remain. The action soon takes place on a wide double bed and develops into the wildest of orgies. Admire the girls' breasts and the way they manipulate the mens [sic] rock hard organs. In short, an exciting film, particularly recommended for showing on rainy evenings.[1]

The film was approximately ten minutes long, in colour and silent. In several ways, this film – which I have not seen – may be quite typical of the fare that was screened in the stores and some of the clubs. It was made under the label Expo by the Danish company Color Climax Corporation, which was by far the most dominant production company of the substandard pornographic films shown in Sweden in the 1970s. Judging by the description on the back cover and the description by the Swedish censor at the National Board of Film Censors, it contains heterosexual intercourse indoors on a bed. Furthermore, it sets up a situation in which the sex can take place, but it does not have a more elaborate narrative.

Another film, *Sexual Symphony*, also from Color Climax Corporation but with the label Rodox, and submitted to the National Board of Film Censors in 1973, was described by the censor as 'Three parts: 1.) Group sex with three couples. 2.) Lesbian intercourse on orange couch with bottle as aid. Later a man joins in. 3.) Group sex with three couples, one of which is lesbian.'[2] *Sexual Symphony* was allowed with no cuts. According to the back cover of the film:

This film offers you a 'triple-porno-pleasure'! It is made up of three fascinating short films with 16 sought-after models who deserve to be called 'especially active'. This is not just a series of randomly selected clips, but a real porno experience. It's like a fantastic 'live show' with Lesbian love and hard-core group sex. Every imaginable sexual position is portrayed, everything from A to Z, plus demonstrations of sexual aids, like Coca Cola bottles! This film is not just for those lonely hours of masturbation, but can also be used as an introduction to the so-called 'Married couple seeks married couple' games. This being of course a Rodox film, there are plenty of red-hot close-ups![3]

Notably, both of these films include instructions for its viewing on the back cover. The first is 'recommended for showing on rainy evenings', while the second is 'not just for those lonely hours of masturbation'. That pornography is something other than the quotidian everyday is something often taken for granted. Already in 1966, Steven Marcus described nineteenth-century Victorian pornographic novels as 'pornotopia' – a fictional world which constructs a perfect sexual time, space and ability.[4] However, Marcus uses the word to describe nineteenth-century pornography in particular, and sees a significant difference between it and its twentieth-century equivalent. Writing some twenty years later, Linda Williams agrees that there may be truth in this, but that Marcus 'invokes a curious double standard' when he pits 'a utopian model of nineteenth century (male-economic) pornography, or "pornotopia"' against 'a realistically reflective, dystopian model of twentieth century (female-economic)' pornography.[5] Nevertheless, even twentieth-century porn offers a utopian space for its spectator. As quoted in the previous chapter, one of my informants saw a stark contrast between what was depicted in the films and the impression given by the environment of one of the establishments: 'The quite emancipated atmosphere of the Danish porn films which signalled open-minded and shameless female students, the liberation of women and sexuality as a life-affirming, pleasure-filled party, which you did not have to be secretive about'.[6] In my informant's account, porn might even be seen as constructing a utopian, sexual space in which the viewer can enter and thus leave the sordid surroundings for as long as the film lasts, generating a space within the space.

Swedish porn scholar Magnus Ullén has claimed that pornography elicits a certain mode of reading, a quality which he terms 'pornographicity'. His argument is that pornography's attraction lies in 'its ability to engage us not through the temporal structure of a narrative, but through the immediate presence of narrating';[7] that is, its 'here-and-now' quality, its propinquity to the spectator established by its capacity to arouse a physical and thus highly tangible response. However, Ullén concentrates exclusively on what he believes is the main response to porn, namely arousal and masturbation. This is obviously a very significant aspect of pornography, but in excluding other aspects – such as humour, illicitness, shame, disgust, political satire, taboo-breaking, bad taste and many others – provides a somewhat reductive interpretation of the readings elicited by porn, condensing them into what is instinctive and automatic rather than intellectual. Nevertheless, noting the significance of the porn spectator's body is unavoidable, which is evident in discussions by scholars such as Linda Williams, Peter Lehman, Magnus Ullén, Susanna Paasonen, Ingrid Ryberg, and several others.[8] As I discussed earlier, psychophysiological and medical sex research use porn because of its direct reflection onto the body of the subject.[9] To deny the more or less reflex, sometimes involuntary, bodily reaction to pornography goes against not only common sense, but also much scholarship. With this aspect in mind, pornography is thus highly haptic in the sense that it can provide us with a strong sensory experience. This does not need be positive – if you do not, or even if you do, feel aroused by pornography, you may very well feel disgusted or powerfully uncomfortable – but it is very palpable.

This in turn affects the space in which they were consumed. As I discussed in the previous chapters, the exhibition venues of pornographic films in Malmö between 1971 and 1976 were not only shaped by their environment (e.g. the physical streets, buildings, interiors), their context (e.g. the striptease and live shows), the patronage and the potential prostitution that took place in the same space, but also by the haptic aspects of the visceral spectacle of filmed intercourse. In this chapter, I will map out what was on the screen – what the films showed, where they came from and how they were censored. Focusing on the 8mm films, my aim is to reconstruct the content of the pornographic screen in the stores and clubs of Malmö in particular, and of Sweden in general. Since the material brings on special methodological issues that have to do with its unwanted status, the chapter begins with a discussion of what is sometimes called 'orphan films' and the sources available to me. In addition, the implications of adding the 8mm films to the historiography of this period will be briefly touched upon. The chapter continues with a general overview of companies and a description of the films. Finally, I will discuss what ended up on the screens after censorship and how these depictions can be said to affect their spatial circumstances.

The 8mm films were produced by single individuals as well as by companies, in both professional and more amateurish settings, and distributed to a large degree through mail order lists and catalogues.[10] They were not screened in cinemas, but in sex clubs, sex stores and at home. To private persons, they were sold or rented out through mail order adverts in newspapers and magazines, or through the sex stores.

Orphan films and the National Board of Film Censors

The 8mm film format was developed in the early 1930s and became popular among hobbyists and home movie-makers.[11] In the 1960s, when the Super 8 format was released, amateur film-making became even easier. As the format was used by private persons to make (non-pornographic) home movies, the films may very well be used as ethnographic or ethnological source material, but they may also be analysed as films.[12]

Distinguishing between the hardcore stag reel and the erotic 8mm films for home viewing, American film scholar Eric Schaefer describes films made and sold between 1930 and 1969 in the United States, and the development from 'nudie' films to more explicit fare. He also points out that even though the porn boom began in the early 1970s, the format was in its final phase because the video cassette was looming in the near future.[13] Since pornographic 8mm films are both a substandard gauge and have dubious content, they have rarely been valued enough to be properly archived.[14] Anecdotal evidence tells of boxes of films handed in to archives containing home movies (vacations, Christmases, birthdays, etc.) with one or two pornographic films among them. One of the films I have studied here belonged to such a collection, and six of them were found by a colleague in the basement of a new apartment, probably left there by the previous owner. Even the most comprehensive archives of films such as these – the stag collection and the Swedish Erotica collection at the Kinsey Institute – are based on donations and discontinuous selection.

Accordingly, the haphazard way these films are saved or archived makes research difficult. Nevertheless, according to the Swedish Cinema Ordinance, between 1911 and 2011 all publicly exhibited films were required to pass through the National Board of Film Censors, where they were provided with an age limit, and in some cases edited or completely forbidden.[15] The guiding principles for the National Board of Film Censors were whether a film (or scenes, or even brief shots in a film) could be regarded as harmful to children's psychic health (in which case they should be provided with an age limit of either fifteen or eleven), or 'harmfully exciting', 'brutalizing' and/or 'inveigle into crime' (in which cases they should be either banned or cut).[16] Before the removal of the obscenity clause in the penal code, most pornographic films were deemed obscene and thus disallowed, despite film censorship becoming more liberal in sexual matters during the 1960s. A handful of 8mm films with pornographic content were submitted before 1971 and actually allowed with a fifteen age limit.

At the National Board of Film Censors, records were kept for each submitted film. Thus, the archives of the National Board of Film Censors – now held by the National Archive – are a unique source for film scholars. Although it is an archive of censorship rather than a film archive, and therefore contains no full films, it does have records for all films publicly exhibited in Sweden between 1911 and 2011. Some 2500 pornographic 8mm films, sent in between 1968 and 1982, have thus been registered and censored at the National Board of Film Censors. Although censorship was generally extremely systematic, this number of 8mm pornographic films is probably only an approximation of all such films screened in Sweden. Some films were submitted more than once without the censors noticing, which means that there is more than one register card for them. On the other hand, it can also be surmised that some films were screened without having been submitted for censorship. At least in the early days of legalized pornography, some store owners did not find it reasonable to send in films for scrutiny: 'Since we never allow more than 5–6 people in here at a time, I don't count this as a public screening', said the owner of one establishment (Grottan) in an article in the tabloid *Kvällsposten*.[17] However, as the clubs and stores in Malmö were hard-pressed by the police later on in the 1970s, it probably became more important to follow the law in more trivial but somewhat obvious matters. In order to hide the illegal activities going on backstage, what existed on the surface or as a 'front' needed to be in accordance with the law. The fact that the number of films submitted increases dramatically in 1973 testifies both to the expanding 8mm porn industry and, I believe, to the growing awareness that 8mm screenings were now regarded as public screenings by the law. Of all films submitted, ninety-four per cent were submitted between 1973 and 1980, with an average of 313 films per year and a somewhat paradoxical peak in 1980 with 356 films. The remaining six per cent are made up mainly by films submitted in the years 1971 and 1972 (i.e. immediately following legalization [five per cent]), but also three films submitted in 1969 and 1970 and eight in 1981 and 1982. The end of submissions of 8mm pornographic films to the National Board of Film Censors is thus more clearly demarcated than the beginning. Submissions of 8mm pornographic films came to an abrupt stop around the breakthrough of the VCR, which in Sweden can be dated quite precisely to December 1980.[18]

Furthermore, until 1989, every single copy of a film that would be screened publically had to be submitted to the National Board of Film Censors. Usually, a distribution company would send in a film for the number of copies that were to be released, but with the 8mm porn films, one or more copies of the film were sent in by several different persons or companies.[19] As such, distribution does not seem to have been nationally centralized, but rather in the hands of individual club and store owners and local companies.

The golden age and 'plotless ruttings'

Judging by this approximated number and by the number of screening contexts, I would consequently contend that 8mm films were a common way to consume pornographic films during this period. This calls into question some of the basic assumptions about the 1970s pornographic cinema. For example, the entire notion of a 'golden age' of pornographic cinema is based on a number of 'classics' – feature-length, narrative porn films such as *Deep Throat*, *The Devil in Miss Jones*, *Behind the Green Door* and *The Opening of Misty Beethoven* (Radley Metzger, 1976). The Swedish equivalents of these American classics would be for instance *The Second Coming of Eva* and *Justine and Juliette*, and in Denmark the *Bedside* and *Zodiac* films. The history of pornographic film is far from comprehensive, and although the shorthand version (from stag films for more or less exclusively male consumption via hardcore narrative feature films to video and eventually streamed clips) does have some validity, it does not begin to describe in-depth the moving image pornography of the twentieth and twenty-first centuries.

Media and porn scholars Susanna Paasonen and Laura Saarenmaa discuss the notion of a golden age in 'The Golden Age of Porn: Nostalgia and History in Cinema'. They claim that a number of feature films and documentaries produced in the 1990s and early 2000s have perpetuated a popular notion that the 1970s was a time of 'innocence, authenticity and struggle for freedom of speech', an era of 35mm, feature-length, narrative porn classics.[20] Their analyses of the films *Boogie Nights* (Paul Thomas Anderson, 1997), *Rated X* (Emilio Estevez, 2000) and the documentary *Inside Deep Throat* (Fenton Bailey & Randy Barbato, 2005) frames them as nostalgic celebrations of a time before the eradication of the 'adventure and exploration' of early porn by issues of finance, AIDS and the 'soulless' medium of videotape.[21] These films deal mainly with the narrative, feature-length porn films ('I want to make a film that makes people stay in their seats after they've come', says porn director/ producer Jack Horner in *Boogie Nights*; *Rated X* is about the Mitchell brothers, whose most famous film is *Behind the Green Door*; and the documentary's title is self-explanatory), again aligning the period above all with its 35mm films.

Other scholars have questioned or nuanced the understanding of the 1970s as a golden age of porn based on empirical material from that era. For instance, Schaefer has conducted extensive work on the sexploitation film and studied 16mm as well as 8mm films, concluding that the 16mm format had an important function in paving the way for hardcore pornographic 35mm films.[22] Since 16mm films were cheaper to make, the stakes in the gamble of challenging the American obscenity laws were lower. Schaefer's previously quoted claim that the 'feature-length hardcore narrative constituted merely an entr'acte between reels of essentially plotless underground stag movies in the years 1908 to 1967 and the similarly plotless ruttings of porn in the videoage' is undeniably correct. In addition, it seems to be the case that the 'plotless ruttings' continued during the entr'acte, but also that they were not always as 'plotless' as one would imagine.

From other perspectives, Peter Lehman and Chuck Kleinhans have – with all due respect to her seminal work – challenged notions put forward by Linda Williams, such as the emphasis on narrative in her analysis of the porn genre.[23] In considering that porn films were rarely seen from the beginning to the end (even at the time they were released), Lehman argues that the narrative is of secondary importance, perhaps not even of any significant importance at all: 'narrative patterning is at best a disrupted aspect of theatrical porn watching'.[24] Nevertheless, I would still maintain that some films actually were seen from beginning to end and that, from a perspective that includes the 8mm films, some of them – like some of the Lasse Braun films that will be discussed further on – had a tightly constructed, efficiently presented narrative.

Kleinhans notes that since *Hardcore* was researched and written in the mid-1980s, Williams',

[…] discussion rests on assumptions that now often must be reversed because of the shift to video and quasi-documentary. […] Even tracing the most aesthetically/erotically accomplished hardcore work of the 1990s such as that of Andrew Blake [well-known porn director], we find Blake's films display a non-narrative spectacle that approximates the high-gloss upscale porn of *Penthouse* magazine. All show, no story.[25]

Nevertheless, show or spectacle was a significant aspect of 1970s porn. For instance, in some of the Danish *Zodiac* films (but also in the 8mm films) there is not necessarily any contradiction between narrative and spectacle. Some pornographic films mainly consist of numbers – be they mundanely or elaborately staged – others have more or less complex narratives, while in others the narrative is what creates the spectacle.

Although I have only been able to see a fraction of all those 2500 films, based on the descriptions I have read and those films that I have seen, I would argue that the stag film's special properties did not disappear, but in fact continued through the 1970s. The format of five-, ten- or twenty-minute films showing various versions of intercourse, perhaps with a rudimentary narrative set-up or an anecdotal story, prevailed even during the so-called golden age of feature-length, narrative hardcore porn. The sheer number of 8mm films submitted to the National Board of Film Censors indicate that this was indeed a common way of consuming pornographic moving image material, especially taking into account that it is unlikely every store or club owner submitted every film for censorship. Furthermore, this indicates that – as both Lehman and Kleinhans seem to implicitly suggest – the number/ narrative structure that Williams compares to the narrative structure of the musical has never been the dominant part of pornographic film. This is also indicated by the fact that many of the feature-length pornographic films that were imported into Sweden were cut up into brief intercourse films, and shown on 16mm in porn cinemas and sex clubs.[26]

In addition, as Linda Williams has pointed out, the historiography of pornographic films is a fragile undertaking. Speaking of the archived stag films at the Kinsey Institute, Williams observes that commercially released DVD collections of early porn are rarely representative, but usually contain films that are unexpected, funny or contain reverse gender roles.[27] To claim anything about the early pornographic films based on these DVD collections is thus problematic. Instead, they are found quaint or cute, or less sexist and misogynist than modern porn. Indeed, even watching a sample of films not selected because of their perceived qualities demands a balancing of what seems representative and what stands out as particular. The films from the Kinsey archive used in this study are selected from the list of films from the National Board of Film Censors described below, and thus screened in Sweden (except the one film that was banned). Nonetheless, the risk of emphasizing those films that mark themselves as different is always imminent: rapes and coercion; a particularly creative use of a carrot as a dildo; a cat sneaking up while some people are having sex; unexpected twists; a woman trying to penetrate a man from behind with a strap-on. In the following, I have attempted to be as impartial as possible – while still making note of the spectacular – to describe a somewhat representative selection yet also pointing to the remarkable.

Sources and selections

From the material available to me, I have chosen to base this chapter on the following:

Material from the National Board of Film Censors

The censorship cards from the National Board of Film Censors contain brief descriptions of the films; for instance: 'An intercourse during which the female part thinks about a lesbian encounter' (*Sweet Lips*). In some cases, the censors have let the succinct 'intercourse' suffice (e.g. *A Sexy Supper*). The descriptions also depend on which censor watched and described the film. One film that was submitted twice is described by one censor as 'Servant girl masturbates outside of room with loving couple but continues with intercourse with man in room', while another elaborates: 'A servant girl watches intercourse through keyhole and

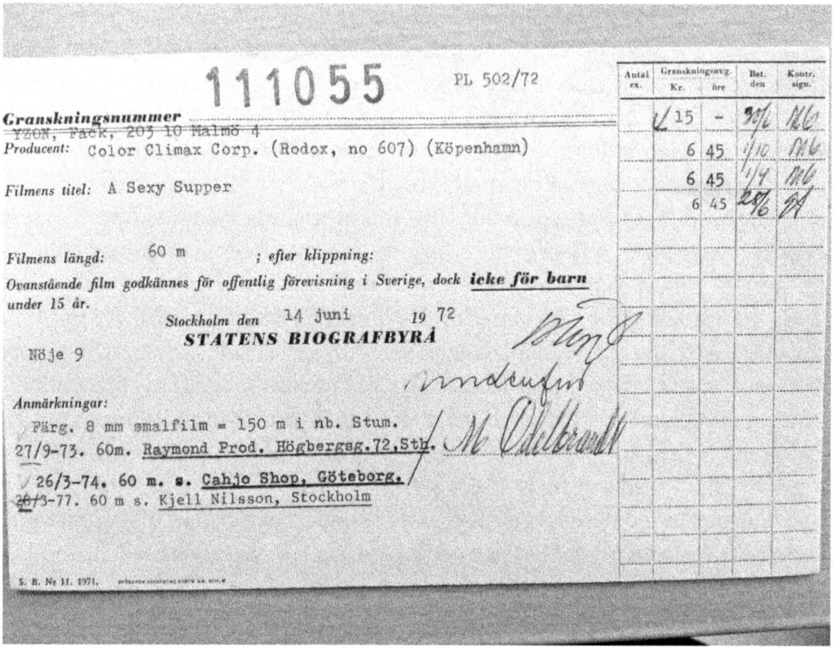

111055   PL 502/72

Antal ex.	Granskningsavg. Kr.	öre	Bet. den	Kontr. sign.
15	–			
	6	45		
	6	45		
	6	45		

Granskningsnummer ....
YZON, Pack, 203 10 Malmö 4
Producent: Color Climax Corp. (Rodox, no 607) (Köpenhamn)

Filmens titel: A Sexy Supper

Filmens längd: 60 m   ; *efter klippning:*
Ovanstående film godkännes för offentlig förevisning i Sverige, dock **icke för barn**
under 15 år.
                Stockholm den 14 juni   19 72
                   STATENS BIOGRAFBYRÅ
  Nöje 9

Anmärkningar:
  Färg. 8 mm smalfilm = 150 m i nb. Stum.
  27/9-73. 60m. Raymond Prod. Högbergsg.72,Sth.
  26/3-74. 60 m. s. Cahjo Shop, Göteborg.
  26/3-77. 60 m s. Kjell Nilsson, Stockholm

S. B. Nr 11. 1971.

Samlag

Figure 1: 'Intercourse': *Sexy Supper* described on the back of the censorship card (111 055). Images by Mariah Larsson.

starts to masturbate, for instance with a flower stalk. A guest enters, and then he and the girl go into the room where group sex with four persons ensues'.[28]

Although admittedly often meagre, my most significant sources of information are censorship cards, register cards and other material (such as lists of films) from the National Board of Film Censors. The original submitter is indicated on the register cards, but in order to know whether the film was submitted by others, one has to look at the censorship cards. Some films are only submitted by one person or company, whereas others are submitted by several persons or companies. I have created a database with all the films indicated on the register cards, and then made a selection with particular relevance for this study. Films submitted before 1971 and after 1976 have been eliminated, creating a list of 1321 entries. Furthermore, I have watched the clips that were censored; these were archived at the Board and are now held by the National Archive. For quantitive information about the cutting and banning of films, I have used a list of films compiled by one of the archivists at the National Archive, and then cross-referenced with the database at the Swedish Media Council, which took over some of the functions of the National Board of Film Censors in 2011 after the abolishment of censorship for people over fifteen. The strength of this material is its quantity, from which I have been able to draw conclusions mainly about production companies and distribution practices.

Films from the Kinsey Institute

A rare collection of stag films and 8mm porn is archived at the Kinsey Institute. By comparing the information in the catalogue of the stag collection and the Swedish Erotica collection, I identified fourteen films that matched, and thus were very likely to have been screened in Sweden (except one that was disallowed for public screening). Most of the fourteen films are cleanly identified (all information matches), but some are a bit ambiguous regarding company and/or year. In addition to these fourteen films, I watched a handful of films from the stag collection that were dated to the late 1960s, since some of these might have been shown very early on in the period without having been submitted to the Board.

Abandoned films

Additionally, I have a collection of seven films. Six of these were found by a colleague in the basement of her new apartment, in all likelihood left there by the previous owner. These films are all (bar one – 'Eros film 1970') untitled and undated, but I have identified one of them as a Lasse Braun film, and judging by hairstyles and furniture, they likely come from the period in question. They are in a sense the epitome of 'orphan' films: unwanted, unacknowledged and abandoned in a cardboard box. These six films have been supplemented with another untitled and undated film, which had been handed in to the 8mm archive in Grängesberg, Sweden.

Lasse Braun DVDs

The fourth source is a collection of Lasse Braun films on six DVDs. These are easily identifiable and, since some have been submitted by persons or companies in Malmö, can be tied to this location. I have chosen these films not because they are representative (as the Danish and German films supposedly are), but because the Lasse Braun films seem to have been popular, with many of them submitted several times by several different persons and companies.

Bonus material

On Klubb Super8's DVD release of *Rapport från Stockholms sexträsk* (Arne Brandhild, 1974), six 8mm films from the Swedish company Party Film and five from Venus Film are included as bonus material. Of these, only five were submitted to the Board.[29]

Adult Loop Database

Another important aid in my mapping of the content of the pornographic screens of Malmö has been the Dutch website Adult Loop Database, which lists films and companies. Many of the films listed also have photos taken of their front and back covers, providing images and descriptions of the films. Here, I have been able to cross-reference titles from the Kinsey Institute and the National Board of Film Censors.

The Internet

Finally, I made some searches on porn sites using the terms 'Danish vintage' and 'German vintage'. The main site that was used was xhamster.com, which came up with more results than xtube.com, porntube.com or youporn.com. The reason for my choice of search entries is that the majority of 8mm films in the period came from Denmark or West Germany. However, when I have been able to identify any of these films, they seem to be from a later date than 1976. Consequently, I have used them carefully as a general reference. It will be clearly stated when any of those films are cited.

These films and descriptions form the empirical material for this chapter. Contrary to the popular perception of porn films, the material suggests quite a diversity – from simple intercourse films to quite advanced narrative short films, conveyed effectively and ingeniously while leaving plenty of time for sexual activities.

General overview

The films from the stag collection at the Kinsey Institute bear evidence to their own history: badly scratched, bleached by the projector lamp and sometimes extremely blurred. Some are copies of copies; others have simply deteriorated because of age. Although all of them were described as black-and-white in the catalogue, some had likely been in colour but had since faded. In one, only magenta remained, giving a stark and somewhat avant-garde impression. As orphan films, they had been neglected; as forbidden films, they had been capitalized on by being screened again and again, as well as by being copied.

A certain progression can be discerned in the films from the Kinsey archive. The later 8mm films were more professionally produced. For instance, in one of the stag films, *College Tuition A Go-Go*, the camera is placed at an angle directed towards the bellies and hips of the performers, resulting in a framing in which very little can be seen. In another, *Love Scene Part I & II*, the intercourse (with a man on his back and the woman on top) is filmed from the foot of the bed, but in order to create a close-up, the camera has zoomed in on the genitals. Through this zoom, an impression is created that the man has extremely short legs, and, in addition, his feet (in black socks) sometimes enter the frame in a disconcerting way. When pornography was legalized and obscenity laws were liberalized in the late 1960s and early 1970s, this kind of technical mishap disappears. Another change is that the performers in some of the older films wear sunglasses, probably to make identification more difficult.

At the National Board of Film Censors, the censors who registered the films are not completely reliable; for instance, the various labels used by Color Climax Corporation (Rodox, Pussycat, etc.) are sometimes indicated as company and sometimes indicated as part of the title. Some of these companies operated under different names, and perhaps changed their name over the course of the years 1971 to 1976.[30] However, with these reservations, a careful but fair estimate is that more than one hundred companies had produced the films that were submitted. The companies are most frequently Danish (38%), West German (36%), and less frequently Swedish (5%), American (3%) and Dutch (1.4%), but as many as 24% are indicated as 'unknown' in regards to their country of origin. By far the most common company was the Danish Color Climax Corporation, representing approximately 20% of the submitted films between 1971 and 1976. About 6% are from Danish Playboy Film Production, 5% from West German Love-film (located in Bochum), and 5% from Lasse Braun. American Adult Cinema represents about 3% of the films. Even accounting for the possibility that not all films were submitted to the National Board of Film Censors, it is probably fair to state that Color Climax Corporation was a dominating producer of the 8mm films shown in Sweden. Supporting this notion, one of my informants claims that many films on display in the Malmö stores and clubs were from Color Climax Corporation.[31]

Color Climax Corporation

The Danish company Color Climax Corporation was founded by the Theander brothers, Jens and Peter, in the 1960s. They produced magazines and films. Even with some cursory glances at the register cards at the National Archive and Adult Loop Database,[32] the sheer size of the production is apparent. Although they have since ceased to produce, Color Climax Corporation is still in existence today, and thus has a history of almost fifty years in the porn business.[33]

Color Climax Corporation was an early and highly enterprising company, and their output also consisted of things such as urolagnia, bestiality, S&M and, more problematically, child pornography. This makes the inquiry into older Color Climax Corporation films tricky, not only because of the ethical and legal complications, but also because, for obvious legal reasons, the Adult Loop Database does not cover the child porn titles. I have come across warnings for 'unauthorized' Color Climax Corporation material on forums and in other contexts, not only because it might be child pornography consciously made for an audience with that particular preference, but also that the performers may be underage even though it might not show. The American Child Protection and Obscenity Enforcement Act of 1988, also referred to as regulation 2257, states that all producers must keep records of the ages of performers in order to be able to prove that performers are not underage. The legal age for performing in pornography also differs between countries. Regulation 2257 – and other similar regulations in other countries – did not exist in the 1970s. In general, and as I have discussed earlier, laws against child pornography have become stricter since 1980, when both Sweden and Denmark outlawed it. On Wikipedia, the talkpage about the Color Climax Corporation entry focuses to a large extent on Color Climax Corporation's production of child porn and how to deal with it.[34] Adult Loop Database explicitly states: 'Known is that in the spirit of the time Color Climax released some material that they shouldn't have. A handful of underage films were published on this label. Those will not be listed'.[35]

Although it lies outside of the scope of this project to discuss child pornography, I cannot completely disregard the issue, since it most definitely was produced during the relevant period. The extent of it, however, is uncertain. Referring to a Norwegian study, Danish criminologist Berl Kutchinsky states that:

[A] number of short 8-mm films with a child pornographic content have been produced along with and often overlapping the magazines. Pettersen (1990) has identified 26 different movies produced by Color Climax in the 1970s and later transferred to videotapes. Additionally a smaller number of private films and videotape recordings of unknown origin existed in pedophile collections.[36]

This number is very small in relation to the output of Color Climax Corporation films in the 1970s, which according to Adult Loop Database amounts to some 630 films (of which more than 500 were submitted to the National Board of Film Censors), not including the illegal material.[37] Including the illegal material, if Kutchinsky's number is correct, would amount to more than 650 films.

The issue of child porn is highly inflammatory and rarely treated with disinterest.[38] In the mid-eighties, a scandal concerning Denmark and the Netherlands as centres for the production of child pornography erupted in the United States, and the moral panic still surrounding child pornography risks both exaggerated numbers and statistics, and a downplaying of its role in order to counter such a moral panic.[39] In general, Kutchinsky seems to emphasize how few examples of child porn there were, how in some cases the models looked young but were fifteen (and therefore legal by being above the age of consent in Denmark), and that much of it was nude posing rather than hardcore porn. This is not to discredit Kutchinsky (whose research spanned many years and has been very informative), but rather to point to the difficulty in knowing exactly what these images were. However, what seems to validate Kutchinsky's number is that twenty-six out of some 650-plus films amounts to slightly less than four per cent, which is not unreasonable considering that it caters to a rather narrow interest group of paedophiles.

The sheer quantity of Color Climax Corporation's films – averaging more than one film per week for the entire decade – is in itself quite impressive, and also explains why Color Climax Corporation represents one fifth of the films submitted to the National Board of Film Censors in Sweden.[40] Color Climax Corporation released films under several different labels, including Rodox, Blue Climax, Danish Hardcore, Masturbation, Pussycat, Sexorama, Exciting, Teenage Sex and Expo. It seems that Rodox was such a prominent label that people sometimes refer to Rodox rather than Color Climax Corporation. One of my informants talked about Rodox and Kutchinsky uses Rodox instead of Color Climax Corporation. (The confusion surrounding labels and companies is actually quite abundant in Kutchinsky's work.) According to Kutchinsky, Rodox was for several years 'one of the largest substandard porno-film producers in the world, but with growing competition from West Germany, France, and the U.S.A. as well as videos taking over, the demand for new Rodox film productions diminished gradually'.[41] Kutchinsky furthermore states that in the early 1970s, the company 'developed the largest and most modern Super 8-mm color film laboratory in Scandinavia, producing 4000 copies of a new film each week'.[42] Kutchinsky claims that these films were made under the label Candy Film. However, according to the Adult Loop Database, Candy Film was a Swedish company, whereas Danish Candys Climax and Candys Studio only has one film listed (the same for both labels).[43] In the records from the National Board of Film Censors, Candy Film is indicated as Swedish. As far as I can make out, however, Color Climax Corporation (which is by far the most common company indicated by the censorship register cards) is the general name for the company, whereas Rodox was one of the labels. This concurs with the description on Adult Loop Database, as well as with Jack Stevenson's account of the Theander brothers' venture in his study *Scandinavian Blue*.[44] In addition, I would contend that Candy

Film is Swedish, although it might be that they were made by Color Climax Corporation and released as Swedish. However, the number of Candy Film productions as indicated at the Adult Loop Database does not match the output that Kutchinsky specifies for that label.

In the early years, most of Color Climax Corporation films were around sixty metres (approximately ten minutes), but later one hundred metres became more common (approximately fifteen minutes), although some, like the masturbation films, were only thirty metres (approximately five minutes). Furthermore, most of them were silent in the early years, whereas the ones produced after the mid-seventies had sound. Those that I have found on porn websites which are from after 1976 (at least the ones that I can identify) have post-synchronized (or at least post-added) German dialogue. Nonetheless, my impression is that when there was sound, the films were dubbed in different languages (for instance, the text on the back cover in English, German and French), although West Germany was an important target for export.

Of the films in the Kinsey archive, three were definitely from Color Climax Corporation and a further one could potentially be. These films are *Motorcycle Mamas* (submitted to the Board in 1971), *Private Club* (submitted in 1971) and *Wedding Night Orgy* (1975).[45] The copy of *Wedding Night Orgy* at the Kinsey Institute was released by Swedish Erotica, but according to the Adult Loop Database, it is the same as the Color Climax Pussycat release with the same title. Color Climax Corporation and Swedish Erotica exchanged footage, which also explains the ambiguous fourth film, *Big John Part I*, a John Holmes film quite obviously shot in California and submitted to the Board (if it is the same film) as an Adult Cinema release in 1974.[46] According to Adult Loop Database, it was released in 1975 as an Expo film (Color Climax Corporation) with the title *Super Stud*. However, it was submitted to the Board under the title *Big John*.

Motorcycle Mamas begins with two bikers on the road. Two women are hitchhiking and the bikers pick them up. Shots show them riding fast on the road, before turning onto a small dirt road where they stop and have sex. Afterwards, the men ride off on the road. The film is quite fast-paced, fetishizing the motorbikes and foregrounding the skull on one of the bikers' helmet.

In *Private Club*, the setting is indoors, in a room with a bed. A number of people – five men and two women – sit on and around the bed. They are fully dressed and watch a third woman, who is strip-dancing on the bed. There is a large poster of a nude woman in the background. The stripper uses a vibrator and starts to caress some people in the audience. Eventually, the audience engages in sex in various constellations. There are two cum shots, both oral and facial, notwithstanding that there are five men present.

Wedding Night Orgy tells a complicated story of a wedding couple checking into a hotel and starting to have sex. The bellboy is spying and masturbating outside. Another couple checks into the room next door and invites the bellboy to join in. The cleaning woman starts spying and masturbating, alternating between the doors. Somehow, she joins in with the newlyweds. The film is a bit confusing and features at one point a split-screen cum shot, split three ways. However, it also contains subtitles, although there is no sound. All films feature oral sex (fellatio to a large extent), vaginal intercourse, and, at one point in *Motorcycle Mamas*, some kind of rod is used as dildo (see image on back cover).

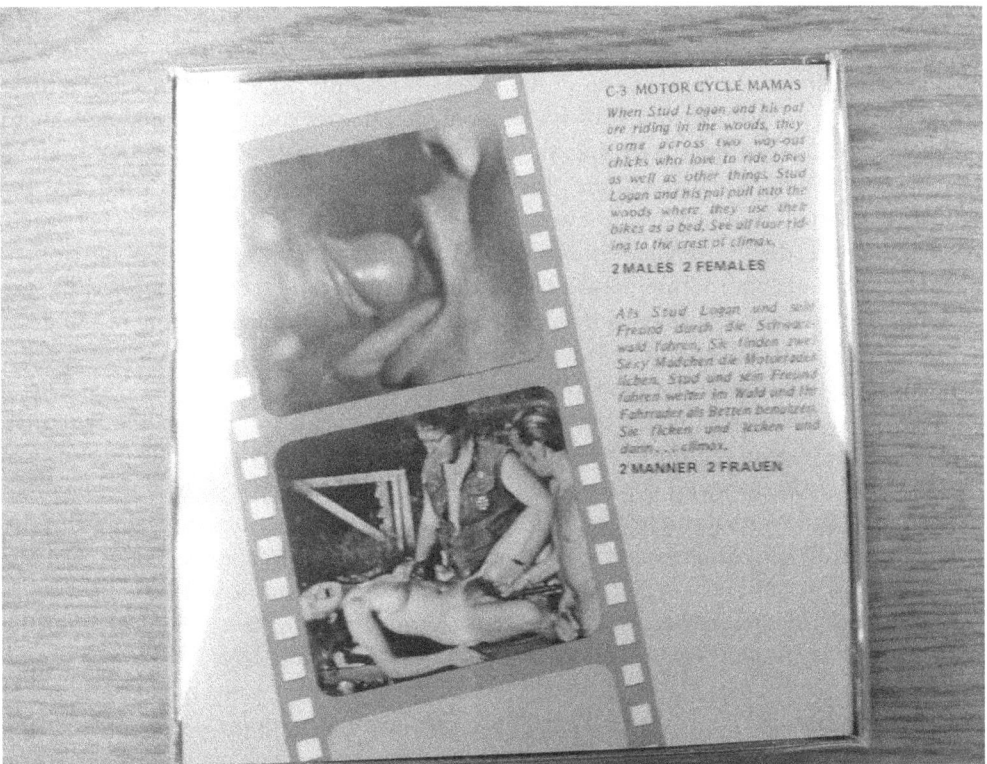

Figure 2: Back cover of *Motorcycle Mamas*. Image by Mariah Larsson.

One of the films found via xhamster.com is *Always Prepared* with Tiny Tove Jensen. *Always Prepared* is listed on the Adult Loop Database as Teenage Sex Film number 708 from 1978 (submitted to the National Board of Film Censors in 1979).[47] Another example is *Young Anal Pissing* from Diplomat, which was submitted to the National Board of Film Censors in Sweden in 1978.[48] A third, *Annette's Climax*, was submitted in 1977. There is still something to be gleaned from these films though. Like the films from the Kinsey Institute, they have a rudimentary narrative framework – *Always Prepared*, for instance, is about two girl scouts who wake up a man when they ring his door to sell raffle tickets – but it is usually limited to setting up a situation in which sex can unfold.

Sexual variations

All the films from the Kinsey Institute – regardless whether they are from Color Climax Corporation or any other company – set up a situation in which sex can occur. It might be a pool man finding a woman sunbathing in the nude in her pool (*Big John Part I*); a car that is not working (*Stalled Rear End*);[49] a hitchhike (*Motorcycle Mamas*); a wedding night (*Wedding Night Orgy*); or a sex club (*Private Club* and *Zum Knutschkeller*).[50] In some, such as *College Playmate* and *Sweet Smell of Ass*, couples meet for sex.[51] *Hot Pants* has a more elaborate story: two women stroll down a shopping street, spot some hot pants and want to try them on. Since the store is closing, the shopkeeper reluctantly lets them in. A cleaning woman is swabbing down the floors. They try on the shorts, but it takes time, and the shopkeeper checks his watch. Cut to a woman standing in the street also checking her watch. Back in the store, the shopkeeper knocks on the fitting room door, which one of the women opens in hot pants and nothing else. She beckons for him to enter. Sex ensues while the cleaning woman masturbates outside the fitting room and the woman waiting in the street smokes one cigarette after another. When they finally leave, the woman in the street sees the women exiting the store and walks away in anger.

Young Anal Pissing features, as the title suggests, both anal sex and urination. The man urinates on the woman and the woman then urinates towards the camera. Kutchinsky claims that urolagnia, together with coprophilia, belonged with those types of pornography that 'catered directly to sexual minorities'.[52] However, Kutchinsky describes magazines that are straightforwardly and exclusively focusing on urination and defecation.[53] The occurrence of 'pissing' in an otherwise regular hardcore film may imply that it was not regarded as deviant to such a degree, although the anal sex performed might have rendered it among the more extreme films. During this period, anal sex does not seem to have been as commonly represented as it is today. However, a more quantitive analysis of a much larger sample of films would be needed in order to say anything about this with certainty. As one of the many sexual activities presented, urination occurs in other films inside the time frame of this study, such as the Lasse Braun film *Ky-Sen – the Vietnamese* (submitted in 1972).[54] There are a handful with titles indicating urination in the register cards from the National Board of Film Censors, such as the Lasse Braun film *Lady Piss* (submitted in 1976), and the Color Climax films *Piss Party*, *Pee Pleasure* and *Golden Showers* (submitted in 1975).[55] One film, simply specified as *Star Film no 3* (1973) has the following content described on its censorship card: 'Group sex: Two men and one woman. Intercourse on table in garden. Woman urinates, two men drink the urine from glass. One man urinates. The woman shits in the face of one man, the other licks'.[56] According to the Adult Loop Database, Unipress released a series of eight films under the label Star Film. Some of them have been submitted to the National Board of Film Censors, and of these, only *no 3* seems to contain urination and defecation.

Of the fourteen films from the Kinsey archive, two contain scenes of women being raped. In one, *Sex and the Gun*, from Danish Films International (recorded at the Board as Cinema Classics in 1973), a woman is coerced into sex at gunpoint.[57] As soon as they begin to have sex, however, her initial resistance turns into acquiescence, and she is depicted as enjoying the act. Although this one was not censored, those films that began with a woman being coerced into sex and continued with her acquiescence were usually cut by the Board, leaving the part with the mutual sex untouched, but deleting the introductory threat and/or violence. However, *Rosa and the Men*, from Pussi Film (submitted in 1972), was disallowed for public screening. It depicts the rape of a waitress by a number of men in a pub. There is no acquiescence in the film at all. Pussi Film released another title that was banned by the Board – *Violated in the Forest* (1973), which also was a rape film.[58] A third film from the Kinsey Institute, *The Sadists* (submitted 1972), includes some coercion, and the spanking and tying up of a man by two women. This film was cut by a few minutes to exclude the spanking and tying. *The Sadists* was from Candy Film, and one of the few Swedish films among the films submitted to the Board.[59]

Although these instances are striking, they are also rare. The remaining eleven films from the Kinsey Institute do not depict any violence or coercion, and only three of the fourteen films contain anal sex. However, from a feminist perspective, the rape films are particularly challenging, not least the ones in which a 'no' turns into a 'yes', implying that if a man persists, the woman will begin to enjoy having sex with him. Given the historic context of these films, wherein they were targeted to male consumers, the conception of (hetero)sexuality, and of women as passive victims and enjoying it, comes across as extremely problematic. Highlighting these particular films, however, runs the risk of misrepresenting the absolute majority of 8mm porn. On the other hand, it also demonstrates that the claim from the anti-porn movement that pornography has become increasingly violent in recent years is fundamentally incorrect.

Judging from the descriptions on the censorship cards, most of the films submitted to the Board contain various forms of heterosexual intercourse, mainly oral and vaginal, with two or more parties, girl-on-girl numbers and masturbation scenes. From the films submitted to the National Board of Film Censors, one can mention for instance *Weekend Sex* from Danish Flesh Film (submitted in 1972), described simply as 'Intercourse outside of tent'; or *Sex de Luxe: Lizzie and Greta in Private Action* from Danish Private Film (submitted in 1973), described as 'Lesbian, two girls, two men of whom one is a negro, are added. Group sex on a Rococo table'.[60] Another example would be the film described in the beginning of this chapter, Color Climax Corporation's *Teenage Sex Game*, which is described thusly by the censor: 'Two couples exercise group sex against a backdrop of a zebra skin' (submitted in 1973).[61] Furthermore, the abandoned films found in the basement, which indeed make up a random sample of films, do not contain any urination, defecation or violence, although persuasion and seduction may occur.

The abandoned films

Some of the abandoned films seem to be compilation films, consisting of a number of different scenes – indoors, outdoors, couples or threesomes, performing vaginal, oral and anal intercourse. Most of them are silent, and the ones that are not (like the compilation films) are overdubbed with music and moaning sounds of pleasure, but have no dialogue. Repeatedly, the sex begins *in medias res* and is quite fragmented. Others have simple narratives, such as the one with a young woman spying on an elderly couple (her parents?), who have sex in the bedroom next door while she masturbates; or the one in which two sisters are being recorded singing in a studio when the sound mixer seduces them. The one with the two sisters is quite complex: it begins with the sisters looking at pop magazines in an apartment; they receive an invitation by phone to the studio, where there is a prolonged seduction; the sisters start out quite reluctantly (the 'no-becoming-yes' scenario) before succumbing (the sex scene). It ends with the two sisters looking at their record, called 'Orgasmus' by Sexy Sisters, and playing it. The song title might imply that the film is German, but there are no other indications as to its nationality.

Others again only set up a situation, such as the one in which a waiter is called to a hotel room, starts having sex with the female guest before his girlfriend joins in upon discovering them; or the one in which one man and two women smoke pot and have sex. One film – identified as a Lasse Braun film called *Women* – depicts a bathing woman who has sex with a female friend. The sexual activities performed in this film include fisting and the use of a strap-on dildo.

Lasse Braun

Sometimes credited as Alberto Ferro, Lasse Braun's reason for working with pornography is claimed to be a protestation against obscenity laws and hypocrisy. He is one of those figures of the 1960s and 1970s – like Berth Milton Sr, who started the magazine *Private*, or Ole Ege and Leo Madsen in Copenhagen – whose entrepreneurial spirit is fuelled by ideology; or, vice versa, whose ideology is fuelled by entrepreneurial spirit. In one of the early issues of *Private*, Milton famously published four photographs, three of them depicting images of violence and murder and one of hardcore sexual intercourse, asking in his editorial why society condemns and outlaws the one image that portrays a natural and loving human behaviour.[62]

According to various sources on the Internet, Lasse Braun also had ideological aspirations, namely to challenge authority through obscenity. For a while he operated out of Stockholm. He produced and directed porn films, but also owned and ran sex clubs in West Germany. One of the women in the prostitution research project in the 1970s describes him thus:

> All the guys in the porn business I hold in little esteem except for Lasse Braun. Because he makes the best films that come out in the world. He does. Because they are very beautiful films. If you can say that about a porn film. They are very beautiful. Because there is a feeling in them and they have fine people performing in them. And sometimes they are exciting films.[63]

From some point in the 1970s, his films were distributed by Reuben Sturman in the United States as loops for peep show booths. In the late 1960s and early 1970s, he made a number of 8mm films. These films are made in series of three, such as the *Tropical* (shot in Trinidad),

Vikings or *Top Secret* (James Bond/spy spoofs) series. They are approximately ten minutes long and most of them (but not all) are narrative. For example, in *Dr. Wu* (1970), one of the *Top Secret* films, a woman arrives at Copenhagen airport and drives off in her car. Before she does, however, she hides a small gadget in her vagina. She is overtaken by a group of men in dark suits, who abduct her, take her to a room and handcuff her to a pole by a bed. They proceed to rape her; although she struggles at first, she then, in line with the cliché of no-becoming-yes, seems to enjoy the activities. Meanwhile, the boss looks on. At the end of the sex, one of the men finds the little gadget inside her and gives it to the boss, who leaves with a smile. This film was disallowed for public screening in Sweden.[64]

Delphia – the Greek (1970), from the *Nymphomania* series, features anal sex and double penetration, without much of a story or setting; another film in the series, *Ulla – the Swede* (1970), sets up a situation on a beach in which two women engage in girl-on-girl activities before two men show up and join in. The double penetration of *Delphia – the Greek* was cut by the National Board of Film Censors.[65] Another film, *Imagination*, from the *Satisfaction* series, shows two women in what looks like a furnished attic.[66] They both look at a photograph of a young man while masturbating and fantasize – visualized in the film – about sex with him. Even though there is no real narrative, the set-up is conveyed through reverse shots of the photograph and special effects (e.g. a kaleidoscope lens). It appears to have passed the censor by, as the film is simply described as 'Intercourse in attic room'. However, in my opinion, the notion of imagination or fantasy is communicated quite efficiently. Sexual fantasy seems to be a common trope in the Lasse Braun films in general, both in the films I have seen and in the ones of which I have only read descriptions.

Which perhaps brings an explanatory frame to the fact that the rape scenario, such as the one in *Dr. Wu*, is not uncommon. In one of the *Vikings* films, *Victory for the Queen* (1971), two nuns are guarding a herd of sheep while enjoying some female-to-female sex, as Vikings descend upon them and rape them. One of them seems to enjoy it, whereas the other struggles throughout the scene. The Viking queen, however, becomes so excited by watching the activities that she commands one of her men to perform cunnilingus on her. The other two Viking films also have rape scenarios, with *In the Name of Odin* (1971) concluding with one woman being sacrificed after having being gang raped by a group of Vikings. The more violent *In the Name of Odin* was banned by the National Board of Film Censors, whereas *Victory for the Queen* was allowed with no cuts.[67] And in *White Fantasies* (1969), one of the *Tropical* films submitted with the title *Black Power* to the National Board of Film Censors, a white man is having sex with two black women. Two black men dressed in T-shirts with the text 'Black Power' enter, tie the man up and proceed to rape the black women, after which they cut the white man's throat. The final fourth of this film, which featured the attack by the black men, was cut by the Swedish censors.[68]

These films are a far cry from those films which only depict various kinds of intercourse, as with some of the abandoned films. They have a smart, countercultural look to them, show good-looking male and female performers, and tell efficiently driven stories without holding back on the sexual action. There are plenty of close-ups of genitalia during oral and vaginal intercourse, and the 'money shot' is shown as a general rule. Anal intercourse and double penetration are also featured to some extent, although the National Board of Film Censors edited out some of these images.

One of the films from the Kinsey Institute was *Hotel Amour* or *Hotel Amore*.[69] This film is also included in the Lasse Braun collection, as one of the three *Oh Paris!* films. However, the film on the DVD and the film at the Kinsey Institute were clearly made from the same footage, and told basically the same story: two women stroll the streets of Paris; they kiss and then enter a hotel, where they undress in a room and begin to have sex. A hotel waiter shows up and has sex with them. The version of the film at the Kinsey Institute is much longer (nearly twelve minutes long), and contains a scene in which we see the waiter entering the room with a tray holding champagne and glasses, looking shocked and surprised. It also contains footage in which one of the women – the Asian performer Ky-Sen – attempts to penetrate the man from behind with a strap-on dildo while he is having sex with the other woman in the missionary position. He makes aversive hand gestures and, after a couple of attempts, she stops. The film is only six minutes long on the DVD, and the waiter somewhat miraculously simply appears in the room, already involved in sex. At the end of the film, a quick montage of images from the story contains one shot of him entering the room.

That there are several versions of the same film is unsurprising. Even today, porn scenes are sometimes re-edited and released on different compilation DVDs. Moreover, the Lasse Braun films were sold both as loops in the United States and as individual films in Europe. Furthermore, the description on the Adult Loop Database indicates that there might be a third version. Here, 'peeping' is mentioned as part of the narrative, yet there is no peeping in any of the two films I have seen.

What ended up on the screens

Due to censorship, the films that were submitted do not equal what was finally screened. For instance, the violent content of the Lasse Braun films was, in those cases that the screenings were preceded by submission to the National Board of Film Censors, often edited or outright banned. During the period 1971–76, twenty-one of the 1324 films submitted were disallowed completely for public screening (i.e. less than two per cent); another forty-six were cut.[70] In all, approximately five per cent of all submitted pornographic 8mm films were censored either by being cut or by being disallowed for public screening (that is, contained material that was regarded as potentially harmful).

It is interesting to note that there was a strict and bureaucratic censorship which (at least in theory) encompassed all films for public screening. On the other hand, this censorship was extremely liberal in regards to sexual depictions. It seems that violence had to be quite explicit and/or unconventional in order to be censored. At the National Board of Censors, the cuts made were saved and archived. However, some cuts are missing. In all, there should be fifty-nine cuts (some of the forty-six films had more than one part cut), but there are only forty-two cuts saved. According to the descriptions of the deleted scenes, the most common cause for cutting was violence, which is also confirmed by watching the archived clips.[71] Many of them depict violence or threats of violence including weapons (a woman forcing two men to undress at gunpoint, for instance, but also knifings and gunshots) and assaults (one or more men overpowering a struggling woman, for example). The assault films most often have their beginnings cut out. Since they continue with the woman succumbing and enjoying the sex, which puts a stop to the coercion, there was no reason to ban the entire film. This means that some films screened must have begun *in medias res* due to a decision of the Board, although they did in fact have some set-up. There are ten such cuts preserved. However, in addition, the Board zeroed in on any association to bestiality (there is one clip which includes dogs, although these are not involved in the intercourse), and BDSM practices such as bondage and spanking. Since BDSM at this time was not an accepted sexual variation, these practices were simply regarded as non-consensual violence. Early in the period, some scenes of double penetration were cut, as was one instance of what is described as 'gross manipulation of vulva', which refers to images showing what in modern porn jargon would be called 'gaping'.[72]

Of the titles sent in to the National Board of Film Censors, it is very hard to make out whether any of the films were child pornography or not. Even by using the descriptions on the censorship cards it is difficult to ascertain; I only came across one instance in my random sample that comments on the age of one of the performers. The film was not edited or banned, but allowed for public screening for those aged over fifteen. This one comment refers to a male performer in gay film *Boys with Boys*.[73] None of the cut films have a description which indicate age as a reason for cutting, although one of the clips I saw at the archive contained a young girl at the bedside of a bandaged man; this clip was unlisted and thus had no description. Some titles imply youth by using words like 'Lolita', 'teenage' or 'young'. However, without having seen the films, it is impossible to determine whether these featured underage girls or simply grown women with pigtails and lollypops. Since it was not illegal to distribute, screen or watch pornography containing minors, it may very well be that there were some such films which the Board did not make any particular fuss about. Then again, it might be that those who submitted films to the Board hesitated to submit child pornography because they would risk becoming involved in investigations into the illegal production of the material in question.

Another interesting observation that can be made is that although the peak for submissions to the Board is later in the decade (with 1977 and 1980 having the highest numbers – 337 and 356, respectively), the major year for cuts and bans was 1973. As many as nine films were banned this year, and twenty-eight had one or more cuts made to them. It is hard to say whether this was due to the censors being overwhelmed (1973 is the first year with a large number of submissions), or whether it was due to a change in the content of the product. However, I would say that it is probable that the censors grew accustomed to the material, since the cases of censored double penetration and the one containing the 'gross manipulation of vulva' all occur before 1973.

A problematic aspect of the censorship of pornographic films during this time is that the banning of the combination of sex and violence by the National Board of Film Censors would superficially appear to provide a less misogynist pornography. At first glance, the idea of censoring violence in pornography seems sympathetic. However, it carries with it several preconceived assumptions that in themselves construct a normative view of sexuality.[74] This is particularly apparent in the early censoring of 'gross manipulation of vulva', as well as of double penetration and anal sex. But evaluating the cuts made and those banned films that I have been able to see, one can tentatively note that it takes more violence towards women to ban a film than it does towards men. For instance, *Rosa and the Men* (banned by the Board and discussed earlier in this chapter), featuring the gang rape of a waitress in a bar by several men, is, in my opinion, a lot more violent and revelling in the woman's subjection than the suggestive Lasse Braun film *Cerimony* (also banned by the Board), in which a crucified man (tied, not nailed, to the cross) is raped by a group of witches.[75] *Rosa and the Men* contains a realistic scenario – a situation that waitressing women could actually find themselves in – whereas *Cerimony* is staged as a fantasy, being set in a dungeon or a crypt, with women in wigs and make-up. There is nothing to indicate that Rosa acquiesces at any point in the film, whereas the first few minutes of *Cerimony* focus on getting the man's penis erect. I am quite aware that my interpretations of these two films are subjective, and there is a lot in *Cerimony* that could be read as spooky or even scary, especially in a cultural climate that favours realism before fantasy. However, *Victory for the Queen* also featured rape, but was allowed with no cuts.[76]

Then again, one could argue that pornography in itself is violent towards women, an argument often heard from the anti-porn movement.[77] The commonly occurring facial cum shot, for instance, could be regarded as, if not violence, at least a degradation and dehumanization of the woman. In one of the films featuring anal sex, *College Playmate Part II*, the subtitles show the woman saying 'It hurts! It hurts!' while being penetrated anally, which also happens in the 35mm film *The Devil in Miss Jones*. In *Big John Part I*, vaginal intercourse causes the same line of dialogue from the woman, supposedly referring to the size of John Holmes' penis. Apparently, the notion of penetration as violence and the penis as an instrument of harm is not completely unfounded, although it might imply that to say that something hurts in a fictional sexual situation – to the performer saying it, to the spectator watching it – is quite open to interpretation.

What ended up being screened in the clubs and stores of Malmö could be a variety of sexual expressions and practices, ranging from paedophilia and Lolita interest to urolagnia and coprophilia, via a vast majority of heterosexual vaginal intercourse with two or more parties, but also masturbation, and oral and anal sex. Of the submitted films, a handful is gay porn. Some films are animated. And although the majority of performers are white, interracial sex was not uncommon, treated and most likely regarded as an interesting, exotic fetish. However, if my suspicion that not all films were submitted is correct, there may very well have been instances of screenings with films which did contain violence, rape and bestiality, although these instances were most likely rare.

Sexual entertainment

To sum up, there was a prolific and vital industry that produced a vast amount of films which depicted many various sexual practices. The films were hardcore and showed sexual activities in close-up; in other words, very honestly and straightforwardly pornographic. They were screened in several venues, sold and rented out, and can without doubt be said to form a significant share of the pornographic moving images consumed at the time. What can also be deduced from the information at the National Board of Film Censors is that, for the most part, they were produced, distributed and exhibited by small-scale enterprises; Color Climax Corporation is the exception, at least in this collection of film metadata. Apart from Color Climax Corporation, there are more than one hundred companies represented. As can be understood from the submitters indicated on the censorship cards, distribution was usually handled by the store and club owners themselves, most likely by ordering films from catalogues.

The fact that these films existed and were screened to such an extent implies that the notion of what a pornographic film is must have been dependent on whether or not a person had seen these films or not. Those who frequented the stores and clubs where these films were screened would most likely not call a film like *Swedish Nymphet* pornographic – maybe softcore, but not 'real' pornography. Neither were these films originally any more 'innocent' than what can be seen today, although the film censorship entailed that (most of) what ended up on-screen was devoid of violent rape scenarios, bestiality, BDSM and, in the first few years, particular forms of double penetration. On the other hand, those who never saw anything other than what was screened in the regular cinemas most probably defined anything nude or softcore as pornographic, and may very well state that pornography in the 1970s was a more innocent affair than what it is today. This is especially true given that, when referring to the feature-length films shown at theatres, the 1970s have been described as a decade of more or less pornographic films in Swedish film historiography.

Furthermore, the descriptions on the back covers of some of the 8mm films paint a stark contrast between the quotidian mundane and the joys that are promised in the film. Although many covers do not have any reference to a viewing situation, those that do construct a viewer who needs or even deserves a break from the non-pornographic everyday. One of the important things about these films, then, seems to be how they function as a kind of escape, constructing a space of their own into which the spectator can move. This space is in turn highly dependent on the haptic aspects of the moving images.

I have previously discussed how performers in the clubs moved among the audience, and how this functioned to dissolve the boundary between audience and performer. In a similar manner, the films can be said to reach out and touch the spectator by invoking a bodily response reflecting the one taking place on-screen.[78] To a certain extent, the sexual space constructed in the stores and clubs seem dependent on this crossing over of the boundary between observer and the observed, with the performance acted out onstage or on-screen actually performed on the body of the spectator.

Notes

1   Cover from http://adultloopdb.nl/ [Accessed March 14, 2014].
2   *Sexual Symphony* (Rodox 615), censorship card no. 112 543, decision October 16, 1973.
3   http://adultloopdb.nl/ [Accessed March 14, 2014].
4   Steven Marcus, *The Other Victorians: A Study of Sexuality and Pornography in Mid-nineteenth Century England*, London: Weidenfeld & Nicolson, 1966.
5   Linda Williams, *Hardcore: Power, Pleasure, and the 'Frenzy of the Visible'*, Berkeley, CA & London: University of California Press, 1999 [1989], p. 109.
6   Informant Z.
7   Magnus Ullén, 'Pornography Remediated', *ejumpcut*, no. 51, Spring 2009.
8   Linda Williams, 'Film Bodies: Gender, Genre, and Excess', *Film Quarterly*, vol. 44, no. 4, 1991; Peter Lehman, 'Revelations about Pornography', in Peter Lehman (ed.) *Pornography: Film and Culture*, New Brunswick, NJ: Rutgers University Press, 2006; Magnus Ullén, *Bara för dig: Pornografi, konsumtion, berättande*, Stockholm: Vertigo förlag, 2009; Susanna Paasonen, *Carnal Resonance: Affect and Online Pornography*, Cambridge, MA: MIT Press, 2011; Ingrid Ryberg, *Imagining Safe Space: The Politics of Queer, Feminist, and Lesbian Pornography*, Stockholm: Stockholm University, 2012.
9   Erick Janssen (ed.), *The Psychophysiology of Sex*, Bloomington, IN: Indiana University Press, 2007.
10 Informant Y.
11 Eric Schaefer, 'Plain Brown Wrapper: Adult Films for the Market, 1930–1969', in Jon Lewis & Eric Smoodin (eds), *Looking Past the Screen: Case Studies in American Film History and Method*, Durham & London, 2007, p. 203.
12 Cf. Erik Hedling & Mats Jönsson (eds), *Välfärdsbilder: Svensk film utanför biografen*, Stockholm: Royal Library, 2008.
13 Schaefer, 'Plain Brown Wrapper', 2007, p. 221.
14 Schaefer, 'Plain Brown Wrapper', 2007, p. 202.
15 SFS 1959:348. http://www.riksdagen.se/sv/Dokument-Lagar/Lagar/Svenskforfattningssamling/Kungl-Majts-Forordning-1959_sfs-1959-348/ [Accessed May 23, 2012]. In the relevant period, the age limits were fifteen and eleven. In 1977, an age limit of seven was established. Those hardcore pornographic films which were not banned received as a rule a fifteen age limit, while films that only contained nudity and were not otherwise deemed harmful to children were allowed for all ages.
16 In the beginning, there was only an age limit of fifteen. The eleven-year-old limit was established in the 1960s. SFS 1959: 348, §3. http://www.riksdagen.se/sv/Dokument-Lagar/Lagar/Svenskforfattningssamling/Kungl-Majts-Forordning-1959_sfs-1959-348/

[May 23, 2012]. Cf. Jan Holmberg, 'Censorship in Sweden', in Mariah Larsson & Anders Marklund (eds.), *Swedish Film: An Introduction and Reader*, Lund: Nordic Academic Press, 2010.

17 S-O Gunnarsson, 'Är sexklubbarna i Malmö farliga?", *Kvällsposten*, January 19, 1971.

18 In December 1980, a Swedish television programme, Studio S, aired a debate about 'video violence', causing a moral panic about films such as *The Texas Chainsaw Massacre* (Tobe Hooper, 1974) and *The Toolbox Murders* (Dennis Donnelly, 1978). The programme led to a new law being passed in 1981 which forbade the spreading of violent videos, but also, paradoxically, to a drastic increase in the sales of VCR.

19 For instance, the Lasse Braun production *Imagination* (1971) in the *Satisfaction* series was submitted by Rolf Wiklund at Funny Girl, Stockholm, April 13, 1972; Bo Wikström, YZON, Malmö, May 8, 1972; Porno-Center, Stockholm, October 4, 1972; Bengt Carenborg, Tobaksaffären, Stockholm, March 23, 1973; Kjell Nilsson & Wilhelm Karlsson, both Stockholm, May 15, 1973; Pic-Up in Malmö, August 21 & September 20, 1973; Ulrich Geismar Prod, Stockholm, October 23, 1973; B Thibblin, July 15, 1975; and Club Miami, Helsingborg, June 9, 1976.

20 Susanna Paasonen & Laura Saarenmaa, 'The Golden Age of Porn: Nostalgia and History in Cinema', in Susanna Paasonen, Kaarina Nikunen & Laura Saarenmaa (eds), *Pornification: Sex and Sexuality in Media Culture*, Oxford & New York: Berg, 2007, p. 23.

21 Paasonen & Saarenmaa, 'The Golden Age of Porn', 2007, pp. 27–30.

22 Eric Schaefer, 'Gauging a Revolution: 16mm and the Rise of the Pornographic Feature', in Linda Williams (ed.) *Porn Studies*, Durham: Duke University Press, 2004, pp. 371–400.

23 Lehman, 'Revelations about Pornography', 2006.

24 Lehman, 'Revelations about Pornography', 2006, p. 88.

25 Chuck Kleinhans, 'The Change from Film to Video Pornography: Implications for Analysis', in Peter Lehman (ed.), *Pornography: Film and Culture*, New Brunswick, NJ: Rutgers University Press, 2006, p. 161.

26 Bertil Wredlund & Torsten Jungstedt, *Filmårsboken: 1973/74*, Stockholm: Proprius, 1974.

27 Linda Williams, '"White Slavery", or the Ethnography of "Sex Workers": Women in Stag Films at the Kinsey Archive', in Claire Hines & Darren Kerr (eds.), *Hard to Swallow: Hard-Core Pornography On Screen*, London: Wallflower Press, 2012.

28 Pornorama film *Mathematik: Mangelhaft. Vögeln: sehr gut*, censorship card no. 113 255, decision April 2, 1974 (A. Svensson); censorship card no. 113 403, decision June 6, 1974 (R. Häggbom).

29 These are *Chambermaid's Orgy*, censorship card no. 111 072; *Wedding Night for Three*, censorship card no. 111 340; and *Even Thieves Do It*, censorship card no. 111 341.

30 Schaefer calls these different names for the same person or company DBA's ('doing business as'). Cf. Schaefer, 'Plain Brown Wrapper', 2007, p. 217.

31 Informant Z.

32 http://adultloopdb.nl/ [Accessed May 5, 2012].

33 See http://www.colorclimax.com/ [Accessed May 5, 2012].

34 See http://en.wikipedia.org/wiki/Talk:Color_Climax_Corporation [Accessed May 7, 2012].

35 http://adultloopdb.nl/category/color-climax/ [Accessed May 7, 2012].

36 Berl Kutchinsky, *Law, Pornography and Crime: The Danish Experience, Scandinavian Studies in Law* (edited by Annika Snare), vol. 16, Oslo: Pax Forlag A/S, 1999, p. 100. The study referred is by Kåre T. Pettersen, 'Rapport om barnepornografi', Oslo: stencil, 1990.

37 This is according to an account of Color Climax Corporation labels at the Adult Loop Database. Some films were re-released, so this number does not equal the actual production. More than 500 Color Climax Corporation films were submitted to the National Board of Film Censors during the period 1968–82.

38 Berl Kutchinsky has also been the subject of severe criticism from the anti-porn movement, not least because his report on the Danish example was used by the Commission of Obscenity in the late 1960s and early 1970s in order to make the point that the legalization of pornography did not lead to an increase in sexual violence towards women. Cf. Kutchinsky, 1999; Diana E. H. Russell (ed.), *Making Violence Sexy: Feminist Views on Pornography*, Buckingham: Open University Press, 1993.

39 In 1984, a television show aired by NBC made the allegation that Denmark and the Netherlands exported large amounts of child porn. The show led to a Senate hearing in the United States. Cf. Kutchinsky, 1999, pp. 101–02.

40 Looking at the entire period (1968–82), Color Climax Corporation produced more than twenty per cent of the films.

41 Kutchinsky, 1999, p. 103.

42 Kutchinsky, 1999, p. 102.

43 Adult Loop Database, http://adultloopdb.nl/category/candy-film, http://adultloopdb.nl/category/candys-climax-studio/ and http://adultloopdb.nl/category/candys-climax-film/ [Accessed May 8, 2012].

44 Adult Loop Database, http://adultloopdb.nl/category/rodox/ [Accessed May 24, 2012]; Jack Stevenson, *Scandinavian Blue: The Erotic Cinema of Sweden and Denmark in the 1960s and 1970s*, Jefferson, NC: McFarland, 2010, p. 117.

45 *Motorcycle Mamas*, censorship card no. 110 652; *Private Club*, censorship card no. 110 815; and *Wedding Night Orgy*, censorship card no.114 208.

46 *Big John*, censorship card no. 113 515.

47 *Always Prepared*, censorship card no. 120 505.

48 *Young Anal Pissing*, censorship card no. 119 171.

49 *Stalled Rear End*, censorship card no. 113 461.

50 *Zum Knutschkeller*, censorship card no. 112 621.

51 *College Playmate*, censorship card no. 113 531; *Sweet Smell of Ass*, censorship card no. 113 534.

52 Kutchinsky, 1999, p. 96.

53 Kutchinsky, 1999, p. 98.

54 *Ky-Sen – the Vietnamese*, censorship card no. 110 892.

55 *Lady Piss*, censorship card no. 116 478; *Piss Party*, censorship card no. 114 391; *Pee Pleasure*, censorship card no. 115 288; and *Golden Showers*, censorship card no. 114 666.

56 *Star Film no 3*, censorship card no. 112 586.

57 *Sex and the Gun*, censorship card no. 112 302.

58 *Violated in the Forest*, censorship card no. 111 499.

59 *The Sadists*, censorship card no. 111 508.

60 *Weekend Sex*, censorship card no. 110 943; *Sex de Luxe: Lizzie and Greta in Private Action*, censorship card no. 112 358. The latter can also be found on Adult Loop Database, http://adultloopdb.nl/private-film-no-3-sex-de-luxe/ [Accessed May 21, 2012].

61 *Teenage Sex Game*, censorship card no 112 241.

62 *Private*, no. 8; cf. Klara Arnberg, 'Synd på export: 1960-talets pornografiska press och den svenska synden', *Historisk Tidskrift*, vol. 129, no. 3, 2009, pp. 482–83. Those who have seen the Milos Forman film *The People vs. Larry Flynt* (1996) will recognize the argument. Since Milton's editorial was published in the 1960s, there is no question who made it first. Nevertheless, what is important here is the connection between free speech and pornography, and the early porn entrepreneurs as avid defenders of free speech (although obviously with an economic interest). Cf. Paasonen & Saarenmaa, 'The Golden Age of Porn', 2007.

63 Sex worker interviews from the 1970s.

64 *Dr Wu*, censorship card no. 111 501, decision November 9, 1972.

65 *Delphia – the Greek*, censorship card no. 110 925, decision April 11, 1972.

66 *Imagination*, censorship card no 110 935, decision April 13, 1972.

67 *Victory for the Queen*, censorship card no. 111 375, decision October 9, 1972; *In the Name of Odin*, censorship card no. 112 649, decision November 1, 1973.

68 *Black Power*, censorship card no. 112 344, decision September 14, 1973.

69 *Hotel Amour*, censorship card no. 111 120. The version submitted to the National Board of Film Censors was almost eleven minutes long.

70 These numbers are calculated using a list of films from the National Archive, with data on which decisions were made. Films that had been sent to the Advisory Board (mandatory in the case of a ban) were then selected and compared with a search in the database at Statens Medieråd (which has taken over some of Statens Biografbyrås work after the abolishment of censorship for people over fifteen).

71 The descriptions are also noted in the list from the National Archive.

72 Quotation is taken from Marmalade Films' *MF 16/1970*, censorship card no. 110 722, decision January 27, 1972, which was cut from sixty to fifty meters. Apparently, there is some spanking which was not cut. The description reads: 'Group sex: one man, two women. Woman spanks other woman. Rummaging in genitals'.

73 *Boys with Boys*, censorship card no. 112 603, decision October 25, 1973. The description reads 'Homosex scene in the jungle with two boys, one a minor, and a rhesus monkey. Begins with an image of a red rose'.

74 The National Board of Film Censors' normative view of sexuality is also discussed in Elisabet Björklund, 'The Limits of Sexual Depictions in the Late 1960s', in Elisabet Björklund & Mariah Larsson (eds), *Swedish Cinema and the Sexual Revolution: Critical Essays*, Jefferson, NC: McFarland, 2016, pp. 126–138.

75 *Cerimony*, censorship card no. 112 779, decision November 29, 1973.

76　Rape in pornography and the Swedish censorship of *Cerimony* and *White Fantasies* is extensively discussed in Mariah Larsson, 'Lasse Braun, Rape Scenarios, and Swedish Censorship: A Case Study of Two 8mm Porn Films Featuring Rape', forthcoming.

77　Cf. Andrea Dworkin, *Pornography: Men Possessing Women*, London: Women's Press, 1981; or Gail Dines, Robert Jensen & Ann Russo, *Pornography: The Production and Consumption of Inequality*, New York: Routledge, 1998.

78　Cf. Williams, 'Film Bodies', 1991.

Chapter 6

A regional, national and transnational cinema?

A n issue that has been touched upon in this study but not further elaborated is the transnational character of both sex films and pornography. Since World War II, mainstream film has been dominated by American production companies, or rather Hollywood.[1] The market share for the domestic cinema in various European countries is generally low – around twenty to twenty-five per cent in Sweden.[2] The remaining percentage consists of American output, with the exception of a few other imported films. This is the reason why many European countries have installed various protective measures in order to stimulate or ease the production of national cinema, such as subsidiaries or tax reliefs to support national film production, or quotas to restrict the import of foreign films. Although pornography seldom has benefitted from these protective measures, various European pornographic industries are quite prolific. Porn industries, however, should be understood differently from film industries, since they rarely rely solely on films, but produce, distribute and sell merchandise like sex toys and magazines as well. A company like German Beate Uhse began by selling condoms, and the films produced by their various subsidiaries today are not connected to the merchandise sold in the Beate Uhse stores. *Private* magazine began in Sweden as a magazine, but is today a multinational corporation with many different products to sell. So both diversity in products and transnationality characterize contemporary successful porn industries.[3] The basis for today's situation was formed during the early boom of porn entrepreneurs, whose local practices were exported to the world. Nevertheless, nationality played and still plays an important role.

As Andrew Higson noted many years ago, there are a number of ways in which the concept of national cinema is used: it can be based on the domestic film industry – the 'who' and 'where' of the films; it can take into account those national characteristics that may be expressed; it can focus on audience consumption; and finally, it can refer to a 'quality art cinema', which relates to a particular national cultural heritage.[4] Yet, as Thomas Elsaesser points out, a national cinema 'most often presupposes a perspective that takes the point of view of production' (i.e. where is the film produced and by whom is it directed).[5] Art cinema or mainstream (non-pornographic) popular genres are most often the focus of discussions of national cinema. In a sense, the sex film and the pornographic film mirror art cinema, since they are both national and international in character. In contrast to art cinema, they function in a commercial market, the conditions of which are quite different from the market for art cinema.

In the following, I will discuss the transnationality of the sex film and pornographic film, looking at production companies and marketing strategies, as well as the significance of the region Malmö-Copenhagen. I will argue that the transnationality of pornography and sexually explicit material has its roots in pornography's historically legally and morally ambiguous status, and that the transnational elements of the material in question are dependent on their nationality, and vice versa.[6] Accordingly, this chapter deals both with the national stereotypes used to market and sell the material abroad, other strategies deployed, and a discussion of various national and international networks. One could say that the sex film 'transcended the national as an autonomous cultural particularity while respecting it as a powerful symbolic force'.[7] To a certain degree, this implies 8mm porn film as well, although the two formats operated under different circumstances regarding production and distribution.

The chapter begins with a discussion of national stereotypes, in particular the Swedish or Scandinavian one, aligning itself with the discussion of sex and the welfare state in Chapter 1. Both the sex film and 8mm porn film are included here. It continues with a description of the networks, collaborations and strategies used in the production and distribution of the sex film, before moving on to the 8mm film and the regional situation for Malmö and Copenhagen.

National stereotypes

In a well-known scene from Martin Scorsese's *Taxi Driver* (1976), Travis Bickle (Robert de Niro) asks Betsy (Cybill Shepherd) out on a date. They go to a movie, but the movie theatre advertises *Swedish Marriage Manual*, and the posters outside openly disclose what kind of a movie it is. By claiming that 'couples come here all the time', Travis persuades Betsy to enter, but after having seen a few brief scenes of the film, Betsy leaves. 'Taking me to a movie like this is about as exciting as saying "Let's fuck!"' she exclaims.

It has been said that the clips shown in *Taxi Driver* are from the Swedish sex education film *Language of Love* (Torgny Wickman, 1969). This, however, is not correct: as Elisabet Björklund has demonstrated, the clips are taken from the American film *Sexual Freedom in Denmark* (John Lamb, 1970), but with an added Swedish soundtrack. However, that this incorrect fact has spread, Björklund explains, not least in Sweden, testifies to the obdurateness of the conception of a Swedish sexual licentiousness.[8] Additionally, when an American film about Denmark becomes a Swedish 'marriage manual' (an American genre) film, it demonstrates how national stereotypes transmute and travel.

Some twenty years after *Taxi Driver* and on the other side of the Atlantic, the BBC production *Our Friends in the North* (1996) detailed the lives of four friends from Newcastle from the early 1960s to the early 1990s. One important theme in the mini-series is corruption, and we are shown corrupt politicians that contract cheap housing construction and go on trips to Sweden to learn more about building cheaply for the working class. Needless to say, the buildings start to mould and decay almost as soon as they are built. One of the four friends leaves Newcastle for London, where he starts working for a crime lord whose empire of porn stores and strip clubs is protected by bribing the police force. The magazines and the films for the stores and clubs are imported from Denmark. However, *Our Friends in North* is a bit of an exception in actually pointing to Denmark, as Sweden had become the more (in)famous of the countries in this particular respect. It has been argued that this comes out of Sweden's position as a neutral nation (in contrast to NATO member Denmark), 'in-between' the two powers of the Cold War, choosing the 'middle way' between socialism and capitalism.[9]

Within pornography, national and ethnic stereotypes are highly marketable. That various nationalities and ethnicities are associated with different sexual practices, varying sexual prowess and endowment, and also often gendered, is not in any way limited to Swedishness or Scandinavianism. The issue of race within pornography (usually in a US context and from an American perspective) has been discussed by Jennifer C. Nash, Linda Williams, Daniel Bernardi and José B. Capino, among others.[10] In the case of the blonde Scandinavian woman, whiteness – otherwise positioned as an unquestioned and therefore invisible norm – becomes foregrounded, and although that norm is still privileged in relation to other racial stereotypes, Scandinavian whiteness carries with it a notion of a gendered Other.[11]

The fact that stereotypes are used in a genre which needs to communicate efficiently, and to a certain extent with little or no dialogue, is unsurprising. Visual markers like blonde hair or dark skin function to add a charge to a sexual situation, and these sexual stereotypes – for instance, of primitive and well-endowed black men, blonde and licentious Scandinavian women, submissive and erotically sophisticated Asian women – work (with variations) across national boundaries in themselves. As such, the ascribed national or ethnic characteristic is a transnational marketing strategy.

According to Klara Arnberg, the use of the stereotype of the sexual Swedish woman began to be utilized by Swedish porn magazines in the 1960s. With titles or slogans like *Stripping Sweden, Spanking Sweden, Loving Sweden*, 'Like to meet Sweden's sweetest girls?' and 'Biggest selection of Swedish beauty', nationality moved to the foreground.[12] However, as Arnberg points out, in some cases photos were bought from abroad, which means that the women in the pictures were not necessarily Swedish at all.[13]

The notion of what historians Nikolas Glover and Carl Marklund have termed 'the Sweden-sex nexus' came, as several scholars have pointed out, from the decision to introduce mandatory sex education in schools in 1955.[14] A notorious article in *Time* magazine entitled 'Sin and Sweden' can be said to be the starting point for a reputation that grew during the 1960s.[15] At approximately the same time, two films became famous abroad for their depiction of young sexuality and nudity. *One Summer of Happiness* and *Summer with Monika* both told stories of young love in the summertime, connecting this youthful sexuality with the warmth and light of summer, as well as nude swimming in lakes and the sea.[16] In both films, the summer ends and autumn brings with it harsh realities; but one lasting impression from them was of a natural and paradoxically innocent sexuality taking place outdoors in the summer landscapes.

During the 1960s, attention increased with regards to the liberalization of censorship in Denmark and Sweden, evident in a number of films released from those countries.[17] Ingmar Bergman's *The Virgin Spring* (featuring the rape of a young woman) and *The Silence* (with female masturbation, casual sex and nudity) gained renown not only for their artistic endeavour, but for their unflinching narration of sexual matters.[18] Vilgot Sjöman's *I am Curious (Yellow)* was seized by customs and tried in an obscenity case in New York.[19] Early on, the public debate in Sweden concerned the problematic aspects of Sweden being associated with loose sexual morals. Concerning print pornography in the 1960s in Sweden, Klara Arnberg has pointed out that the idea of the sexually emancipated Swedish woman in pornography was something positive, whereas in the debate, this image was described as a blow to the nation's respectability, demonstrating how nationality, female respectability and sexuality were interlinked.[20] As Arnberg notes, 'nationalism and the respectability and sexuality of women were connected. Descriptions of Swedish women as sexually licentious became a blow to the national identity'.[21] Later on, however, as Glover and Marklund have demonstrated, the Swedish Institute, working to promote Sweden abroad, appropriated this image of Swedish sexuality and exploited it in their publicity.[22] However, it was used in such a way as to emphasize 'sexual democracy' – the rational and realist Swedish way – the equality between genders in the welfare state, and to illustrate modernity and progress.[23] Nonetheless, the more unfavourable perception of Sweden as a welfare state that had colonized even the most private and intimate remained ambiguously ensconced in representations such as *Sweden, Heaven and Hell*.

In this manner, the national stereotype became a marketable commodity. Like for art films – often associated with their national origin (e.g. Italian neorealism, the French New Wave, the Swedish bleakness of Bergman) – nationality became a signifier that could provide a taste of form and content. In West Germany, the designation *Schwedenfilm* did not simply mean a film from Sweden, but any dirty picture. In the United States, a production company of 8mm pornography called itself Swedish Erotica. As Eric Schaefer observes, during the late 1960s, sexploitation films with 'Swedish' or 'Danish' in the title, or with the nationalities of the respective countries emphasized in the marketing, became abundant.[24]

On the one hand, then, the Sweden-sex nexus was visually associated with summer and nature; a kind of natural sexuality which had connections to both the history of an agrarian nation and to movements like the German *Freikörperkultur*. On the other hand, it also evoked modernity, rationality, progress and the welfare state.[25] This somewhat unexpected juxtaposition – which is made nationally as well as internationally – is quite obvious in *One Summer of Happiness*, in which the young couple is vehemently opposed by tradition and the church. The male protagonist, Göran, comes from the city and is modern in most ways, but it is not until he comes to the countryside that he understands what life is about. Thus, the countryside, with its fields and forests and rural life is represented as good, and rendered nearly sensual in a voice-over by Göran:

> Slowly, I got to know the countryside. It was like crawling through a quagmire in the spring. It hurt your back and knees and you'd wonder why you were there. But still you

stayed even though you didn't have to. There was something that pulled you forward. The land itself lay there wide open and seemed to say 'come, touch me with your hands'. It was the sun and the summer that came – and then, there was Kerstin.

Yet the countryside is also backward and conservative, since many people who live there are not modern, but religious and puritan. The urban ways of the city, on the other hand, are marked as shallow and superficial, but modernity in the form of knowledge, rationality and science is seen as something positive. Accordingly, *One Summer of Happiness* negotiates the paradoxical juxtaposition of modernity and nature. Although it ends in tragedy, the film, by balancing city and countryside, modernity and tradition, seems to suggest a solution to this opposition.

There is kinship (albeit possibly distant) between Ulla Jacobsson's Kerstin in *One Summer of Happiness* and Ulla in *Ulla – the Swede* by Lasse Braun. *Ulla – the Swede* is a pornographic 8mm film from the *Nymphomania* series, which also contained the two films *Delphia – the Greek* and *Ky-Sen – the Vietnamese*. All three films have, as the titles imply, a woman at the centre. But it is not only a woman, but a nationality as well. Delphia, 'loaded with Mediterranean sensuality',[26] has sex with two men, including anal sex and

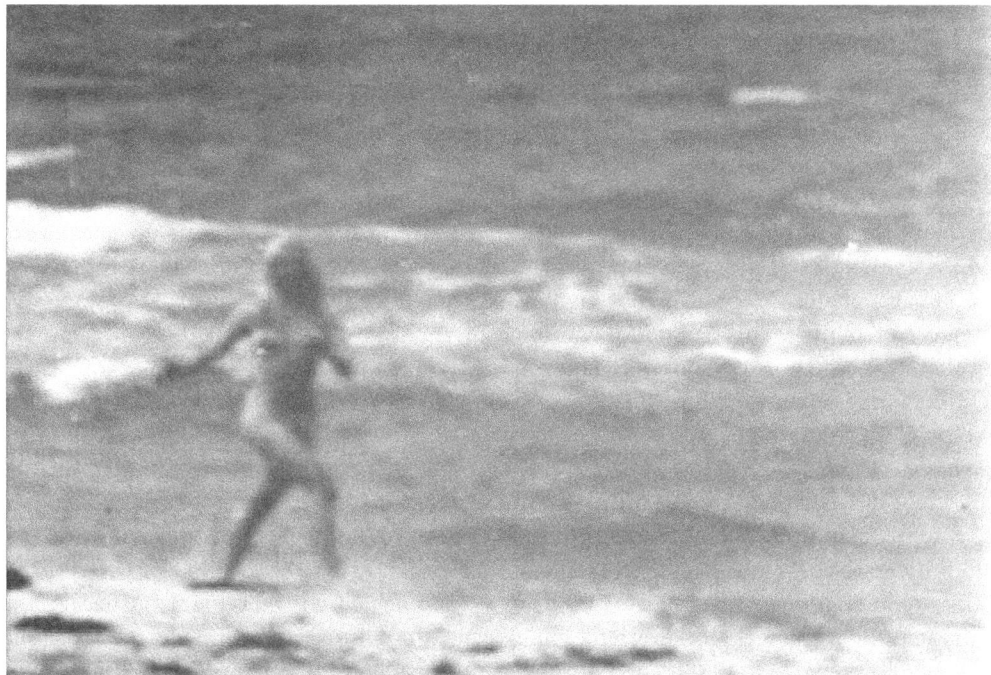

Figure 1: Ulla the Swede running naked along the beach. Frame grab.

double penetration. Ky-Sen, 'with charm and sophistication',[27] has sex with one man and one woman, but the film begins with her watching them and masturbating, and includes urination. *Delphia* takes place indoors, *Ky-Sen* in a garden. In *Ulla*, however, a blonde, naked woman, 'a girl who knows the score – and likes a bit of wrestling',[28] is jogging along a beach. Her breasts are bouncing, her long hair moving in the wind. She has freckles.

She comes across a woman; they begin to have sex and two men soon join them. The sex is not only outdoors, but on a beach, and although none of them go swimming, the association to summer, freedom and wild nature is still there. Another Scandinavian stereotype can be found in the three Lasse Braun films in the *Vikings* series, with Vikings that rape and pillage. In *Victory for the Queen*, the statuesque, blonde Viking queen (looking a bit like Brunhilde with her plaited hair) commands her men to perform cunnilingus on her while she is watching the rapes.

In the Mac Ahlberg/Inge Ivarson production *Justine and Juliette*, the virtuous sister (Marie Forså) is taken out into the archipelago by a man who is courting her. She believes they are in love, but he is actually trying to seduce her into selling sexual services for him. On one island, he films her with his Super 8 camera while she dances in the nude in front of him. Not only is this an archetypal 'Swedish summer' scene, it also quite explicitly references Ingmar Bergman's *Summer with Monika*, as the cliffs are similar to the ones in Bergman's film; moreover, one could argue, the film seems to underscore the relation between the film-maker/pimp and seduced woman/sex worker in a manner that might actually be read as a criticism of the great auteur.[29] That Bergman played an important role not only in the image of Sweden that had circulated since *Summer with Monika* onwards, but also as an inspiration to sex film-makers like Mac Ahlberg, Joe Sarno and Bo A. Vibenius is quite evident considering how many intertextual references there are to the Bergman films in Swedish sex films.[30]

The relationship set up in Ingmar Bergman's *Summer with Monika* – young sultry woman on cliffs, man behind camera – and alluded to in *Justine and Juliette* seems to echo Laura Mulvey's theories of the male gaze, woman as object of desire, and the (film) camera as oppressive, phallic tool.[31] A few Viking rapists aside, the main national/sexual symbol was gendered feminine. This had to do with the centrality of women in general in the sexually explicit films and pornography of the golden age. Women were not only the object of desire, but as Linda Williams has pointed out, her sexual pleasure was the object of investigation as well.[32] Comparing the hardcore American *Deep Throat* with the sexploitation film *Swedish Nymphet*, (both released in Sweden in 1973), one can note that although the narratives are quite different, one important plot point is the same: the acquirement of the elusive female orgasm. Both Linda Lovelace and Anita need to 'untangle their tingle' in order to fulfil themselves. While *Deep Throat* anatomically focuses on the location of the clitoris, Anita's search for full sexual release is more of a psychological and emotional journey. Linda Lovelace undergoes a clinical examination to locate the clitoris in her throat, whereas Anita is treated by a psychology student, but both are subjected to the 'medical gaze'.[33] Both films end in happy coupledom with the respective men who can provide them with orgasms.[34]

Sexploitation, softcore and hardcore films that feature women at the centre of the narrative are abundant in general – from Joe Sarno's *Sin in the Suburbs* (1964) to *Emmanuelle* (Just Jaeckin, 1974) to *Debbie Does Dallas* (Jim Clark, 1978). Nevertheless, in relation to the Swedish films, international stars like Harry Reems or Eric Edwards played the male leads, while the female leads were to a large extent Swedish (some were Danish and German, such as Anne Bie Warburg [*Justine and Juliette*; *Bel Ami*] and Christa Linder [*Bel Ami*]). As object, the Swedish man is remarkably absent in the discourse of the Sweden-sex nexus. His existence comes in the form of director, producer or pornographer – a Vilgot Sjöman, an Inge Ivarson or a Berth Milton Sr.

Scandinavian sexuality became excessively associated with women, creating not only a gendered object of desire, but a gendered gaze from abroad as well. Although the Swedish Institute emphasized the changing sex roles in Sweden and the undermining of a troublesome moralist past, the sexual double standards for men and women, and attempts to turn 'sin' into 'sexual democracy',[35] the alleged progressive equality of Sweden could be said to be countered by the imbalance of gender roles in these films. Conversely, however, these films can also be described as 'participatory and modern', challenging 'normative moral standards that existed in the United States at the time'.[36] In such a reading, the (young) women of these films embody modern and progressive ideals of a liberated sexuality, in particular from a perspective from abroad where such ideals may run counter to prevailing norms.

A network of national and international production

Swedish film historian Leif Furhammar claims that the Swedish sex film was mostly made for export. To a certain extent, and with some qualification, this claim seems to hold true. Although many of these films were submitted to the National Board of Film Censors in order to be allowed to be screened in Sweden, and although they did screen across the country, many of them were also in a sense 'un-Swedish' because they were so clearly aimed at an international market.[37] Looking at the production strategies, one can also say that they were made across national boundaries; more so in some instances than in others (for example, the productions of Saga Film which were co-produced with companies in other countries). In some cases, the national confusion is complete – *Nøglehullet* is included in *Svensk filmografi 7* (with the Swedish title *Nyckelhålet*), but its box-office is listed among foreign films in the annual report of the Swedish Film Institute.

Approximately one third of the Swedish sex films were co-produced across national boundaries, but most of the films also utilized certain strategies in order to be marketable internationally.[38] Consequently, four of the six films made by Filminvest between 1974 and 1977 were based on literary originals, namely *Flossie*, *Justine and Juliette*, *Bel Ami* and *Molly*. These were based on *Flossie: A Venus of Fifteen*; the two novels *Justine ou les Malheurs de la virtu* (1791) and *Histoire de Juliette, ou les Prospérités du vice* (1797–1801) by the Marquis de Sade; *Bel Ami* (1885) by Guy de Maupassant; and *The Fortunes and Misfortunes of the*

Famous Moll Flanders (1722) by Daniel Defoe. These literary originals had some reputation for their erotic content – some, like *Justine* and *Juliette*, can even be said to be infamous for their content – and were well-known outside of Sweden. It is significant that none of them were based on a Swedish literary original, but picking up on the erotic literary traditions of France and the United Kingdom. The films were very freely adapted, with the most obvious change being that *Justine and Juliette* ends well for the virtuous sister rather than the viceful one, as in de Sade's morality tale. Nonetheless, the use of internationally well-known erotic literary originals indicates knowledge of the potentials of 'pre-sold property'[39] in marketing these films not only at home but also abroad.[40]

In addition, the films contained a more or less international cast. They starred Swedish actresses, in particular Marie Forså under the more easily pronounced pseudonym Maria Lynn, but also Danish, German and American actors. Harry Reems and Eric Edwards both performed in a string of films. This, too, increased the marketability of the films abroad, as well as the fact that these films were often dubbed into English.[41] It was not only the films that travelled – their stars did as well. Marie Forså, Marie Ekorre and Christina Lindberg had international careers, starring in West German, French, Tunisian and Japanese films.[42]

In a sense, then, these films can be said to be 'un-Swedish', as Furhammar seems to insinuate.[43] At the same time, however, they enhanced their own Swedishness, emphasizing national stereotypes of the blonde, sexually emancipated but somehow innocent young woman, Stockholm as a northern city of sin, and the Swedish summer landscapes where sexuality could be natural and free.

Country unknown: 8mm films and the problem of origin

In comparison with the 8mm pornographic film, however, the sex film was cumbersome to export. The 35mm films had a dialogue that needed to be dubbed or subtitled and posters printed with the title in the relevant language. Sometimes editing was needed which allowed for different national censorship regulation and marketing considerations, and several large canisters of films had to be transported. Despite this, these films were often made with distributors who were already interested (according to Inge Ivarson, the *Language of Love* was made partly on the initiative of a West German company),[44] and had a kind of established infrastructure of distribution circuits and exhibition venues. These looked different from the 8mm films, which were forbidden in some of the countries to which they were exported, and thus had a completely different kind of network for distribution and exhibition.

Many of the 8mm films had no sound, or a soundtrack consisting of music and sounds of pleasure. At any rate, the dialogue was not really necessary to understand what was happening. The film reels were quite small and could fit into a padded envelope or something similar. Marketing consisted of lists of titles, still images and short texts. Looking at the available back covers at the Adult Loop Database, most have a text in three different

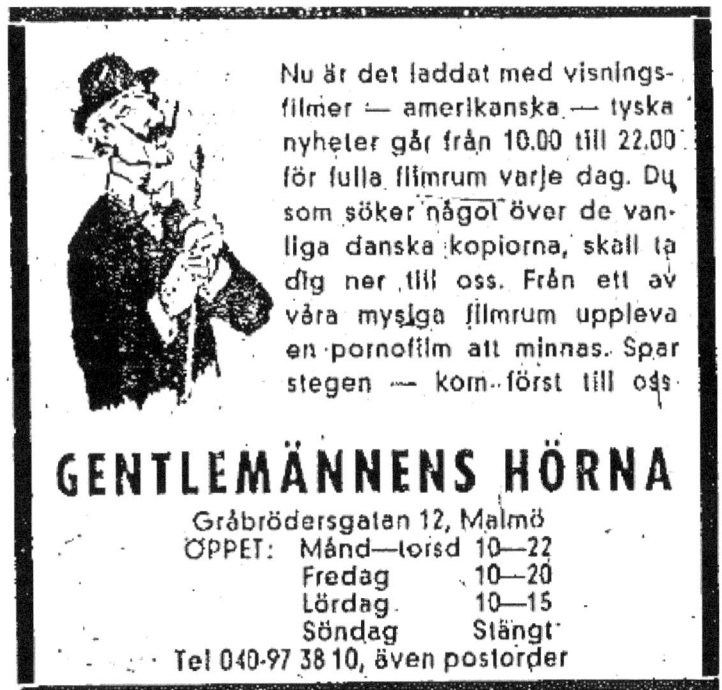

Figure 2: 'Now we are loaded with films for screening – American – German new films are shown from 10.00 to 22.00 in full exhibition rooms every day. You who are looking for something beyond the usual Danish copies should come to us. In one of our cozy film rooms experience a porn film to remember. Save your steps – come first to us.' Advertisement from *Kvällsposten*, October 20, 1975.

languages – English, French and German – none of which are necessarily the language of the country where the film was produced. This is similar to how the early pornographic magazines like *Private* were made. It was established and run by Berth Milton Sr., and had an international approach from the outset, with texts in Swedish, English and German.[45] The transnational features of the 8mm film, however, did not make nationality redundant. (See for instance the advert for Gentlemännens hörna from 1975 in Figure 2.)

Among the 8mm films submitted to the National Board of Film Censors, a large share (seventeen per cent) was indicated as 'country unknown' on the register card. During the period 1971–76, 1321 films were submitted, and of these, 217 were marked with a question mark or simply a blank in the space for nationality. This is interesting given that some of the films were made by companies which in other cases had been indicated as Danish, West German or some other country of origin, which means that the censor would have only had to check another film from the same company in order to set a country of origin.

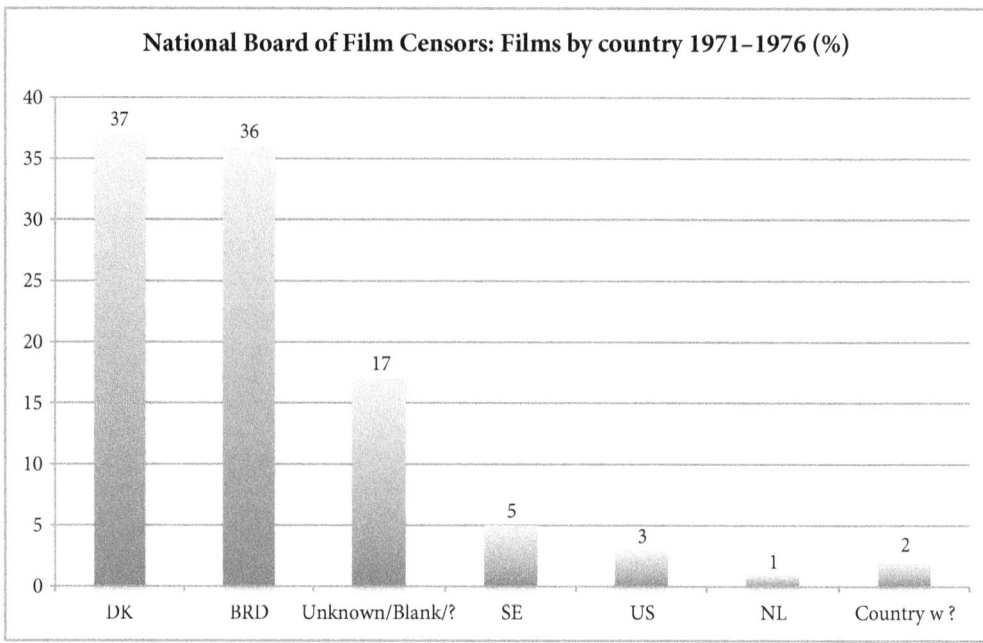

Figure 3: Number of films by country as indicated by the National Board of Film Censors.

As I mentioned in the previous chapter, most films came from Denmark (37%) and West Germany (36%). The third largest category was unknown.

Perhaps this is not surprising considering the tedious work of censoring pornographic 8mm films. Before censorship of films for people over fifteen was abolished, Swedish censors complained for a long time about the copious amounts of pornography they had to watch; not only having to see the films and make a decision based on the contents, but also filling out one register card and one censorship card for each film. If the nationality of the film was not readily available through a note on the back cover or as part of the credits, leaving the space blank or with a question mark would be the easy way out.

Nonetheless, it also testifies to the ambiguous national status of these films. For instance, although outside the time frame of this investigation, the US label Swedish Erotica (submitted 1978–80) proves an interesting case (see Figure 4). According to the Adult Loop Database, Swedish Erotica exchanged footage with Danish Color Climax Corporation, which means that some films were released by Color Climax Corporation (and thus not included in this diagram), while other films were made by Color Climax Corporation but released through Swedish Erotica.[46] This seems to be confirmed by the films from the Kinsey Institute's archive, which, although from Swedish Erotica, matched films from Color Climax Corporation. The name of the label capitalized on the marketability of the national stereotype without having any actual connection to Sweden, but added to the mix-up of nationality – especially since some footage was from a neighbouring Scandinavian country.

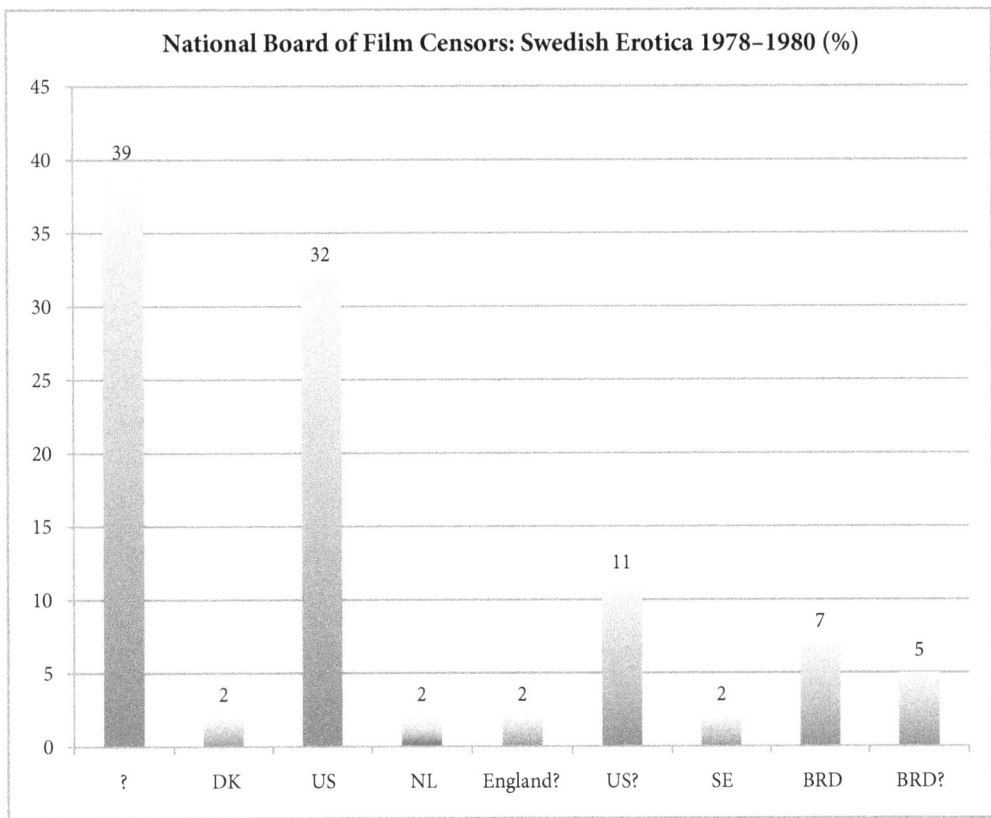

Figure 4: Swedish Erotica films by country as indicated by the National Board of Film Censors.

As evidenced by these diagrams, national confusion for these films was profuse. Of fifty-seven films, less than a third (32%, eighteen films) were definitely identified as American. As many as twenty-two films (39%) were given a question mark, six films (11%) were indicated as 'US?', while other countries given as potential home countries for these productions included West Germany (7%, four films) and 'West Germany?' (5%, three films), Denmark (2%, one film), 'England?' (2%) and Sweden (2%).

Another example of this national ambiguity is Lasse Braun productions. As mentioned in the previous chapter, Lasse Braun is a pseudonym for Alberto Ferro. The pseudonym, consisting of one very Swedish-sounding first name (Lasse is a wholesomely Swedish nickname for Lars) and a German-sounding last name (Braun, meaning brown, is a common surname in Germany), intimates a transnational identity which is further reinforced by Braun's/Ferro's background. Together they provide a mix of Northern Europe and Mediterranean countries.[47] Furthermore, Lasse Braun worked in various countries, among them Sweden, Denmark, the United States and West Germany, and his films were shot in

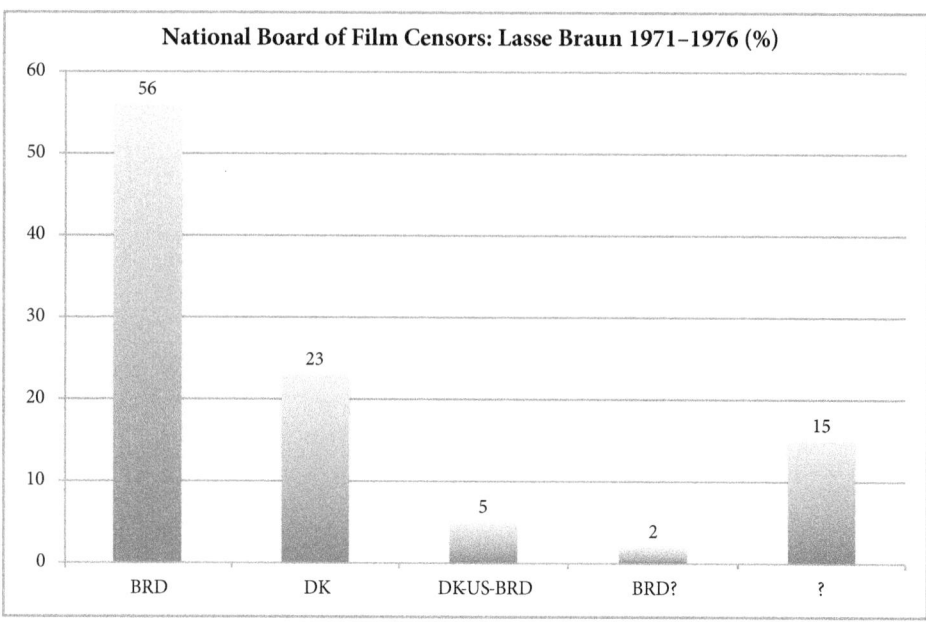

Figure 5: Lasse Braun films by country as indicated by the National Board of Film Censors.

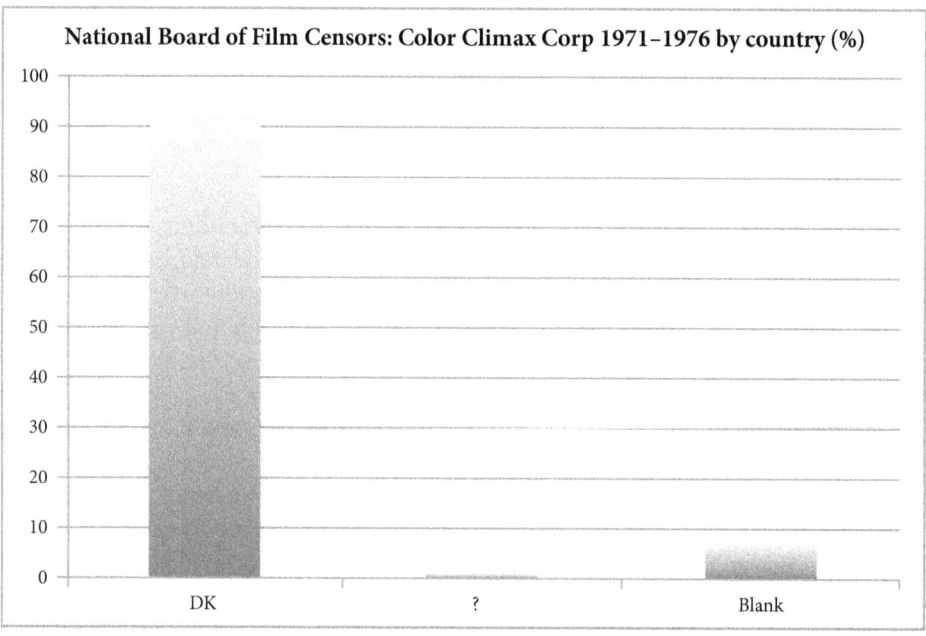

Figure 6: CCC country of origin as indicated by the National Board of Film Censors.

several more. Here, almost fifteen per cent (or nine out of sixty-two films) are indicated as unknown in origin.

One instance of a quite definite country of origin is Color Climax Corporation and its various labels. Between 1971 and 1976, 257 films were submitted. Of these, 237 were identified as Danish by the National Board of Film Censors. Approximately eight per cent (or twenty films) were either given a question mark or had the space for nation left blank. Color Climax Corporation had back cover texts in three languages, none of them Danish, and thrived on export. Those Color Climax films that can be found on porn sites like xhamster.com, although of a later date (1978 onwards), are dubbed into German.

Another (albeit weaker) indication of these films' transnationality is how they travelled. That several of the films submitted to the National Board of Film Censors could also be found in the archive at the Kinsey Institute – more than a quarter of the globe away – is not surprising, but quite telling, especially since the films at the Kinsey Institute have not been collected systematically. That the 8mm films were quite easy to send by mail (although liable to be stopped at customs, depending on national laws on obscenity) or to carry with you in a bag made them itinerant in a way that the 35mm film could never be. They were also smuggled (see below); they were, so to speak, handy, and their narrative never dependent on dialogue, but either quite redundant or conveyed efficiently in images.

The regional situation

This had a bearing on the situation in Malmö. Today, Malmö and Copenhagen are connected through the bridge across Öresund. The bridge was built in the late 1990s and inaugurated in the summer of 2000. The train ride between the central stations of Malmö and Copenhagen takes thirty-five minutes. Before the bridge, ferries or hovercrafts took traffic across the sound, and travel time was approximately one hour. Because of the Nordic Passport Union, passports were not necessary to travel between Sweden and Denmark.[48] However, there were (and still are) customs checks on passengers and vehicles leaving the ferries, although much less since Sweden entered the European Union in 1995. Nonetheless, communications have been quite unproblematic between the two countries, although Sweden has regarded Denmark and the connection across Öresund as a potential site for contagion of various inflictions on the continent.

By the 1960s, Danish pornography was starting to be smuggled into Sweden. As the gateway to Sweden, Malmö had close ties with Copenhagen. Yet the import of Danish pornography was usually quite informal and small-scale: either Danish salesmen brought a trunk or two to Malmö where the material was then sold, or Swedes crossed Öresund to buy material in Copenhagen which they brought back.[49] Furthermore, although Copenhagen held a promise of a Nordic capital of sin for Swedes living in the south of Sweden, far from the Swedish capital Stockholm, sex workers travelled across the sound to work in both cities, from strippers and vaudeville artists to prostitutes.[50] Since Denmark legalized pornography earlier than Sweden, sex stores and sex clubs proliferated in Copenhagen both on Istedgade and Strøget, and in Nyhavn.[51] Jack Stevenson describes Copenhagen around 1971 as 'a giant pornographic freak show', and for many Swedes, Copenhagen epitomized a city of sin, somewhat displacing their own progression towards sex stores, sex clubs and porn cinemas onto their Nordic neighbour.[52] The development in Denmark – which was earlier, bigger and more prolific – influenced what happened in Sweden. Denmark's earlier legalization led to several production companies which made pornographic 8mm film starting up during the 1960s. In addition, more upscale 35mm sex films were also produced in Denmark.[53] The milieu of Copenhagen spilled over into much smaller Malmö, with *Kvällsposten* frequently reporting from Copenhagen and the streets where sexual commerce took place at that time.

In 1972, Danish sex clubs were under scrutiny for tax evasion and connections to criminality, and several clubs had to close down. In January 1972, *Kvällsposten* reported that Malmö might be the new 'sex center' – that as clubs closed down in Copenhagen, tourists would come to Malmö instead.[54] Some two weeks later, a headline read '"Persecuted" porn chicks escape across the Sound!' According to the article, experienced Danish strippers and live show artists were sought after in Malmö, and since there were no jobs in Copenhagen, they accepted job offers from the Swedish clubs.[55] The Swedish clubs and stores were also under scrutiny, both for activities related to procuring and for tax evasion. According to Erik Stahre, the man responsible for evaluating the finances of the clubs and stores at the county authority (Länsstyrelsen), it was an impossible task. He was quoted by *Kvällsposten* as saying that state brothels would be a good thing both because the clubs would be regulated and the state would get a good income, as with taxes gained on tobacco and alcohol.[56] Regardless of the efforts of the police and tax authorities, and notwithstanding that a couple of club owners were indicted, it would take another four years before the clubs were more definitely closed down.

Studying the 8mm films submitted to the National Board of Film Censors can provide some answer to how the flow of imported films moved. Surprisingly, few of the submitted 8mm films were Swedish. This might be because few films were actually produced in Sweden, i.e. the number of submitted films corresponds to the number of films made. But there are two other possible explanations. Firstly, it might be that Swedish-produced films were screened in Sweden but not submitted to the Board for various reasons (such as fear for repercussions, or a false sense that Swedish films could not be 'harmful' in the same manner as foreign films). Supporting this explanation is the fact that, of the 8mm Swedish films included in the DVD *Rapport från Stockholms sexträsk*, only half can be found in the records of the Board.[57] Secondly, it might be that Swedish-produced 8mm films, as Furhammar claims about the 35mm sex films, were made for export and were not included in the domestic exhibition contexts. However, judging by the share of films on Adult Loop Database that are indicated as Swedish, the first explanation seems the most probable: there was only a small production of Swedish 8mm porn. In comparison to the Danish output, the Swedish share is miniscule.

From the list of films submitted to the National Board of Film Censors between 1971 and 1976 (1321 titles), I composed another list of films originally submitted by persons or companies in Malmö. This list only consists of ninety-eight entries. Of these ninety-eight films, twenty-six per cent were from Color Climax Corporation. Compared to the percentage of Color Climax Corporation films in the original 1971–76 list (twenty per cent), this is somewhat larger. An even more convincing number to underline the connection between Malmö and Copenhagen/Denmark is that half (forty-nine) of the films on the list of films originally submitted from Malmö are indicated as Danish. Accordingly, people involved in the sex store and sex club businesses in Malmö either travelled to Copenhagen to buy films, or had connections with people who came over to Malmö and sold films. The persons and companies indicated on the register cards as submitting films were Kerstin Lindholm, Bo Wikström at YZON, YZON, Pic Up, Tidningsshopen, Lanza AB and Trading bokförlag.

Travelling between Sweden and Denmark with reasonable amounts of pornographic material was legal. However, bringing large amounts of obscene magazines or films into countries where such material was forbidden was not. Three different articles from the summer of 1972 tell of people arrested for smuggling. In Travemünde, a couple from Malmö had been apprehended for 'porn smuggling'.[58] In this case, the couple only carried magazines, but the customs officers in Travemünde claimed to have confiscated 6200 magazines and 630 films, which does not seem to be an extremely large amount given that a Danish man (described as 'bachelor' by the newspaper) had attempted to enter England with 10,000 magazines, 310 films and a number of card decks with pornographic pictures. All in all, according to the article's headline, this amounted to 'half a ton' of porn.[59] The third article told of a Hungarian man, resident in Sweden, who had been caught trying to smuggle 3682 porn films hidden in a secret storage space in his truck into Italy.[60] These reported attempts bear evidence that porn, in the shape of magazines and 8mm films (and card decks), was taken across borders into countries where such material was not allowed, and in quite large quantities as well.

These examples demonstrate that like the sex film, the 8mm film travelled as well. Although some such travel was formalized, as for instance in the exchange of footage between Color Climax Corporation and Swedish Erotica, the transnational distribution of 8mm films did not necessarily go through established networks and production collaborations. Rather, location and opportunity played a role in where the films ended up. Nevertheless, producers demonstrated an awareness and forethought that their product was not simply national but might appeal to consumers worldwide, as indicated by the texts in different languages on the back covers.

Notes

1 Cf. Tomas Elsaesser, *European Cinema: Face to Face with Hollywood*, Amsterdam: Amsterdam University Press, 2005.

2 Statistics from the Swedish Film Institute, 2011–2015. Available online: http://www.sfi.se/sv/statistik/.

3 See Olof Hedling & Mariah Larsson, 'National Boundaries: Notes on the Pornographic Film in 1970s Sweden', in Savaş Arslan, Volkan Aytar, Defne Karaosmanoğlu & Süheyla Kırca Schroeder (eds), *Media, Culture and Identity in Europe*, Istanbul: Bahçeşehir University Press, 2010.

4 Andrew Higson, 'The Concept of National Cinema', in Alan Williams (ed.), *Film and Nationalism*, New Brunswick, N.J.: Rutgers University Press, 2002, pp. 52–53.

5 Elsaesser, 2005, p. 37.

6 Cf. Mariah Larsson, 'National/Transnational Genre: Pornography in Transition', in Tommy Gustafsson & Pietari Kääpä (eds), *Nordic Genre Film: Small Nation Film Cultures*, Edinburgh: Edinburgh University Press, 2015.

7 Hedling & Larsson, 2010, p. 273.

8 Elisabet Björklund, '"This is a dirty movie" – *Taxi Driver* and "Swedish sin"', *Journal of Scandinavian Cinema*, vol. 1, no. 2, 2011.

9 Cf. Nikolas Glover & Carl Marklund, 'Arabian Nights in the Midnight Sun? Exploring the Temporal Structure of Sexual Geographies', *Historisk Tidskrift* vol. 129, no 3, 2009; Lena Lennerhed, *Frihet att njuta: Sexualdebatten på 1960-talet*, Stockholm: Norstedts, 1994; Klara Arnberg & Carl Marklund, 'Illegally Blonde: "Swedish Sin" and Pornography in American and Swedish Imaginations, 1950–1971', in Elisabet Björklund & Mariah Larsson (eds), *Swedish Cinema and the Sexual Revolution: Critical Essays*, Jefferson, NC: McFarland, 2016.

10 Cf. Jennifer C. Nash, *The Black Body in Ecstasy: Reading Race, Reading Porn*, Durham, NC: Duke University Press, 2014; Linda Williams, 'Skin Flicks on the Racial Border: Pornography, Exploitation, and Interracial Lust', in Linda Williams (ed.), *Porn Studies*, Durham, NC: Duke University Press, 2004; Daniel Bernardi, 'Interracial Joysticks: Pornography's Web of Racist Attractions', in Peter Lehman (ed.), *Pornography: Film and Culture*, New Brunswick, NJ: Rutgers University Press, 2006; José B. Capino, 'Asian College Girls and Oriental Men with Bamboo Poles: Reading Asian Pornography', in Peter Lehman (ed.), *Pornography: Film and Culture*, New Brunswick, NJ: Rutgers University Press, 2006.

11 Cf. Richard Dyer, *White: Essays on Race and Culture*, London: Routledge, 1997. Cf. Arne Lunde, *Nordic Exposures: Scandinavian Identities in Classical Hollywood Cinema*, Seattle, WA: University of Washington Press, 2010, pp. 3–15.

12 Klara Arnberg, 'Synd på export: 1960-talets pornografiska press och den svenska synden', *Historisk Tidskrift*, vol. 129, no. 3, 2009, pp. 480–81.

13 Arnberg, 2009, p. 481.

14 Glover & Marklund, 'Arabian Nights', 2009; Lennerhed, 1994; Arnberg, 'Synd på export', 2009.

15 Joe David Brown, 'Sin and Sweden', *Time*, April 25, 1955. Cf. Frederick Hale, 'Time for Sex in Sweden: Enhancing the Myth of the "Swedish Sin" During the 1950s', *Scandinavian Studies*, vol. 75, no. 3, 2003; Eric Schaefer, '"I'll Take Sweden!" The Shifting Discourse of the "Sexy Nation" in Sexploitation Films', in Eric Schaefer (ed.), *Sex Scene: Media and the Cultural Revolution*, Durham, NC & London: Duke University Press, 2014. Arnberg & Marklund, 'Illegally Blonde', 2016.

16   Cf. Eric Schaefer, *Bold! Daring! Shocking! True!: A History of Exploitation Films, 1919–1959,* Durham, NC: Duke University Press, 1999, pp. 335–36.

17   Cf. Jack Stevenson, *Scandinavian Blue: The Erotic Cinema of Sweden and Denmark in the 1960s and 1970s,* Jefferson, NC: McFarland, 2010; Schaefer, "I'll Take Sweden!", 2014.

18   Linda Williams, *Screening Sex,* Durham, NC: Duke University Press, 2008; Maaret Koskinen, *Ingmar Bergman's The Silence: Pictures in the Typewriter, Writings on the Screen,* Seattle, WA: University of Washington Press, 2010.

19   See Kevin Heffernan, 'Prurient (Dis)Interest: The American Release and Reception of *I am Curious (Yellow)*', in Eric Schaefer (ed.), *Sex Scene: Media and the Sexual Revolution,* Durham, NC & London: Duke University Press, 2014; Anders Åberg, *Tabu: Filmaren Vilgot Sjöman,* Lund: Filmhäftet förlag, 2001.

20   Arnberg, 2009, p. 484.

21   Arnberg, 2009, p. 484 (my translation).

22   Glover & Marklund, 'Arabian Nights', 2009.

23   Glover & Marklund, 'Arabian Nights', 2009.

24   Schaefer, "I'll Take Sweden!", 2014, p. 227.

25   Glover & Marklund, 'Arabian Nights', 2009; Schaefer, "I'll Take Sweden!", 2014.

26   Back cover text taken from Adult Loop Database: http://adultloopdb.nl/up/lassebraun/lasse-braun-lb307-nymphomania-delphia-the-greek-1970-2.jpg [Accessed October 26, 2012].

27   Back cover text taken from Adult Loop Database http://adultloopdb.nl/up/lassebraun/lasse-braun-lb308-nymphomania-ky-sen-the-vietnamese-1970-2.jpg [Accessed October 26, 2012].

28   Cover text taken from Adult Loop Database: http://adultloopdb.nl/up/lassebraun/lasse-braun-lb309-nymphomania-ulla-the-swede-1970-2.jpg [Accessed October 26, 2012].

29   Mariah Larsson, 'Ingmar Bergman, Swedish Sexploitation, and Early Swedish Porn', *Journal of Scandinavian Cinema,* vol. 5, no. 1, 2015.

30   Larsson, 'Ingmar Bergman', 2015.

31   Laura Mulvey, 'Visual Pleasure and Narrative Cinema', in Bill Nichols (ed.), *Movies and Methods: An Anthology vol II,* Berkeley, CA, London: University of California Press, 1985. Originally published in *Screen,* vol. 16, no. 3, 1975.

32   Linda Williams, *Hardcore: Power, Pleasure, and the 'Frenzy of the Visible',* Berkeley, CA & London: University of California Press, 1999 [1989].

33   Cf. Mary Ann Doane, *The Desire to Desire: The Woman's Film of the 1940s,* Houndmills & London: MacMillan Press, 1987, pp. 37–59.

34   Cf. Mariah Larsson, 'Contested Pleasures', in Mariah Larsson & Anders Marklund (eds), *Swedish Film: An Introduction and Reader,* Lund: Nordic Academic Press, 2010.

35   Glover & Marklund, 'Arabian Nights', 2009.

36   Schaefer, "I'll Take Sweden!", 2014, p. 216.

37   Mariah Larsson & Olof Hedling, 'Skandinavische Lust und europäisches Kino: Eine schwedische Filmographie', *Montage AV,* February 18, 2009; Hedling & Larsson, 2010.

38   Larsson & Hedling, 'Skandinavische Lust', 2009; Hedling & Larsson, 'National Boundaries', 2010.

39   Justin Wyatt, *High Concept: Movies and Marketing in Hollywood,* Austin, TX: University of Texas Press, 1994.

40 Larsson & Hedling, 'Skandinavische Lust', 2009; Hedling & Larsson, 'National Boundaries', 2010.

41 Larsson & Hedling, 2009; Hedling & Larsson, 2010.

42 Larsson & Hedling, 2009; Hedling & Larsson, 2010.

43 Mariah Larsson, 'Practice Makes Perfect? The Production of the Swedish Sex Film in the 1970s', *Film International*, vol. 8, no. 6, 2010.

44 Interview with Inge Ivarson, conducted by Elisabet Björklund & Mariah Larsson, Stockholm November 8, 2010. See also Elisabet Björklund, *'The Most Delicate Subject': A History of Sex Education Films in Sweden*, diss. Lund: Lund University, 2012.

45 Klara Arnberg, *Motsättningarnas marknad: den pornografiska pressens kommersiella genombrott och regleringen av pornografi i Sverige 1950–1980*, Lund: Sekel bokförlag, 2010, p. 140.

46 Adult Loop Database, http://adultloopdb.nl/category/swedish-erotica/ [Accessed October 24, 2012].

47 One reader of my blog expressed surprise that Lasse Braun (whose films he was well acquainted with) was not Swedish.

48 The Nordic Passport Union was established in the early to mid-1950s. At the time of writing (January 2016), however, border controls have been introduced again between Sweden and Denmark for travelers into Sweden due to the refugee situation that arose during autumn 2015.

49 Arnberg, 2010, pp. 210–11.

50 Sven-Axel Månsson, *Könshandelns främjare och profitörer: om förhållandet mellan hallick och prostituerad*, Lund: Doxa, 1981; Gunilla Ekroth, *Gunilla af Halmstad: ett annat liv i Sverige*, Stockholm: Hjalmarson & Högberg, 2009.

51 Stevenson, 2010; Berl Kutchinsky, *Law, Pornography and Crime: The Danish Experience, Scandinavian Studies in Law* (edited by Annika Snare), vol. 16, Oslo: Pax Forlag A/S, 1999.

52 Stevenson, 2010, p. 163.

53 Stevenson, 2010.

54 'Malmö nytt sexcentrum', *Kvällsposten*, January 13, 1972.

55 '"Förfölja" porrbrudar på flykt över Sundet!', *Kvällsposten*, January 28, 1972.

56 'Han har Malmös omöjligaste jobb: skatte-razzia bland sexklubbarna', *Kvällsposten*, January 20, 1972.

57 *Rapport från Stockholms sexträsk*, DVD released by Klubb Super 8, 2013. Bonus material.

58 'Malmömakar greps för porrsmuggling', *Kvällsposten*, July 5, 1972.

59 'Försökte smuggla in halvt ton porr i England', *Kvällsposten*, June 29, 1972.

60 'Fast med 3682 porrfilmer', *Kvällsposten*, June 16, 1972.

Conclusion

The porn scene in Sweden, 1971–1976

There are several conclusions to be drawn from this study; some tentative and others quite definite. For all Sweden's reputation of promiscuity and permissiveness, the amount of pornographic films produced was not actually that significant: sexually explicit films, yes; hardcore porn, not so much. Nevertheless, there were plenty of sites for the consumption of sexual entertainment, merchandise and, in some cases, services, so there was most definitely a 'porn scene' that included film screenings and other kinds of sexual entertainment. Furthermore, the material screened in stores, clubs, porn cinemas, as well as regular cinemas, travelled readily across borders and/or was produced in transnational collaborations, with various strategies deployed in order to increase the international marketability of the material – from the use of the Swedish or Scandinavian stereotypes, to dubbing into English and the inclusion of foreign stars, to the print on the back cover being in three different languages.

This porn scene extended to all of Sweden, but was more pronounced in the larger cities of Stockholm, Gothenburg and Malmö. In addition, the proximity of Malmö to Copenhagen influenced not only the supply of films on offer, but the general urban sexual space as well, as sex workers and film distributors travelled back and forth across Öresund to work, find ideas and buy films.

Furthermore, although the legalization of pornography resulted from a discussion about sexuality that took its point of departure in visionary ideas about a society free from prejudice, inhibition and ignorance, the consequences of decriminalized pornography were quite soon perceived of as unwanted. Where previously arguments (such as those in the 1960s) had focused on better pornography and sexually free and independent human beings, they began (in the 1970s, in particular from the mid-seventies onwards) to emphasize misery, criminality, prostitution, drinking and drug abuse, and the abuse of minors.[1] The women's movement attacked pornography for its capitalist, patriarchal objectification and exploitation of women, and the small-time, more or less grey-zone operating sex business entrepreneurs were at odds with the ideals of the welfare state. Although the sex stores and sex clubs offered a space beyond the 'power-knowledge grid'[2] this same space was regarded, by social workers and police authorities, as an opportunity for predators to prey on socially vulnerable people, most often women. And true enough, the space occupied by stores and the lower-end clubs were places of urban decay and neighbourhoods of unrest, thereby simultaneously reinforcing and being reinforced by it, perpetuating the delinquency of the streets and buildings, but also filling them with 'lived space'. This space was not necessarily an exclusively heterosexual one with woman as the object of desire – although many customers were heterosexual – but could offer a space for sexual encounters between men. Furthermore, although some of the sites were used for procuring and providing sexual services beyond entertainment, women who worked there found working conditions safer than on the streets. However, some of them found the required performances onstage – dancing and stripping – embarrassing and awkward. In addition, some of the establishments were run or owned by women, couples or as family enterprises. While both clubs and stores most certainly were places of exploitation, crime and/or destitution, their functions and meanings for the people who worked and went there were more complex than the general picture allows.

The backlash for sexual liberation – or at least the renegotiation of its meaning – coincided with the oil crisis and the downward trajectory of the economy that ensued. In the beginning of this period, articles in *Kvällsposten* that dealt with stores and clubs in Malmö could have a kind of slightly condescending jokey attitude towards the sex business. The news items were often accompanied by advertisements featuring naked women (the 'naked' sound of a hi-fi system) or by the ubiquitous 'Evening post chick' [*Kvällspinglan*], a young, pretty woman photographed, for instance, perched on top of a copying machine in a mini-skirt, on the beach in a bikini, or otherwise enticingly dressed. Towards the end of this period, articles and editorials about the sex business are serious in tone and use words and phrases like 'exploitation', 'women as sexual objects' and 'male society'.[3] The connection to a criminal underworld with drugs and criminality, and the violence and manipulation used by the pimps to exploit the women, were emphasized.[4] A discursive change has taken place, and although prostitution seems to be regarded as unavoidable, it is also regarded as exploitative and leading to drugs and misery.[5]

One of the most jarring paradoxes of porn is that it contains both the misery described by social workers, police and journalists, as well as a 'lived space'; a space for 'deviants' or, in a different terminology, people who could not really fit into welfare society's grid-like and all-encompassing benevolence. Its visual presence in society provokes a debate – or several debates – about sexuality, and as Brian McNair claims in *Porno? Chic!*, societies that allow pornography generally have a more liberal view on issues of women's rights and the rights of sexual minorities.[6] This, I would argue, somewhat in line with McNair, does not have to do with pornography per se, but with the openness that allows it and the debates that follow, and that must, in consequence, also be allowed. The 'post-pornographic' years in Swedish cultural history were, on the one hand, a brief parenthesis and, some would say, a failed experiment, a sexual liberation gone wrong. On the other hand, they opened up a debate; and although (as described in Chapter 1) Sweden did not have any actual 'sex wars' like those in the United States, the debate was still vicious. In addition, not all of the liberation had gone wrong, as pornography forced the women's movement to explicitly express a desire for a free female sexuality.

Accordingly, the Swedish porn scene encompasses all those paradoxes of porn that have been discussed in this volume: liberation and exploitation; emancipation and objectification;

innocence and hard-minded entrepreneurism; a place for radicals and reactionaries; a 'lived space' for people who were regarded as deviants and a hegemonic male space that dominated the urban cityscape. It carved its own place just on the borders of the social welfare state, dependent on its liberal-mindedness, but abhorrent to the good intentions of its all-encompassing benevolence.

Notes

1   'Alf Svensson till attack mot barnpornografi', *Kvällsposten*, October 16, 1977; Lars Christiansson, 'Utan kunder – ingen prostitution', *Kvällsposten*, October 20, 1977.
2   Henri Lefebvre, *The Production of Space*, Malden, MA: Blackwell, 2005 [1991], as quoted in Marilyn Adler Papayanis, 'Sex and the Revanchist City: Zoning Out Pornography in New York', *Environment and Planning D: Society and Space*, vol. 18, 2000, p. 351.
3   Christiansson, 'Utan kunder', 1977; 'Man träffar en hallick – och blir kär!', *Kvällsposten*, October 29, 1977.
4   'Knarket leder till "träsket"'; 'Man träffar en hallick – och blir kär!', *Kvällsposten*, October 29, 1977.
5   'Samhället blir framtidens hallick?', *Kvällsposten*, October 19, 1977.
6   Brian McNair, *Porno? Chic!: How Pornography Changed the World and Made It a Better Place*, London: Routledge, 2013.

References

Archival material

Material from the National Board of Film Censors Archive 420285:D2

109 472. *Mera ur kärlekens språk*, Inge Ivarson, Torgny Wickman. Minutes for meeting held September 15, 1970.

110 072. *Chambermaid's Orgy*. Venusfilm. Decision date May 25, 1971.

110 652. *Motorcycle Mamas*. Color Climax Corp. Decision date December 30, 1971.

110 722. *MF 16/1970*. Marmalade film. Decision date January 27, 1972.

110 815. *Private Club*. Color Climax Corp. Decision date February 29, 1972.

110 818. *Ulla – the Swede*. Lasse Braun Production. Decision date February 29, 1972.

110 892. *Ky-Sen – the Vietnamese* (registered as *Ky Son the Vietnamese*). Lasse Braun Production. Decision date March 27, 1972.

110 925. *Delphia – the Greek*. Lasse Braun Production. Decision date April 11, 1972.

110 935. *Imagination*. Decision date April 13, 1972.

110 943. *Weekend Sex*. Flesh film. Decision date April 14, 1972.

111 055. *Sexy Supper*. Color Climax Corp. Decision date June 14, 1972.

111 120. *Hotel Amour*. Lasse Braun Production. Decision date July 7, 1972.

111 264. *Party Film nr. 3: Hairdresser*. Party Film. Decision date September 13, 1972.

111 303. *Party Film nr. 2: Easy Riding*. Party Film. Decision date September 20, 1972.

111 340. *Wedding Night for Three*. Simona. Decision date September 28, 1972.

111 341. *Even Thieves Do It*. Simona. Decision date September 28, 1972.

111 375. *The Vikings – Victory for the Queen*. Lasse Braun Production. Decision date October 9, 1972.

111 499. *Violated in the Forest*. Pussy Film. Decision date November 9, 1972.

111 501. *Dr. Wu*. Lasse Braun Production. Decision date November 9, 1972.

111 502. *Rosa and the Men*. Venus Film. Decision date November 9, 1972.

111 508. *The Sadists*. Candy-Film. Decision date November 10, 1972.

112 083. *Behind the Green Door*. Artie Mitchell, Jim Mitchell. Decision date July 10, 1973.

112 241. *Teenage Sex Game*. Color Climax Corp. Decision date August 21, 1973.

112 302. *Sex and the Gun*. Cinema Classics Inc. Decision date September 4, 1973.

112 344. *Black Power*. Lasse Braun Production. Decision date September 14, 1973.

112 358. *Sex de Luxe: Lizzie and Greta in Private Action*. Private Film. Decision date September 17, 1973.

112 543. *Sexual Symphony* (Rodox 615). Color Climax Corp. Decision date October 16, 1973.

112 586. *Star Film no 3.* Star Film. Decision date October 25, 1973.

112 603. *Boys with Boys.* Erlipo Film. Decision date October 25, 1973.

112 621. *Zum Knutschkeller.* Tabu Film Production. Decision date October 29, 1973.

112 649. *In the Name of Odin.* Lasse Braun Production. Decision date November 1, 1973.

112 779. *Cerimony.* Decision date November 29, 1973.

113 255. *Mathematik: Mangelhaft. Vögeln: sehr gut,* Pornorama Film. Decision date April 2, 1974 (A. Svensson).

113 403. *Mathematik: Mangelhaft. Vögeln: sehr gut,* Pornorama Film. Decision date June 6, 1974 (R. Häggbom).

113 461. *Stalled Rear End.* Adult Cinema Fanny Film. Decision date July 3, 1974.

113 515. *Big John.* Adult Cinema. Decision date July 11, 1974.

113 531. *College Playmate.* Adult Cinema. Decision date July 12, 1974.

113 534. *Sweet Smell of Ass.* Adult Cinema Fanny Film. Decision date July 12, 1974.

114 208. *Wedding Night Orgy.* Color Climax Pussycat 414. Decision date January 24, 1975.

114 391. *Piss Party.* Unknown (acc. to submitter Screw 4). Decision date March 14, 1975.

114 666. *Golden Showers.* Flesh Film Production. Decision date June 26, 1975.

115 288. *Pee Pleasure.* Color Climax Corp. Decision date December 30, 1975.

116 478. *Lady Piss.* Lasse Braun. Decision date January 3, 1977.

118 215. *Annette's Climax.* Beauty Film. Decision date August 31, 1977.

119 171. *Young Anal Pissing.* Diplomat Films. Decision date June 20, 1978.

120 505. *Always Prepared.* Color Climax Corp. Decis ion date August 30, 1979.

420285:A1A

109 472. *Mera ur kärlekens språk,* Inge Ivarson, Torgny Wickman. Attachment to the minutes from the meeting held September 29, 1970.

109 472. *Mera ur kärlekens språk,* Inge Ivarson, Torgny Wickman. Minutes from the meeting held September 15, 1970.

Articles from newspapers and magazines

Brown, Joe David, 'Sin and Sweden', *Time*, April 25, 1955.

Görling, Lars, 'Förbud mot verkligheten', *BLM*, no. 1, 1964, pp. 26–28.

Kvällsposten, January 10, 1969 [Advertisement].

Borglund, Tore, 'Ömhet och politik hör ihop', *Kvällsposten,* April 20, 1970.

Edström, Mauritz, 'Rolig dansk fräckis', *Dagens Nyheter*, December 27, 1970.

Behring, Bertil, 'Mazurkan går över Sverige: Fnissporr ger bion 1 miljon', *Kvällsposten*, February 7, 1971.

Ekselius, Eva, 'Hur man botar sexångest', *Dagens Nyheter*, July 9, 1971.

Gunnarsson, S-O, 'Är sexklubbarna i Malmö farliga?", *Kvällsposten*, January 19, 1971.

'Malmö nytt sexcentrum', *Kvällsposten*, January 13, 1972.

'Han har Malmös omöjligaste jobb: skatte-razzia bland sexklubbarna', *Kvällsposten*, January 20, 1972.

'"Förföljda" porrbrudar på flykt över Sundet!', *Kvällsposten*, January 28, 1972.

'Fast med 3682 porrfilmer', *Kvällsposten*, June 16, 1972.

'Försökte smuggla in halvt ton porr i England', *Kvällsposten*, June 29, 1972.

'Malmömakar greps för porrsmuggling', *Kvällsposten*, July 5, 1972.

Kvällsposten, October 1972. [Advertisement]

Hellbom, Thorleif, 'Danska gladporren en saga blott', *Dagens Nyheter*, August 14, 1973.

Kvinnobulletinen, nos 3–4, 1973.

Sydsvenska Dagbladet Snällposten, December 24, 1973.

Tunbäck-Hanson, Monica, *Göteborgsposten*, January 22, 1974.

FiB/Aktuellt, no. 39, 1975, pp. 26–33.

Kvällsposten, January 18, 1975.

Kvällsposten, October 20, 1975.

Sedvallson, Kerstin, 'Inte bara gladporr i dagens danska filmer', *Dagens Nyheter*, December 18, 1975.

Axelquist, Ulla, 'Försvar för våldtäkt', *Dagens Nyheter*, July 3, 1976.

Bylund, Leif, 'Skyddet mot våldtäkt', *Dagens Nyheter*, April 28, 1976.

Dagens Nyheter, April 20, 1976.

Engström, Lars-Göran, 'Svar på tal', *Dagens Nyheter*, June 23, 1976.

Sangregorio, Inga-Lisa, 'Våldtäktslagen', *Dagens Nyheter*, May 9, 1976.

'Alf Svensson till attack mot barnpornografi', *Kvällsposten*, October 16, 1977.

'Samhället blir framtidens hallick?', *Kvällsposten*, October 19, 1977.

'Kopplerimålet: Drar sig ur de påstådda samlagen?', *Kvällsposten*, October 26, 1977.

'Knarket leder till "träsket"', *Kvällsposten*, October 29, 1977.

'Man träffar en hallick – och blir kär!', *Kvällsposten*, October 29, 1977.

'Unikt beslut i kopplerimålet: Lyckta dörrar', *Kvällsposten*, October 29, 1977.

Christiansson, Lars, 'Utan kunder – ingen prostitution', *Kvällsposten*, October 20, 1977.

magasin defect (1995–1997).

Lindberg, Tomas, 'Kungliga biblioteket har låst in barnpornografisk bok', sverigesradio.se, http://sverigesradio.se/sida/artikel.aspx?programid=106&artikel=5805061 [Accessed April 23, 2014].

Interviews

Bergström-Walan, Maj-Briht, interviewed by Elisabet Björklund & Mariah Larsson, Stockholm, November 9, 2010.

Informant U, interviewed by Mariah Larsson, Lund, March 26, 2009.

Informant V, interviewed by Mariah Larsson, Malmö, May 29, 2009.

Informant X, interviewed by Mariah Larsson, Malmö, September 2, 2009.

Informant Y, telephone conversation with Mariah Larsson, September 4, 2009.

Informant Z, e-mail correspondence with Mariah Larsson, November 2010–May 2012.

Ivarson, Inge, interviewed by Elisabet Björklund & Mariah Larsson, Stockholm, November 8, 2010.

Lindberg, Christina, interviewed by Mariah Larsson, Malmö University, February 19, 2009.
Sex worker interviews from the 1970s, conducted by Stig Larsson & Sven-Axel Månsson.

Literature

Åberg, Anders, *Tabu: Filmaren Vilgot Sjöman*, Lund: Filmhäftet förlag, 2001.

Åhlander, Lars (ed.), *Svensk filmografi 7: 1970–1979*, Stockholm: Norstedts/SFI, 1989.

Ahlmark-Michanek, Katarina, *Jungfrutro och dubbelmoral*, Malmö: Cavefors, 1962.

Altman, Rick, *Film/Genre*, London: BFI Publishing, 1999.

Andersson, Lars Gustaf, 'Peter Weiss: Underground and Resistance', in Mariah Larsson & Anders
Marklund (eds), *Swedish Film: An Introduction and Reader*, Lund: Nordic Academic Press,
2010, pp. 229–38.

Arnberg, Klara, 'Synd på export: 1960-talets pornografiska press och den svenska synden',
Historisk Tidskrift, vol. 129, no. 3, 2009, pp. 467–86.

Arnberg, Klara, *Motsättningarnas marknad: den pornografiska pressens kommersiella genombrott
och regleringen av pornografi i Sverige 1950–1980*, Lund: Sekel bokförlag, 2010.

Arnberg, Klara & Carl Marklund, 'Illegally Blonde: "Swedish Sin" and Pornography in American
and Swedish Imaginations, 1950–1971', in Elisabet Björklund & Mariah Larsson (eds),
Swedish Cinema and the Sexual Revolution: Critical Essays, Jefferson, NC: McFarland, 2016,
pp. 185–200.

Arnberg, Klara & Tommy Gustafsson, *Moralpanik och lågkultur: genus- och mediehistoriska
analyser 1900–2012*, Stockholm: Atlas, 2013.

Arnberg, Klara & Mariah Larsson, 'Benefits of the In-Between: Swedish Men's Magazines and
Sex Films 1965–1975', *Sexuality & Culture*, vol. 18, no. 2, 2013, pp. 310–30.

Arnstberg, Karl-Olov, *Miljonprogrammet*, Stockholm: Carlsson, 2000.

Axelsson, Christina, *Hemmafrun som försvann: Övergången till lönearbete bland gifta kvinnor i
Sverige 1968–1981*, Stockholm: Institutet för social forskning, 1987.

Baschiera, Stefano & Francesco Di Chiara, 'Once Upon a Time in Italy: Transnational Features of
Genre Production 1960s–1970s', *Film International*, vol. 8, no. 6, 2010, pp. 30–39.

Båvner, Per, 'En reproducerad debatt: Svenska ståndpunkter om pornografi', *Res Publica*, vol. 43,
1999, pp. 85–103.

Bejerot, Nils, *Barn – serier – samhälle*, Stockholm: Folket i bild, 1954.

Berkowitz, Dana, 'Consuming Eroticism: Gender Performances and Presentations in
Pornographic Establishments', *Journal of Contemporary Ethnography*, vol. 35, no. 5, 2006,
pp. 583–606.

Bernardi, Daniel, 'Interracial Joysticks: Pornography's Web of Racist Attractions', in Peter
Lehman (ed.), *Pornography: Film and Culture*, New Brunswick, NJ: Rutgers University Press,
2006, pp. 220–42.

Biasin, Enrico, Giovanna Maina & Federico Zecca (eds), *Porn After Porn: Contemporary
Alternative Pornographies*, Mimesis International, 2014.

Bjurling, Oscar, Rolf Ohlsson, Bo Malmsten, P. D. Lindeberg & Lars Hamberg (eds), *Malmö stads
historia. D. 7, 1939–1990*, Malmö: Malmö stad, 1994.

Björkin, Mats, '*Fäbodjäntan*: Sex, Communication and Cultural Heritage', in Alf Björnberg (ed.), *Frispel: festskrift till Olle Edström*, Göteborg: Institutionen för musikvetenskap, 2005.

Björklund, Elisabet, '"This is a dirty movie" – *Taxi Driver* and "Swedish sin"', *Journal of Scandinavian Cinema*, vol. 1, no. 2, 2011, pp. 163–76.

Björklund, Elisabet, '*The Most Delicate Subject': A History of Sex Education Films in Sweden*, diss. Lund: Lund University, 2012.

Björklund, Elisabet, 'The Limits of Sexual Depictions in the Late 1960s', in Elisabet Björklund & Mariah Larsson (eds), *Swedish Cinema and the Sexual Revolution: Critical Essays*, Jefferson, NC: McFarland, 2016, pp. 126–138.

Björklund, Elisabet & Mariah Larsson (eds), *Swedish Cinema and the Sexual Revolution: Critical Essays*, Jefferson, NC: McFarland, 2016.

Boëthius, Maria-Pia, *Skylla sig själv: en bok om våldtäkt*, Stockholm: Liberförlag, 1976.

Brownmiller, Susan, *Against Our Will: Men, Women and Rape*, New York: Fawcett Books, 1993 [1975].

Capino, José B., 'Asian College Girls and Oriental Men with Bamboo Poles: Reading Asian Pornography', in Peter Lehman (ed.), *Pornography: Film and Culture*, New Brunswick, NJ: Rutgers University Press, 2006, pp. 206–19.

Champagne, John, '"Stop Reading Films!" Film Studies, Close Analysis, and Gay Pornography', *Cinema Journal*, vol. 36, no. 4, 1997, pp. 76–97.

Coulmont, Baptiste & Phil Hubbard, 'Consuming Sex: Socio-legal Shifts in the Space and Place of Sex-shops', *Journal of Law and Society*, vol. 37, no. 1, 2010, pp. 189–209.

Dahlerup, Drude, *Rødstrømperne: den danske Rødstrømpebevægelses udvikling, nytænkning og gennemslag 1970–1985*, Copenhagen: Gyldendal, 1998.

Dalquist, Ulf, *Större våld än nöden kräver? Medievåldsdebatten i Sverige 1980–1995*, Ph.D. diss. Lund Univeristy, Umeå: Borea, 1998.

Dean, Tim, Steven Ruszczycky & David Squires (eds), *Porn Archives*, Durham, NC & London: Duke University Press, 2014.

Dellamorte, Daniel, *Svensk sensationsfilm: en ocensurerad guide till den fördolda svenska filmhistorien, 1951–1993*, Malmö: Tamara Press, 2003.

Dines, Gail, Robert Jensen & Ann Russo, *Pornography: The Production and Consumption of Inequality*, New York: Routledge, 1998.

Doane, Mary Ann, *The Desire to Desire: The Woman's Film of the 1940s*, Houndmills & London: MacMillan Press, 1987.

Duggan, Lisa & Nan D. Hunter, *Sex Wars: Sexual Dissent and Political Culture* (10th anniversary edition), New York: Routledge, 2006.

Dworkin, Andrea, *Pornography: Men Possessing Women*, London: Women's Press, 1981.

Dyer, Richard, *White: Essays on Race and Culture*, London: Routledge, 1997.

Edenborg, Carl Michael, 'Utgivarens förord', in *Anonym: Flossie: En sextonårig Venus. Av en som känt denna tjusande gudinna och dyrkat vid hennes helgedom*, Stockholm & Sala: Vertigo förlag, 2013, pp. 5–10.

Ekeroth, Daniel, *Swedish Sensationsfilms: A Clandestine History of Sex, Thrillers, and Kicker Cinema*, New York: Bazillion Points, 2011.

Ekroth, Gunilla, *Gunilla af Halmstad: ett annat liv i Sverige*, Stockholm: Hjalmarson & Högberg, 2009.

Elsaesser, Thomas, *European Cinema: Face to Face with Hollywood*, Amsterdam: Amsterdam University Press, 2005.

Ezra, Elizabeth & Terry Rowden, *Transnational Cinema: The Film Reader*, London: Routledge, 2006.

Foucault, Michel, *The Will to Knowledge – The History of Sexuality Volume I* (translated by Robert Hurley), London: Penguin 1998 [1976].

Friberg, Joakim, *Erotikens ideologi*, Stockholm & Lund: Symposium bokförlag, 1987.

Furhammar, Leif, *Filmen i Sverige: En historia i tio kapitel*, Höganäs: Wiken, 1991.

Gagnon, John H. & William Simon, *Sexual Conduct: The Social Sources of Human Sexuality*, Chicago, IL: Aldine Pub. Co., 2005 [1973].

Garpe, Margareta & Suzanne Osten, *Jösses flickor: Kärleksföreställningen: två kvinnopjäser*, Stockholm: Gidlund, 1977.

Gerhard, Jane, *Desiring Revolution: Second-wave Feminism and the Rewriting of American Sexual Thought, 1920 to 1982*, New York: Columbia University Press, 2001.

Glover, Nikolas & Carl Marklund, 'Arabian Nights in the Midnight Sun: Exploring the Temporal Structure of Sexual Geographies', *Historisk Tidskrift*, vol. 129, no. 3, 2009, pp. 487–510.

Goffman, Erving, *The Presentation of Self in Everyday Life*, Edinburgh: Edinburgh University Social Sciences Research Centre, 1956.

Goffman, Erving, *The Presentation of Self in Everyday Life*, London: Penguin, 1990 [1959].

Gorfinkel, Elena, 'Wet Dreams: Erotic Film Festivals of the Early 1970s and the Utopian Sexual Public Sphere', *Framework: The Journal of Cinema and Media*, vol. 47, no. 2, 2006, pp. 59–86.

Gustafsson, Tommy, 'The Open Secret: Illegal Screenings of Pornographic Films for Public Audiences in Sweden 1921-1943', in Elisabet Björklund & Mariah Larsson (eds), *Swedish Cinema and the Sexual Revolution: Critical Essays*, Jefferson, NC: McFarland, 2016, pp. 101–15.

Gustafsson, Tommy & Mariah Larsson, 'Porren inför lagen: Två fallstudier angående den officiella attityden till offentligt visad pornografisk film 1921 och 1971', *Historisk tidskrift*, vol. 129, no. 3, 2009, pp. 445–65.

Hagener, Malte (ed.), *Geschlecht in Fesseln: Sexualität zwischen Aufklärung und Ausbeutung im Weimarer Kino 1918–1933*, München: Edition Text + Kritik, 2000.

Hägg, Maud & Barbro Werkmäster, *Kvinnor och sex*, Göteborg: Författarförlaget, 1973.

Hale, Frederick, 'Time for Sex in Sweden: Enhancing the Myth of the "Swedish Sin" During the 1950s', *Scandinavian Studies*, vol. 75, no. 3, 2003, pp. 351–74.

Hedling, Erik, 'Breaking the Swedish Sex Barrier: Painful Lustfulness in Ingmar Bergman's *The Silence*', *Film International*, vol. 6, no. 6, 2008, pp. 17–27.

Hedling, Erik & Mats Jönsson (eds), *Välfärdsbilder: Svensk film utanför biografen*, Stockholm: Royal Library, 2008.

Hedling, Olof & Mariah Larsson, 'National Boundaries: Notes on the Pornographic Film in 1970s Sweden', in Savaş Arslan, Volkan Aytar, Defne Karaosmanoğlu & Süheyla Kırca Schroeder (eds), *Media, Culture and Identity in Europe*, Istanbul: Bahçeşehir University Press, 2010, pp. 271–79.

Heffernan, Kevin, 'Prurient (Dis)Interest: The American Release and Reception of *I am Curious (Yellow)*', in Eric Schaefer (ed.), *Sex Scene: Media and the Sexual Revolution*, Durham, NC & London: Duke University Press, 2014, pp. 105–25.

Heffernan, Kevin, 'Many of Your Finer Nudie Films: Saga Film, Swedish National Cinema, and Seventies Transnational Erotic Film', in Elisabet Björklund & Mariah Larsson (eds), *Swedish Cinema and the Sexual Revolution: Critical Essays*, Jefferson, NC: McFarland, 2016, pp. 216–32.

Henriksson, Benny, *Risk Factor Love: Homosexuality, Sexual Interaction and HIV Prevention*, Göteborg: Institutionen för socialt arbete, 1995.

Henriksson, Benny & Sven-Axel Månsson, 'Sexual Negotiations: An Ethnographic Study of Men Who Have Sex with Men', *Culture and Sexual Risk: Anthropological Perspectives of AIDS*, Amsterdam: Gordon and Breach Publisher, 1995, pp. 157–82.

Herzog, Amy, 'In the Flesh: Space and Embodiment in the Pornographic Peep Show Arcade', *Velvet Light Trap*, no. 62, Fall, 2008, pp. 29–43.

Higson, Andrew, 'The Concept of National Cinema', in Alan Williams (ed.), *Film and Nationalism*, New Brunswick, NJ: Rutgers University Press, 2002, pp. 52–67.

Holmberg, Jan, 'Censorship in Sweden', in Mariah Larsson & Anders Marklund (eds), *Swedish Film: An Introduction and Reader*, Lund: Nordic Academic Press, 2010.

Holmström, Charlotta & May-Len Skilbrei, 'Prostitution in the Nordic Countries' (Conference report, Stockholm, October 16–17, 2008), Copenhagen: Nordic Council of Ministers, 2009.

Hubbard, Phil, Roger Matthews, Jane Scoular & Laura Agustín, 'Away from Prying Eyes? The Urban Geographies of "Adult Entertainment"', *Progress in Human Geography*, vol. 32, no. 3, 2008, pp. 363–81.

Hunt, Lynn, 'Introduction: Obscenity and the Origins of Modernity', in Lynn Hunt (ed.), *The Invention of Pornography: Obscenity and the Origins of Modernity, 1500–1800*, New York: Zone Books, 1996, pp. 9–45.

Ilshammar, Lars, Pelle Snickars & Per Vesterlund (eds), *Citizen Schein*, Stockholm: Kungliga biblioteket, 2010.

Jackson, Erika, 'Swedish Beauties or Feminists with Dragon Tattoos? A History of Sexualizing Nordic Feminine Qualities in American Popular Culture', Paper presented at *Society for the Advancement of Scandinavian Studies*, San Francisco, May 2–4, 2013.

Jacobs, Jane, *The Death and Life of Great American Cities*, London: Pimlico, 2000 [1962].

Janssen, Erick (ed.), *The Psychophysiology of Sex*, Bloomington, IN: Indiana University Press, 2007.

Janssen, Erick, Deanna Carpenter & Cynthia A. Graham, 'Selecting Films for Sex Research: Gender Differences in Erotic Film Preference', *Archives of Sexual Behavior*, vol. 32, no. 3, 2003, pp. 243–51.

Johansson, Birgitta, *Befrielsen är nära: feminism och teaterpraktik i Margareta Garpes och Suzanne Ostens 1970-talsteater*, Stockholm: Östlings bokförlag Symposion, 2006.

Juffer, Jane, *At Home with Pornography: Women, Sex, and Everyday Life*, New York: New York University Press, 1998.

Kääpä, Pietari, 'Transnational Approaches to Ecocinema: Charting an Expansive Field', in Tommy Gustafsson & Pietari Kääpä (eds), *Transnational Ecocinema: Film Culture in an Era of Ecological Transformation*, Bristol and Chicago: Intellect, 2013, pp. 21–43.

Karp, David A., 'Hiding in Pornographic Bookstores: A Reconsideration of the Nature of Urban Anonymity', *Journal of Contemporary Ethnography*, no. 1, 1973, pp. 427–51.

Kendrick, Walter, *The Secret Museum: Pornography in Modern Culture*, Berkeley, CA: University of California Press, 1996 [1987].

Kipnis, Laura, *Bound and Gagged: Pornography and the Politics of Fantasy in America*, New York: Grove Press, 1996.

Klein, Norman, *The History of Forgetting: Los Angeles and the Erasure of Memory*, London: Verso, 1997.

Kleinhans, Chuck, 'The Change from Film to Video Pornography: Implications for Analysis', in Peter Lehman (ed.), *Pornography: Film and Culture*, New Brunswick, NJ: Rutgers University Press, 2006, pp. 154–67.

Koskinen, Maaret, *Ingmar Bergman's The Silence: Pictures in the Typewriter, Writings on the Screen*, Seattle, WA: University of Washington Press, 2010.

Koskinen, Maaret, 'P(owe)R, Sex, and *Mad Men* Swedish Style – Or How the Personal Can Become the Political', in Elisabet Björklund & Mariah Larsson (eds), *Swedish Cinema and the Sexual Revolution: Critical Essays*, Jefferson, NC: McFarland, 2016, pp. 153–67.

Kulick, Don, 'Four Hundred Thousand Swedish Perverts', *GLQ: A Journal of Lesbian and Gay Studies*, vol. 11, no. 2, 2005, pp. 205–35.

Kutchinsky, Berl, *Law, Pornography and Crime: The Danish Experience, Scandinavian Studies in Law* (edited by Annika Snare), vol. 16, Oslo: Pax Forlag A/S, 1999.

Laplanche, Jean & Jean-Bertrand Pontalis, *The Language of Psychoanalysis*, New York: Norton, 1974.

Larsson, Mariah, 'Making Love Detumescently: Some Preliminary Notes on the Body Language of the Penis', *Kosmorama*, no. 258 (www.kosmorama.org).

Larsson, Mariah, *Skenet som bedrog: Mai Zetterling och det svenska sextiotalet*, Lund: Sekel bokförlag, 2006.

Larsson, Mariah, 'Drömmen om den goda pornografin: Om sextio- och sjuttiotalsfilmen och gränsen mellan konst och pornografi', *Tidskrift för genusvetenskap*, nos 1–2, 2007, pp. 93–111.

Larsson, Mariah, 'Contested Pleasures', in Mariah Larsson & Anders Marklund (eds), *Swedish Film: An Introduction and Reader*, Lund: Nordic Academic Press, 2010, pp. 205–13.

Larsson, Mariah, 'Practice Makes Perfect? The Production of the Swedish Sex Film in the 1970s', *Film International*, Special issue: 'Making Movies in Europe', vol. 8, no. 6, 2010, pp. 40–49.

Larsson, Mariah, '"Vem behöver *den här* yttrandefriheten?" Om filmcensur och rörliga bilders farlighet', in Sara Johnsdotter & Aje Carlbom (eds), *Goda Sanningar? Debattklimatet och den kritiska forskningens villkor*, Lund: Nordic Academic Press, 2010. pp. 155–182.

Larsson, Mariah, 'Svarta affärer som blev vita: Om sexbutiker som sexuella rum då och nu', in Lars Plantin & Sven-Axel Månsson (eds), *Sexualitetsstudier*, Stockholm: Liber, 2012.

Larsson, Mariah, 'Ingmar Bergman, Swedish Sexploitation, and Early Swedish Porn', *Journal of Scandinavian Cinema*, vol. 5, no. 1, 2015, pp. 49–61.

Larsson, Mariah, 'National/Transnational Genre: Pornography in Transition', in Tommy Gustafsson & Pietari Kääpä (eds), *Nordic Genre Film: Small Nation Film Cultures*, Edinburgh: Edinburgh University Press, 2015, pp. 217–29.

Larsson, Mariah, 'Lasse Braun, Rape Scenarios, and Swedish Censorship: A Case Study of Two 8mm Porn Films Featuring Rape', forthcoming.

Larsson, Mariah & Olof Hedling, 'Skandinavische Lust und europäisches Kino: Eine schwedische Filmographie', *Montage AV*, February 18, 2009.

Larsson, Stig, 'Könshandeln: om prostituerades villkor', Stockholm: Skeab förlag, 1983.

Lefebvre, Henri, *The Production of Space*, Malden, MA: Blackwell, 2005 [1991].

Lehman, Peter (ed.), *Pornography: Film and Culture*, New Brunswick, NC: Rutgers University Press, 2006.

Lehman, Peter, 'Introduction: "A Dirty Little Secret" – Why Teach and Study Pornography?', in Peter Lehman (ed.), *Pornography: Film and Culture*, New Brunswick, NJ: Rutgers University Press, 2006, pp. 1–24.

Lehman, Peter, 'Revelations about Pornography', in Peter Lehman (ed.), *Pornography: Film and Culture*, New Brunswick, NJ & London: Rutgers University Press, 2006, pp. 87–98.

Lennerhed, Lena, 'Fäbodjäntan och hennes systrar', in Lars Åhlander (ed.), *Svensk filmografi 7: 1970–1979*, Stockholm: Norstedts (SFI), 1989, pp. 38–44.

Lennerhed, Lena, *Frihet att njuta: Sexualdebatten i Sverige på 1960-talet*, Stockholm: Norstedts, 1994.

Lennerhed, Lena, '491 and the Censorship Controversy', in Elisabet Björklund & Mariah Larsson (eds), *Swedish Cinema and the Sexual Revolution: Critical Essays*, Jefferson, NC: McFarland, 2016, pp. 116–25.

Lindholm, Margareta & Arne Nilsson, *En annan stad: manligt och kvinnligt homoliv 1950–1980*, Göteborg: AlfabetaAnamma, 2002.

Listerborn, Carina, 'Understanding the geography of women's fear: Toward a reconceptualization of fear and space', in Liz Bondi (ed.), *Subjectivities, Knowledges, and Feminist Geographies*, Lanham, MD: Rowman & Littlefield, 2002, pp. 34–43.

Listerborn, Carina, 'Våld i staden', in Göran Graninger & Christer Knuthammar (eds), *Makten över rummet: tankar om den hållbara staden*, Linköping: Linköping University Electronic Press, 2010.

Lunde, Arne, *Nordic Exposures: Scandinavian Identities in Classical Hollywood Cinema*, Seattle, WA: University of Washington Press, 2010.

MacKinnon, Catherine, *Feminism Unmodified: Discourses on Life and Law*, Cambridge, MA: Harvard University Press, 1987.

Mallik, Ira, 'Porr som vapen', in Stina Andersson & Silvia Sjödahl (eds), *Sex – en politisk historia*, Göteborg: Alfabeta/Anamma in collaboration with RFSU, 2003, pp. 149–155.

Månsson, Sven-Axel, *Könshandelns främjare och profitörer: om förhållandet mellan hallick och prostituerad*, Lund: Doxa, 1981.

Månsson, Sven-Axel & Stig Larsson, *Svarta affärer: utredning om vissa klubbars och näringsställens sociala betydelse och struktur*, Malmö: Socialförvaltningen, 1976.

Marcus, Steven, *The Other Victorians: A Study of Sexuality and Pornography in Mid-Nineteenth Century England*, London: Weidenfeld & Nicolson, 1966.

McNair, Brian, *Porno? Chic!: How Pornography Changed the World and Made It a Better Place*, London: Routledge, 2013.

Mulvey, Laura, 'Visual Pleasure and Narrative Cinema', in Bill Nichols (ed.), *Movies and Methods: An Anthology vol II*, Berkeley, CA, London: University of California Press, 1985, pp. 303–15. Originally published in *Screen*, vol. 16, no. 3, 1975.

Nash, Jennifer C., *The Black Body in Ecstasy: Reading Race, Reading Porn*, Durham, NC: Duke University Press, 2014.

Nestius, Hans, *I last och lust: sexuella bilder förr och nu*, Stockholm: Prisma in collaboration with RFSU, 1982.

Nilsson, Arne, *Såna och riktiga karlar: om manlig homosexualitet i Göteborg decennierna kring andra världskriget*, Göteborg: Anamma, 1998.

Paasonen, Susanna, *Carnal Resonance: Affect and Online Pornography*, Cambridge, MA: MIT Press, 2011.

Paasonen, Susanna & Laura Saarenmaa, 'The Golden Age of Porn: Nostalgia and History in Cinema', in Susanna Paasonen, Kaarina Nikunen & Laura Saarenmaa (eds), *Pornification: Sex and Sexuality in Media Culture*, Oxford & New York: Berg, 2007, pp. 23–32.

Pallesen, Henning, *De avvikande*, Stockholm: Bonnier, 1964.

Papayanis, Marilyn Adler, 'Sex and the Revanchist City: Zoning Out Pornography in New York', *Environment and Planning D: Society and Space*, vol. 18, 2000, pp. 341–53.

Pettersen, Kåre T., 'Rapport om barnepornografi', Oslo: stencil, 1990.

Pitzulo, Carrie, 'The Battle in Every Man's Bed: *Playboy* and the Fiery Feminists', *Journal of the History of Sexuality*, vol. 17, no. 2, 2008, pp. 259–89.

Porn Studies Journal, vol. I, nos 1–2, 2014.

Qvist, Per Olov & Tytti Soila, 'Eva – den utstötta/Swedish and Underage', in Tytti Soila (ed.), *The Cinema of Scandinavia*, London: Wallflower Press, 2005, pp. 151–59.

Rubin, Gayle, 'Thinking Sex: Notes for a Radical Theory on the Politics of Sexuality', in Carol Vance (ed.), *Pleasure and Danger: Exploring Female Sexuality*, Boston, MA: Routledge, 1984, pp. 267–319.

Russell, Diana E. H. (ed.), *Making Violence Sexy: Feminist Views on Pornography*, Buckingham: Open University Press, 1993.

Ryberg, Ingrid, *Imagining Safe Space: The Politics of Queer, Feminist, and Lesbian Pornography*, Stockholm: Stockholm University, 2012.

Sarrimo, Cristine, *När det personliga blev politiskt: 1970-talets kvinnliga bekännelse och självbiografi*, Eslöv: Brutus Östlings bokförlag Symposion, 2000.

Schaefer, Eric, *Bold! Daring! Shocking! True!: A History of Exploitation Films, 1919–1959*, Durham, NC: Duke University Press, 1999.

Schaefer, Eric, 'Gauging a Revolution: 16mm Film and the Rise of the Pornographic Feature', in Linda Williams (ed.), *Porn Studies*, Durham, NC & London: Duke University Press, 2004, pp. 370–400.

Schaefer, Eric, 'Plain Brown Wrapper: Adult Films for the Home Market, 1930–1969', in Jon Lewis & Eric Smoodin (eds), *Looking Past the Screen: Case Studies in American Film History and Method*, Durham, NC & London: Duke University Press, 2007, pp. 201–26.

Schaefer, Eric, '"I'll Take Sweden!" The Shifting Discourse of the "Sexy Nation" in Sexploitation Films', in Eric Schaefer (ed.), *Sex Scene: Media and the Cultural Revolution*, Durham, NC & London: Duke University Press, 2014, pp. 207–34.

Schein, Harry, *I själva verket: Sju års filmpolitik*, Stockholm: Norstedts, 1970.

Segal, Lynne, 'Only the Literal: The Contradictions of Anti-*Pornography Feminism', in Pamela Church Gibson (ed.), *More Dirty Looks: Gender, Pornography, Power*, London: BFI Publishing, 2004, pp. 59–70.

Silbersky, Leif & Carlösten Nordmark, *Såra tukt och sedlighet: en debattbok om pornografin*, Stockholm: Prisma, 1969.

Simon, William & John H. Gagnon, 'Sexual Scripts: Permanence and Change', *Archives of Sexual Behavior*, vol. 15, no. 2, 1986, pp. 97–120.

Sjögren, Olle, *Inte riktigt lagom? Om 'extremvåld', filmcensur och subkultur*, Uppsala: Filmförlaget, 1993.

Sjöwall, Maj & Per Wahlöö, *Murder at the Savoy*, New York: Vintage Books, 2009.

Sjöwall, Maj & Per Wahlöö, *Polis polis potatismos*, Stockholm: Norstedts, 1970.

Skytte, Göran, *Porrens profitörer: två reportage om porr- och kontaktbranschen*, Stockholm: Ordfront, 1979.

Smith, Clarissa, *One for the Girls!: The Pleasures and Practices of Reading Women's Porn*, Bristol: Intellect, 2007.

Sobchack, Vivian, *Carnal Thoughts: Embodiment and Moving Image Culture*, Berkeley, CA: University of California Press, 2004.

Stauslund, Uffe, *Bio i Malmö: Malmös biografer genom tiderna*, Malmö: Corona förlag, 2001.

Stevenson, Jack, *Scandinavian Blue: The Erotic Cinema of Sweden and Denmark in the 1960s and 1970s*, Jefferson, NC: McFarland, 2010.

Svensson, Arne, *Den politiska saxen: en studie i Statens biografbyrås tillämpning av den utrikespolitiska censurnormen sedan 1914*, Stockholm: Stockholm University, 1976.

Svensson, Bengt, *Heroinmissbruk*, Lund: Studentlitteratur, 2005.

Taormino, Tristan, Celine Parreñas Shimizu, Constance Penley & Mireille Miller-Young (eds), *The Feminist Porn Book: The Politics of Producing Pleasure*, New York: The Feminist Press, 2013.

Tewksbury, Richard, 'Patrons of Porn: Research Notes on the Clientele of Adult Bookstores', *Deviant Behavior*, no. 11, 1990, pp. 259–71.

Thorgren, Gunilla, *Grupp 8 & jag*, Stockholm: Norstedt, 2003.

Timm, Mikael, *Dröm och förbannad verklighet: spelet kring svensk film under 40 år*, Stockholm: Bromberg i samarbete med Svenska filminstitutet, 2003.

Tykesson, Tyke L. & Björn Magnusson Staaf, *Malmö i skimmer och skugga: stadsbyggnad & arkitektur 1945–2005*, Malmö: Architectus Verborum in collaboration with Malmö Stadsbyggnadskontor, 2009.

Ullén, Magnus, *Bara för dig: Pornografi, konsumtion, berättande*, Stockholm: Vertigo förlag, 2009.

Ullén, Magnus, 'Pornography Remediated', *ejumpcut*, no. 51, Spring 2009.

Ullerstam, Lars, *De erotiska minoriteterna*, Göteborg: Zinderman, 1964.

Valentine, Gill, 'The Geography of Women's Fear', *Area 21*, 1989, pp. 385–90.

Vesterlund, Per, 'Vägen till filmavtalet – Harry Scheins politiska aktivitet innan filmavtalet 1963', *Nordisk kulturpolitisk tidskrift*, vol. 16, no. 1, 2013, pp. 45–66.

Vesterlund, Per, 'Instituted Sexploitation? The Swedish Film Institute and the research on effects of cinema in the 1960s', in Elisabet Björklund & Mariah Larsson (eds), *Swedish Cinema and the Sexual Revolution: Critical Essays*, Jefferson, NC: McFarland, 2016, pp. 141–52.

Waugh, Thomas, *Hard to Imagine: Gay Male Eroticism in Photography and Film From Their Beginnings to Stonewall*, New York: Columbia University Press, 1996.

Wertham, Fredric, *Seduction of the Innocent*, New York: Rineheart, 1954.

Williams, Linda, 'Film Bodies: Gender, Genre, and Excess', *Film Quarterly*, vol. 44, no. 4, 1991, pp. 2–13.

Williams, Linda, *Hardcore: Power, Pleasure, and the 'Frenzy of the Visible'*, Berkeley, CA & London: University of California Press, 1999 [1989].

Williams, Linda (ed.), *Porn Studies*, Durham, NC & London: Duke University Press, 2004.

Williams, Linda, 'Skin Flicks on the Racial Border: Pornography, Exploitation, and Interracial Lust', in Linda Williams (ed.), *Porn Studies*, Durham, NC: Duke University Press, 2004, pp. 271–308.

Williams, Linda, 'Porn Studies: Proliferating Pornographies On/Scene: An Introduction', in Linda Williams (ed.), *Porn Studies*, Durham, NC: Duke University Press, 2005, pp. 1–23.

Williams, Linda, *Screening Sex*, Durham, NC: Duke University Press, 2008.

Williams, Linda, '"White Slavery", or the Ethnography of "Sex Workers": Women in Stag Films at the Kinsey Archive', in Claire Hines & Darren Kerr (eds), *Hard to Swallow: Hard-Core Pornography On Screen*, London: Wallflower Press, 2012, pp. 81–100.

Williams, Linda, 'Pornography, Porno, Porn: Thoughts on a Weedy Field', *Porn Studies Journal*, vol. 1, no. 1–2, 2014, pp. 24–40.

Witt-Brattström, Ebba, *Å alla kära systrar!: historien om mitt sjuttiotal*, Stockholm: Norstedt, 2010.

Wredlund, Bertil & Torsten Jungstedt, *Filmårsboken: 1971/72*, Stockholm: Proprius, 1972.

Wredlund, Bertil & Torsten Jungstedt, *Filmårsboken: 1973/74*, Stockholm: Proprius, 1974.

Wredlund, Bertil, & Rolf Lindfors, *Långfilm i Sverige 7: 1970–1979*, Stockholm: Proprius, 1983.

Wyatt, Justin, *High Concept: Movies and Marketing in Hollywood*, Austin, TX: University of Texas Press, 1994.

Other

Annual Reports and Public Inquiries (SOU)

SOU 1969:14. Filmcensurutredningen, *Filmen – censur och ansvar: betänkande*, Stockholm, 1969.

SOU 1969:38. Kommittén för lagstiftningen om yttrande-och tryckfrihet, *Yttrandefrihetens gränser: sårande av tukt och sedlighet: brott mot trosfrid: betänkande*, Stockholm, 1969.

SOU 1976:9. Sexualbrottsutredningen, *Sexuella övergrepp: förslag till ny lydelse av brottsbalkens bestämmelser om sedlighetsbrott: betänkande/avgivet av Sexualbrottsutredningen*, Stockholm, 1976.

SOU 1982:61, 1977 års Sexualbrottskommitté, *Våldtäkt och andra sexuella övergrepp*, Stockholm, 1982.

SOU 2001:14. 1998 års Sexualbrottskommitté, *Sexualbrotten: Ett ökat skydd för den sexuella integriteten och angränsande frågor*, Stockholm, 2001.

Svenska filminstitutets verksamhetsberättelse 1969–70, Stockholm: Swedish Film Institute, 1970.

Svenska filminstitutets verksamhetsberättelse 1970–71, Stockholm: Swedish Film Institute, 1971.

Svenska filminstitutets verksamhetsberättelse 1971–72, Stockholm: Swedish Film Institute, 1972.

Svenska filminstitutets verksamhetsberättelse 1972–73, Stockholm: Swedish Film Institute, 1973.
Svenska filminstitutets verksamhetsberättelse 1973–74, Stockholm: Swedish Film Institute, 1974.
Svenska filminstitutets verksamhetsberättelse 1974–75, Stockholm: Swedish Film Institute, 1975.
Svenska filminstitutets verksamhetsberättelse 1975–76, Stockholm: Swedish Film Institute, 1976.

Internet sources

Adult Loop Database, http://adultloopdb.nl/
Color Climax Corporation: http://www.colorclimax.com/
Ingmar Bergman Face to Face: http://ingmarbergman.se/en/
McDragans website: http://mcdragans.se/
Statens medieråd: http://www.statensmedierad.se/
Svensk filmdatabas [SFI]: http://www.svenskfilmdatabas.se/
Svensk författningssamling at riksdagen.se: SFS 1959: 348, §3. http://www.riksdagen.se/sv/Dokument-Lagar/Lagar/Svenskforfattningssamling/Kungl-Majts-Forordning-1959_sfs-1959-348/
Talk:Color Climax Corporation, Wikipedia: https://en.wikipedia.org/wiki/Talk:Color_Climax_Corporation

Index

Lightning Source UK Ltd.
Milton Keynes UK
UKHW051420080822
407005UK00020B/268